PAKISTAN SOCIETY

ISLAM, ETHNICITY
AND
LEADERSHIP
IN
SOUTH ASIA

PAKISTAN SOCIETY

ISLAM, ETHNICITY
AND
LEADERSHIP
IN
SOUTH ASIA

AKBAR S. AHMED

KARACHI
OXFORD UNIVERSITY PRESS
OXFORD   NEW YORK   DELHI
1986

Oxford University Press

OXFORD NEW YORK
TORONTO MELBOURNE AUCKLAND
PETALING JAYA SINGAPORE HONG KONG TOKYO
DELHI BOMBAY CALCUTTA MADRAS KARACHI
NAIROBI DAR ES SALAAM CAPE TOWN

and associates in

BEIRUT BERLIN IBADAN NICOSIA

OXFORD is a trademark of Oxford University Press

First Edition, 1986
ISBN 0 19 577350 0

Printed at
Kifayat Printers, Karachi
Published by
Oxford University Press
5-Bangalore Town, Sharae Faisal
P. O. Box 13033, Karachi-8, Pakistan.

For Razia, Aisha, Rani,
and Zainab, with love.

Contents

Preface

In the preface to an earlier book I had noted the unceasing process of dynamic change in Pakistan society. The book, *Pieces of Green: The Sociology of Change in Pakistan,* covered the period up to 1974. A decade later, in the eighties, Pakistan society continues to be in a state of flux and change. Some of the main factors are easily identified: the process of the 'Islamization' of Pakistan, the trauma and tension of defining and enacting the Islamic vision; the migrant workers abroad, especially those in the Arab States; the return of these workers to their villages and the consequent socio-psychological problems for them and their society; and the changed situation in Afghanistan with its impact, mainly through the refugees, on Pakistan. These problems are reflected in this volume.

But beneath the rapid and often bewildering changes are stronger, more permanent, features. Of these Islam, ethnicity and leadership are discussed.

Although the ethnographic data in the volume are based on field research two chapters, the first and last, are exploratory. The first attempts to construct a socio-historical framework for the study of Pakistan society drawing from themes in South Asian history. The last chapter grapples with issues in social and economic development keeping before it the Japanese model, so alluring for Asia. Both chapters explore ideas and remain speculatory.

The volume is structured. The papers are grouped around Islam, ethnicity and leadership in society in the first two parts. Other general areas of contemporary interest are covered in the third part.

Pakistan society is complex and diverse. This is clearly illustrated in the volume. Both the unexpected—the ritual deaths at Hawkes Bay, Karachi, for instance—and expected—the prominence of *Mullahs* in the Frontier (in times of crises) Sufism in Sind, Sardars in Baluchistan and peasant-farmers in the Punjab (at all times)—are examined. Omissions and inclusions will raise comment; no collection can be free of this criticism.

The papers were published in the following books, journals, and newspapers which are gratefully acknowledged: 'Islam, Ethnicity and Leadership in South Asia', in *Purusartha: Islam and Society*, Paris, 1986; 'The Islamization of The Kalash Kafirs', in *The Herald*, Karachi, 1985 and *The Illustrated Weekly of India*, 1986; '*Mor* and *Tor*: Binary and Opposing Models of Pukhtun Femalehood', in *The Endless Day: Some Case Material on Asian Rural Women*, Pergamon Press, Oxford, 1981; 'Death in Islam: The Hawkes Bay Case', in *MAN: The Royal Anthropological Institute Journal*, London, 1986; 'Order and Conflict in Muslim Society: A Case-study from Waziristan', in *The Middle East Journal*, Washington, 1982; 'Hazarawal: Formation and Structure of District Ethnicity', in *The Prospects for Plural Societies*, USA, 1984; 'An Aspect of the Colonial Encounter in the NWFP', in *Asian Affairs*, London, 1979; 'Pukhtun Tribes in the Great Game', in *Asian Affairs*, London, 1980; 'The Arain Ethic and the Spirit of Capitalism in Pakistan', in *The Guardian*, London, 8 August 1984; 'The Afghan Refugees', in *The South Syndication Services*, London, 1985; 'An Afghan Refugee Grows Up', in *Royal Anthropological Institute News (RAIN)*, London, 1982; and 'How to Aid Afghan Refugees', in *RAIN*, 1980; 'Baluchistan: Land and People', in *The South Syndication Services*, London, 1985; 'Gilgit: High in the Karakorums', in *Dawn*, Karachi, 4 November 1983; 'The On-Farm Water Management Project: Honour, Power and Agnatic Rivalry in Rural Pakistan', Seminar at the Harvard Institute of

International Development, in *AID, Project Impact Evaluation Report No. 35,* Washington, 1982; 'Nomadism as Ideological Expression: The Gomal Nomads', in *Nomadic Peoples,* Canada, 1981; and 'Can Pakistan be Japan? Social Factors in Economic Development', in *Asian Affairs,* London, 1985.

Ziarat, Baluchistan,
25 May 1986   AKBAR S. AHMED

Part One
Islam in Society

1

Islam, Ethnicity and Leadership in South Asia

Islam, ethnicity, and the state in Pakistan cannot be understood without reference to the history of the Muslims in India. This chapter aims to examine two interconnected points which directly relate to, and help explain, the themes of the subject. First, that Muslims in India confronting a major world religion to which the majority of the people belonged faced a continuing and serious challenge to their religious and cultural identity (not faced by Muslims in Afghanistan and Iran). Second, as a direct consequence of the above, they responded historically by adopting one of two distinct, mutually opposed models of socio-political behaviour: orthodox, legal, formal on the one hand and unorthodox, syncretic, and informal on the other. A third, more recent, model developed as a direct result of the British colonial period and under its fullest impact in the middle of the nineteenth century. These models express defensive positions and find their genesis in the slow decline of Muslim power in the late seventeenth century after centuries of rule. The models reflect the unresolved tensions and dilemmas in Pakistan society—one broadly defined as tribal groups west of the river Indus, and agricultural-peasant groups with urban concentrations of the refugee population from India on the other bank. However, the models are not mutually exclusive. The oscillation from one to the other model is as much a consequence of external political stimuli—especially perception of hostility—as internal developments. Contemporary Islam in Pakistan, and its linkages to political and ethnic problems, will be understood better if we apply this conceptual framework.

The aim of the chapter is, therefore, to elucidate principles which allow us to perceive beneath the surface structure of nations; this is best achieved through relating contemporary politics to the past or 'diachronic sociology'[1] incorporating the use of 'thick description'[2] and 'depth interpretation'.[3] The chapter is speculative and exploratory, suggesting possible future avenues of investigation.

Afghanistan, Iran and Pakistan

In certain important ways Afghanistan, Iran, and Pakistan share a regional identity underlined by a common religion and a similar historical progress. These are medium-sized countries with large rural and tribal populations, coming to terms with central and sometimes Imperial authority. There are figures who feature in the history of all three. Ahmad Shah Abdali, the Afghan ruler, is one such example.[4] Today, each state uneasily contemplates its larger neighbours, who are seen as minatory. Yet in equally important ways Pakistan is different from Afghanistan and Iran.[5]

The difference is fundamental to structure and arises from the thoroughness with which the British colonized India. Apologists for empire enumerate the extensive network of rail, road, and canal among its blessings. More important was the widespread educational system which by the late nineteenth century had established itself firmly. Schools and colleges, using English as the medium of instruction, in almost every district produced a stream of native candidates for service in the army and the civil services.[6] They were the product of Macaulay's historic Minute of Education, 1835, which hoped to create a class 'Indian in blood and colour, but English in taste, in opinions, in morals, and in intellect.' Cricket, which is not played in Iran and Afghanistan, is a national game in Pakistan.

For north Indian Muslims, education at such institutions as Chief's or Aitchison and Government College in Lahore, or Edwardes in Peshawar became a symbol of status and a passport to the services. Even girls, contrary to traditional Muslim practice, were sent to convents and colleges. The Convent of Jesus and Mary in Murree, organized by Catholic nuns, celebrated its centenary a few years ago. Today, the same institutions continue to produce the future elite of the country.

What does this mean for our comparative statement regarding Afghanistan and Iran? As a result of its educational system, the Pakistan ruling elite reflected values which were part westernized and part liberal. These values formed the ethos of the army[7] and the civil services, 'the steel frame' which held the state together and were perpetuated in services clubs. There was thus, an in-built structural mechanism to check extreme forms and expressions of politics in Pakistan.[8]

How, then, are we to explain the current Islamization programme of General Zia-ul-Haq's regime? Is Zia a deviation from the westernized ethos? An isolated visionary imposing his views on society? Are the various ethnic zones in step with him? Or does he represent what western observers call a 'resurgence' or 'revival' of Islam? Are we witnessing the permanent shift away from the westernized liberal ethos? And, finally, does this imply that Islam is not compatible with the liberal ethos? These are complex and important questions requiring diachronic historical perspective if we are to tackle them satisfactorily. An examination of the late seventeenth century in India would assist in illuminating some of the current intellectual, ideological, and political problems of Pakistan.

Social Developments in India in the Late Seventeenth Century

The dilemma facing Aurangzeb, the last great Mughal Emperor of India, in the second half of the seventeenth century was not a new one.[9] All Muslim rulers of India had to confront it to a degree. Simply put: was Aurangzeb the impartial Emperor of a poly-ethnic, multi-religious state or the Muslim leader of the Muslim community in India, the *ummah*, exclusively treating non-Muslims as lowly conquered subjects? But, unlike his predecessors, developments in his century forced Aurangzeb to grapple with the issues around the dilemma. The question is related to fundamental theological issues.

Was Mughal India, for Muslims, the ideal state, *madinat al-tamma*, or the imperfect state, *madinat al-naqisa*? If the latter, was India the *dar al harb*, the land of war, as distinct from *dar al Islam*, the land of Islam? To make matters more complex for Muslims, Islam in India confronted a highly established and sophisticated world religion to which the majority of the people belonged. In India, Islam faced its most interesting set of challenges.

But, what was happening in the seventeenth century to make it different from the previous centuries? A number of factors combined to create the most severe intellectual and socio-political crisis of confidence for the Indian Muslims. It was the beginning of the end of Muslim power in India and corresponded with the emergence of the colonial era in Indian history. The main developments have been briefly touched on:

a. *The political crisis of Mughal India was reaching a climax*. The very size of the Empire, stretching from Kabul to Chittagong, in those days of poor communications foretold its disintegration. At the height of its greatest physical expanse the Empire was at its weakest. Mughal princes, waiting for Aurangzeb's long reign to end, led armies against him and each other, sapping the strength of the empire. But empires have held for centuries, as had the Mughal Empire, and we may turn to other factors behind the crisis.

b. *Important cultural-religious developments applied internal pressure on the Empire*. Assertive Hindu revivalist movements were spreading rapidly in India and often assuming an anti-Muslim shape. Tulsi Das translated the *Ramayana* into Hindi from Sanskrit providing access to it for the majority. In particular, the *bhakti* movement made its impact on northern India. Although the *bhakti* movement had originated with figures like Kabir preaching universal peace, and borrowed certain features of Islam, such as monotheism and egalitarianism, by the late seventeenth century it became an anti-Muslim movement.

c. *Non-Muslim religious movements converted into nationalist-ethnic armed struggle against the Mughals.* The emergence of ethnic identity was a new socio-political phenomenon. Whereas, previously political conflict was based on dynastic, religious, or caste differences now, ethnicity was emerging as a major factor.[10] Ethnicity as a political force was destined to grow over the centuries. Today, it threatens the integrity of the contemporary state in the subcontinent.[11]

Of the ethno-religious movements, those of the Marathas and the Sikhs were the most significant in the part they played in debilitating the Mughals. Their leaders, Sivaji, and Guru Gobind Singh, after his predecessor was killed by Aurangzeb, were personally committed to fighting the Mughals. Aurangzeb spent the entire second half of his long reign in a seemingly futile attempt to crush the Marathas in the south. The Sikhs, until then a syncretist religion between Hinduism and Islam, thenceforth moved towards the former in their ideological and political position. In the eighteenth and early nineteenth centuries they were to rule large Muslim populations in north India—constantly in rebellion—with an iron hand.[12]

d. *The appearance of the Europeans in India.* New ideas, new military techniques, and new technology from a Europe about to launch into the industrial revolution which would change the map of the globe burst upon the Mughals posing an external challenge just when they were at their weakest.[13] By the last decades of the seventeenth century, it was clear that the English were winning the colonial race against other Europeans. They had established important factories, which soon became organized military forts in Bombay, Madras and, by 1690, Calcutta. These were to become the future Presidencies—the nucleus of civil and military activity—of the British Indian Empire.

The combination of these internal and external developments created a deep sense of crisis among Muslims.[14] Their world was beginning to shrink and crumble. The slow process of decadence and political degradation would continue for the next few centuries, providing the major themes of lost glory and sense of despair for Muslim literature (as depicted in the poetry of Ghalib, Hali, and Iqbal). In the late seventeenth century, the Muslims faced two choices: they could either firmly redraw the boundaries of Islam around themselves, shutting out the emerging realities, or allow the boundaries to become elastic and porous thereby effecting synthesis with non-Muslim groups. The two alternatives delineated were clear: legal, orthodox, and formal on the one hand and eclectic, syncretic, and informal on the other. It is no accident that these two clearly differentiated and mutually opposed choices emerged in the person and character of the sons of the Emperor Shah Jahan, Aurangzeb and Dara Shikoh. No such dramatically extreme and opposed positions in the sons of the rulers of Delhi are recorded in earlier Muslim history.[15] One of the two would succeed Shah Jahan to rule India and thereby influence the course of future history, casting shadows on contemporary events in Pakistan.

The A and B Categories

Orientalists perceive two distinct, contradictory, and exclusive alternatives of Muslims and their society: 'westernized modernists' or 'traditional fundamentalists'.[16] a lead followed somewhat uncritically by scholars on Pakistan—Ahmad[17] Binder[18] Bolitho[19] Callard[20] Sayeed[21] Stephens[22] Wilcox[23] and Williams.[24] The former are seen by westerners as 'liberal', 'humanist', 'progressive', and by implication the 'good guys'. The latter are 'fanatic', 'retrogressive', and the 'bad guys'. The application of these western labels best suited for political analysis in western democracies, could be misleading in South Asia. The labels do not take into account the complex and dynamic interplay of local religious, cultural, and ethnic factors. Such simplistic labels cannot satisfactorily illuminate the complexity of South Asian Islam, they may aid in obfuscating it.

To my mind anthropologists, perhaps because they are trained to be sensitive to society and culture, have presented a more satisfactory analysis of Muslim society. Gellner, working in Morocco, suggests a 'pendulum swing theory' between P—urban, puritan, literate society—and C—rural, informal, illiterate society[25] —and 'flux and reflux'[26] in understanding Muslim social groups. Adding data to the Moroccan material from the other end of the Muslim world, Indonesia, Geertz distinguishes *santri* groups (Islamic, traders) in opposition to *abangan* and *prijaji* ones (animistic, peasant), the former seeing the latter as idol-worshippers.[27]

A kind of pendulum swing theory provides us with a useful conceptual framework to understand South Asian Islam. For our exercise, we could list the characteristics of Aurangzeb and Dara Shikoh[28] to provide us with the two models of Muslim leadership in Muslim society between which it oscillates. We may label them *A* and *B* respectively. There is a third type of Muslim model which developed as a direct consequence of western colonialism. We may call it *C*. Another model, *D*, does not concern us in South Asia. *D* is secular and totally committed to modernism in its West European, or more recently, Marxist, shape. Kamal Ataturk is the best example of *D*. The model has not commanded any significant following among South Asian Muslims, perhaps for the reasons outlined earlier.

The chief distinguishing characteristics of Aurangzeb *A* and Dara Shikoh *B* illustrating their anti-thetical nature may be summarized as follows:

Chart 1.1: Chief Distinguishing Characteristics of Aurangzeb *A* and Dara Shikoh *B*

A	B
• orthodox, legalistic, Islam	• syncretic, eclectic, Islam
• emphasis on *ummah*, Muslim community	• universalist humanity
• discouraged art (music, dancing, etc.)	• encouraged art
• supports clergy/*ulema*	• anti-clergy ('Paradise is there, where there is no *mullah*')[b]
• outward signs of orthodoxy: rejects silk clothes and gold vessels, the *Nawroz*—the Persian New Year—the solar year, etc.	• constant company of Sufis, Hindu *yogis* and *sanyasis*: his ring bore the legend *'Prabhu'*, the Sanskrit for god
• patron of *Fatawai-i-Alamgiri*, most comprehensive digest of Muslim jurisprudence ever compiled	• patron/translator of *Upanishads/Bhagavadgita*, classic Hindu texts, into Persian
• favourite reading: Quran, Al-Ghazzali[a]	• favourite reading: mystics
• wished Muslim society to revert to orthodox mould thus drawing boundaries	• wished to expand boundaries of Muslim society into incorporating non-Muslims: equates Michael with Vishnu, Adam with Brahman, etc.

a. In reading Al-Ghazzali, Aurangzeb was following a tradition established by Akbar, his great grandfather, who is accused by the orthodox of drifting away from Islam. So much did Akbar admire Al-Ghazzali that he ordered in a *farman* issued to his governors that they spend their spare time reading the major works of Al-Ghazzali and Maulana Rumi. See Rizvi, S.A.A., *Shah Wali-Allah and his Times*, Marifat Publishing House, Canberra, ACT, Australia, 1980, pp. 34-5.

b. Schimmel, A., *Mystical Dimensions of Islam*, University of North Carolina Press, Chapel Hill, 1975.

A glance at the characteristics of A and B may lead us into the same trap into which the Orientalists have fallen. We may be tempted to reject B as an apostate. There is no problem with A. He is the model of pious orthodoxy. But do we simply reject B as an apostate?

Although the charge sheet drawn up by Aurangzeb on the basis of which Dara Shikoh was executed, centres around apostasy, he, at no point renounces Islam. His understanding of Islam is wildly extravagant and at times incorrect, but, in an earlier phase, his orthodoxy is irreproachable. For all his syncretism, his ideal, like that of Aurangzeb, remained the Holy Prophet of Islam. The dilemma for South Asian Islam becomes acute when both A and B refer to the Prophet. We are thus not talking of two or three types of Islam but different aspects of Islam.

The adventurism comes later in B's life. But even then he wished to extend not reject Islam. Indeed he sees the Hindu holy scriptures—the *Upanishads* and the *Bhagavadgita*—in the Holy Quran. The tragedy of his life is not the lack of commitment to religious ideals but excess of it.

So we have before us two models, created as a consequence of the socio-political crisis in the seventeenth century: A, orthodox, legalistic, formal; and B, unorthodox, mystical, and informal, reflecting two aspects of Muslim society. However, it is not a question of either A or B but a variety of computations of A and B. But the story does not end with the Mughals.

Drawing genealogical lines, from Aurangzeb and Dara Shikoh to the leaders of Pakistan, illuminates the problem further. Mr. Zulfikar Ali Bhutto, the late Prime Minister of Pakistan, in a significant and historical manner, despite Oxford and Berkeley, reflects the conceptual position of B.[29] Both were eclectic and syncretist. While Dara Shikoh wished to include Hinduism in Islam, Bhutto attempted a similar exercise with the dominant rival ideology of his time, socialism, evolving the concept of 'Islamic socialism'.

In particular, the Sufic elements in the character of the two are worth noting. I do not wish to push the argument portraying Bhutto as a mystic Sufi too far, but his devotion to Sufis—especially to Shah Baz Qalandar, the 'saint of the beggars' who traced his spiritual lineage to al-Hallaj—is well-known. His fascination with Shah Baz Qalandar converted the devotional hymn—the *dhammal*—about the saint almost into an informal national song. Audiences at public meetings burst into it, accompanied by clapping and often dancing, on seeing Bhutto.[30] He frequently recited the verses of the other great Sindhi Sufi, Shah Abdul Latif. By his public association with the Sindhi Sufi saints, whose poetry is explicitly populist, he was making a political point to the dispossessed in society and Sindhis in particular. To the former, he appeared as a champion of their rights and to the latter, of their ethnicity. Rural Sind, no matter what his politics, would remain loyal to him.

Bhutto's death at the gallows merely confirmed an established Sufi tradition stretching back to the spiritual mentor of Shah Baz Qalandar, al-Hallaj. The Sufi prepares to meet death, and his Maker, as the famous Persian line on Shah Baz's tomb says, 'dancing on the gallows'.

While many saw Bhutto's behaviour as highly unorthodox, excessive, and at shrines, for instance, ecstatic, others read in it signs of Sufism, no matter that his practical life was not sublimated by mysticism, an observation also made of Dara Shikoh.[31]

Conceptually, General Zia is a spiritual descendant of Aurangzeb. He is personally austere, committed to Islam and the *ummah*, and a regular visitor to the orthodox holy places of Islam in Saudi Arabia. The question of adding to Islam 'socialism', or any 'ism', does not arise for him as Islam is a perfect and complete system in itself. However, his education at St. Stephen's College, Delhi, and career in the elite corps of the army, the Guides, indicate wide networks.

In terms of modern Islam, ethnicity, and the state, the chief distinguishing characteristics of Zia *A* and Bhutto *B* summarized in the following chart provide an interesting comparison with the previous one, and bring into relief the arguments in this chapter.

Chart 1.2: **Chief Distinguishing Characteristics of Zia** *A* **and Bhutto** *B*

A	B
• orthodox formal Islam, prays five times daily, visits holy places in Saudi Arabia regularly	• 'mystical' informal Islam, visits Sufi shrines, dance and ecstatic behaviour
• personally austere	• personally extravagant
• abstains from alcohol	• drinks alcohol ('I drink alcohol not blood like others')
• culture defined by Islam	• ethnic culture ('I will not allow Sindhis to become like Red Indians')
• emphasis on Urdu as national language	• encourages ethnic languages
• *ummah* supreme over ethnicity	• importance of ethnicity
• dress: formal military or formal national (black coat over white muslin shirt)	• western suits or informal worn by common man (usually with Chinese cap)
• public meetings formal, proto-col (wears military dress)	• informal, melee-like (wears informal clothes)
• National Assembly called 'Majlis-e-Shoora', (ideally good Muslims), nominated	• elected National Assembly represents all political shades
• heroes: Prophet and Muslim generals	• Prophet, Napoleon, Mao Tse-Tung
• wishes to draw boundaries firmly around Islam	• wishes to expand Islam (to include, for example, socialism)

Critics of both A^{32} and *B* accuse them of exploiting religion to further political ends. Some anthropologists studying religious behaviour are inclined to be cynical of what they observe. Others[33] are more believing. I am in agreement with the latter position. As social scientists, we are interested in basing conclusions on regularly observed, or recorded, social behaviour. So although their critics would accuse *A* and *B* of manipulating religion, I maintain that Bhutto's tears as a result of listening to Shah Abdul Latif's verses or Zia's when praying in the holy *Kaaba* in Mecca are genuine. In those moments, they are not Prime Ministers and

Presidents but worshippers responding genuinely to deeply felt emotion. For purposes of our analysis, it is interesting to distinguish the different contextual framework of the stimuli that moved them. Both *A* and *B* respond to Islam but, significantly, to different aspects of it.

The question that arises is: how accurate are the stereotypes of *A* and *B*, the one a rigid fanatic, the other a syncretic humanist? Are Aurangzeb[34] and Zia the extreme orthodox fanatics portrayed by their critics? Recent historical research indicates that Aurangzeb was not the destroyer of temples he is popularly pictured as. On the contrary, records exist showing numerous grants to Hindu temples.[35] Similarly, although Zia's image in the western press is that of a harsh Islamic judge ordering criminals to be stoned to death or lashed, and their hands cut off, the facts show a very limited use of this punishment.[36] Type *A* suffers from a bad press.

On the other hand, just how far has *B* drifted, consciously or unconsciously, from religion? Here, too, the answer is interesting. *B* does not see himself as leaving Islam for non-Islamic ideologies, but rather, as bringing the latter into the former. His understanding of Islam may be faulted, not his intentions. With Iqbal, himself a Sufi poet hovering between *B* and *C*, *B* believes 'at critical moments in their history it is Islam that has saved Muslims and not vice versa'.[37]

It appears that the confrontation between *A* and *B* is destined to end in the death of *B* at the hands of *A*. There is no compromise or synthesis between the two. The death warrants signed by Aurangzeb and Zia thus reflect the unresolved dilemmas of South Asian Islam and illustrate the continuity of the tension between *A* and *B* in historical perspective.

Islam, Ethnicity and the State

Do *A* and *B* as the two traditionally anti-thetical, but related models of South Asian Islam, also explain recent Muslim history? I think they do with minor local operations.

Although *A,* in the main remained unchanged over time,*B* adjusted to changing circumstances, both behaving in characteristic structural fashion (one orthodox, the other syncretist). However, the full impact of the colonial era produced a third and almost distinct category, which we are calling *C.* I use 'almost' advisedly, for in certain parts *C* reflected some of the features of *A* and *B. C* may be labelled, indeed it calls itself so—'liberal', 'modern', and 'educated' (usually in English). *C* educated in western institutions and employed in the colonial services, demanded a synthesis between tradition and the contemporary world.[38] *C* is—and remains—scarred by the colonial experience, unlike *A* and *B* who possess internal defensive mechanisms to shut out the world. Most significantly, the concept of 'nationalism' is developed and incorporated in *C* for the first time among South Asian Muslims. *C* remains as uncomfortable with orthodox formal Islam as it does with mystical or ecstatic behaviour.[39] An attempt is made to draw a grand, generalized, genealogical chart relating the major links of Muslim history and making allowances for 'lost' and 'telescoped' ancestors:

Chart 1.3: Genealogy of Major Links of Muslim History

	A	*B*	*C*
seventeenth century	Aurangzeb	Dara Shikoh	
	↓	↓	
eighteenth century	Shah Waliullah	Wali	
	↓	↓	
nineteenth century	Sayyed Ahmad Barelvi	Ghalib	Sayyed Ahmad
	↓		↓
twentieth century	Maulana Maudoodi		M.A. Jinnah
	↓	↓	↓
	Zia-ul-Haq	Z.A. Bhutto	Ayub Khan

Two key educational institutions which came to symbolize
A and *C* in South Asia, and whose alumni were to play an
important role in the creation of Pakistan, are the ones at
Deoband and Aligarh. Generations of Aligarh men have
served in the services and held high office in India, and after
1947 in Pakistan, including that of President. Aligarh, founded
by Sayyed Ahmad, attempted to seek 'modern' answers to
the problems of the Muslims. Compromise with the British, it
was argued by him, would prevent the Muslims from being
swept away by resurgent Hinduism. Sayyed Ahmad was trained
in the orthodox traditions of Shah Waliullah. Deoband
remained an orthodox Islamic centre. The diametrically
opposed positions of the two centres is illustrated by the
behaviour of their leaders during 1857. Sayyed Ahmad
supported the British while Maulana Manawatawi fought
them.

Under British rule in the late nineteenth century, *A, B,* and
C adopted different strategies of survival. *A,* biding their
time, remained hostile and aloof, which discouraged participation in government service. While some of *B* also took the
easy path, lamenting lost glory in intoxicants and verses,[40]
others diverted their energies from pacific Sufi activity to
aggressive movements of rebellion, especially among tribal
groups. Illiterate, ill-armed, and ill-prepared tribal groups
followed their leaders in suicidal encounters with European
armies. *Jihad,* holy war, was declared by Sufi leaders such as
the Sanusi of Cyrenaica, the Mahdi of Sudan, and the Akhund
of Swat, among tribal groups throughout the Muslim world.[41]
C joined the colonial services and in some cases rose to
eminence. Their assimilation was sometimes so successful
that they opened themselves to charges of having become
kala sahib (black Englishman).

Political parties, too, aligning themselves with their leaders
leaned to *A, B,* or *C.* The Muslim League of Mr. Jinnah in the
forties until that of Ayub Khan in the sixties could be classi-
fied as *C.* The League argued for a liberal, democratic, and at
one time, almost secular state. Mr. Bhutto's Pakistan People's

Party falls, like he does, into *B*. The Party is an unresolved mix of populist, socialist, and Islamic ideologies. The ambiguity explains in part its phenomenal success at the polls—it was all things to all men. The Jamaat-e-Islami, like its founder and leader, Maulana Maudoodi, is placed unequivocally in *A*.

The movement for Pakistan in the forties brought out the unresolved problems of Muslim self-perception in India and the inherent tension between *A*, *B*, and *C*. The problems were not resolved with the creation of Pakistan in 1947. Generally speaking, *C* leaders ruled the country imposing their vision of society upon it. Maulana Maudoodi was thus provoked to remark about the first Constitution: 'If a secular and Godless instead of an Islamic Constitution was to be introduced, what was the sense in all this struggle for a separate Muslim homeland?'[42] The Maulana himself was a latecomer to Pakistan as his party had not joined the struggle for Pakistan on ideological grounds and therefore remained suspect as far as *B* and *C* were concerned.

In the end, we may elucidate principles which assist us in understanding Pakistan society and politics in relation to the themes of this chapter which suggest ours is a predictive model. Type *A* focuses on Islam, plays down ethnicity, in the ideal the *ummah* supersedes tribal or ethnic loyalties ('there are no genealogies in Islam', the Prophet had said) and emphasizes a strong centralized state. The concomitants of the last are seen as a highly centralized bureaucracy, consisting mainly of the army and civil services, a national language, Urdu, and a high degree of commitment to Pakistan. The entire package is described as the 'ideology of Pakistan'. *B* and *C*, while not necessarily playing down Islam, also pay attention to other issues emanating from regional or ethnic compulsions. They are supportive of ethnic culture and languages. In general, groups with a strong sense of tribal identity, such as on the west of the river Indus, would be more in harmony with *B* than with A. However, the picture is not so simple. The fighting in Baluchistan by the Pakistan Army to make Baluch leaders malleable to Islamabad was severest in the Bhutto period. Those ruling in Islamabad, whether A, B, or C, would be equally defensive if external threat were perceived. Thus the state emerges as a strong centralizing force under A, B, and C.

Pakistanis, and there is an entire generation that has come of age in Pakistan, cling tenaciously to the 'ideology of Pakistan'. The greater the threat perceived, the more rigid will be the adherence to the ideology and towards A. Indeed, Pakistanis have cause to be apprehensive. The world of the north Indian Muslims since Aurangzeb has been contracting slowly, sometimes punctuated by dramatic, and for Muslims often devastating, events. In 1857, at one stroke they lost an Emperor, a capital, and an Empire.[43] However shrunk in importance these were the last symbols of Muslim Imperial power.

Recent Pakistan history generates similar fears for Pakistanis. In 1971, Pakistan was split in two. External threat and internal strife will continue to create tension but also help to bind different ethnic groups together.

The leaders of Pakistan need to strike a balance and create a synthesis between A, B, and C if they are to create a healthy polity for the future. Ideologically, the issue of *dar al Islam* or *dar al harb* had been settled in 1947. Pakistan, literally land of the pure, is *dar al Islam*. But the repeated collapse of different national governments argues that there is a problem. At times of extreme national crisis aggravated by external hostility, the pendulum will swing with violence from one to the other model, as after the breakaway of East Pakistan in 1971 when it swung from C to B. The severe crisis of 1971 is largely responsible for jolting C out of power, ruling Pakistan since 1947.

The pendulum in the mid-seventies swung again dramatically from B to A, but it may well swing away from A in the future. If it does, some of the internal tensions may be articulated through aggressive ethnicity, particularly in Baluchistan and rural Sind, posing a threat to Pakistan.[44]

The similar, though not identical, intellectual crisis for Muslim Arabs between orthodox and Sufi forms of Islam was resolved by Imam Al-Ghazzali after intense soul-searching in the eleventh century. In addition, Hellenistic intellectual and ideological influences pressurized Islam then, as do western ones now. The genius of Al-Ghazzali,[45] who has often been called 'the greatest Muslim after the Prophet Muhammad',[46] lay in reconciling the three major influences of his time to each other: the more formalistic, orthodox aspects of religion A, to inner Sufic experience which relates worshipper and worshipped B, in the context of external western influences C. Pakistan society, destined to oscillate between seemingly opposed positions, A, B, and C, and surrounded by powers it perceives as less than friendly, awaits its Al-Ghazzali. Until the reconciliation of these fundamental issues takes place the problems of Islam, ethnicity, and the state will remain pressing.

NOTES

1. Evans-Pritchard, E.E., 'Anthropology and History', in *Essays in Social Anthropology*, Faber and Faber, London, 1962.

2. Geertz, C., *The Interpretation of Cultures*, Basic Books, New York, 1973.

3. Lambek, M., *Human Spirits: A Cultural Account of Trance in Mayotte*, Cambridge University Press, 1981.

4. Abdali was the founder of a dynasty in the eighteenth century whose members ruled Afghanistan until the pro-Soviet *coups* in the seventies. See also note 14.

5. The difference is further exaggerated by the social ramifications of Iran's Shia form of Islam. See Fischer, M.J.M., *Iran: From Religious Dispute to Revolution*, Harvard University Press, Cambridge, Massachusetts, 1980.

6. There is an extensive literature on the services in British India. Woodruff, P., *The Men Who Ruled India*, Vols. 1-2, Cape, London, 1953 and 1954 provides a general—if nostalgic—view which is worth consulting. For the continuing colonial impact on Pakistan's administrative structure, see Braibanti, R., *Research on the Bureaucracy of Pakistan*, Duke University, Durham, 1966; and Goodnow, H.F., *The Civil Service of Pakistan*, Yale University Press, 1964; and its examination through an extended case-study see Ahmed, A.S., 'Order and conflict in Muslim society: a case-study from Pakistan', *Middle East Journal*, Vol. 36, No. 2, Spring 1982 and *Religion and Politics in Muslim Society: Order and Conflict in Pakistan*, Cambridge University Press, 1983; and as a consequence the creation of artificial 'district ethnicity', see Ahmed, A.S., 'Hazarawal: formation and structure of district ethnicity in Pakistan', in *Prospects for Plural Societies*, Lewis, M., (editor), American Ethnological Society, Kentucky, Lexington, 1984. See also Part Two, chapter 6.

7. Ayub Khan, President of Pakistan in the sixties, best represents this ethos. Even as a politician he never quite managed to shake off the values and change the behavioural patterns he acquired at the Royal Military Academy, Sandhurst, and in the Indian Army. His impressive bearing, clipped moustache, and haircut—the prototype general—faithfully reflected an inner commitment to these values. At home, shooting grouse on the demesnes of Scottish lords, on the golf-course, and

in a dinner-jacket, he ruled Pakistan as a 'benevolent dictator', a stern but sympathetic schoolmaster. His views clearly reflecting his position are expressed in his autobiography, Khan, M.A., *Friends Not Masters*, Oxford University Press, Karachi, 1967. In him Macaulay stood vindicated. For the changing social structure of the Pakistan Army, see Cohen, S., *The Pakistan Army*, University of California Press, Berkeley, 1984; and Ali, T., *Can Pakistan Survive?* Penguin Books, 1983.

8. My argument does not take into account Bangladesh. The events of 1971 which clearly saw a breakdown in these values require a separate discussion outside the scope of this chapter.

9. Aurangzeb, who ruled India for over forty-eight years, dying in 1707, is particularly well covered in history. For standard references see Datta, K., Chaudhuri, H.R., and Majumdar, R.C., *An Advanced History of India*, Macmillan, London, 1956; Irvine, W., *Later Mughals*, Vols. 1-2, London and Calcutta, 1922; Sarkar, J., *History of Aurangzeb*, Vols. 1-5, Calcutta, 1912-24 and *Fall of the Mughal Empire*, Vols. 1-3, Calcutta, 1938-50; and Spear, P., *A History of India*, Penguin Books, Harmondsworth, 1965.

10. A notable exception are the tribal groups such as the Baluch and Pukhtun for whom tribal identity, or ethnicity, has always been of highest importance in self-perception. See Part One, chapter 3; Part Two, chapter 8; and Part Three, chapter 14.

11. For a perceptive anthropological comment, see Geertz, op.cit., 1973.

12. Archer, J.C., *The Sikhs*, Princeton University Press, 1946; and Singh, K., *History of the Sikhs*, Vols. 1-2, Oxford University Press, 1963-6.

13. The earlier comparative economic position of Mughal India and England is represented by the following figures: the salary of a *mansabdar* of 5,000—the senior troop commander—was equivalent to £24,000 of English purchasing power when the total revenues of England were less than a million pounds. See Spear, op. cit., p. 46.

14. It is no accident that the early eighteenth century produced one of the greatest Muslim reformers in India, Shah Waliullah, who sounded the orthodox alarm as a result of the social condition of the Muslims. He emphasized a reversion to pristine Islam and rejection of Hindu accretions such as tomb worship, consulting Brahmins for omens and celebrating Hindu festivals. Pointedly, he wrote his major contribution to theological dialectics, *Hujjat Allah al-baligha*, in Arabic not Persian. In spite of bitter polemics by the traditional *ulema* he translated the Holy Quran into Persian for it to reach a wider readership; his sons translated it into Urdu. Shah Waliullah's ideas were to shape the Islamic college at Deoband and influence Muslims of all opinions. Significantly, one of his greatest heroes was Aurangzeb.

It is believed that his urgent letters to Ahmad Shah Abdali may have influenced the Afghan ruler to come to India and challenge the rapidly growing and victorious Maratha confederacy. By defeating the Marathas in the third and last battle on the fields of Panipat in 1761, Abdali provided Muslims breathing space for a while. See also note 4.

15. The earlier Mughals move in a more relaxed and more confident world. The threat around them appears containable. If not entirely at peace with their environment, they are ready to come to terms with it. Babar, founder of the dynasty, drunk one night and fired with religious zeal the next, who discusses his most personal problems in his autobiography, symbolizes the earlier position. Babar was somewhat inclined to mysticism, professing he was 'the servant of *derwishes*'. More remarkably, Mughal women established themselves as brilliant poets, painters, and writers. The tension felt so acutely by the later Mughals had not developed.

16. Watt, W.M., *Islam and the Integration of Society*, Routledge and Kegan Paul, London, 1961.

17. Ahmad, A., *Islamic Modernism in India and Pakistan*, London, 1967 and *Studies in Islamic Culture in the Indian Environment*, Oxford University Press, London, 1969.

18. Binder, L., *Religion and Politics in Pakistan*, University of California Press, 1961.

19. Bolitho, H., *Jinnah: Creator of Pakistan*, John Murray, London, 1964.

20. Callard, K., *Pakistan: A Political Study*, Allen and Unwin, London, 1958.

21. Sayeed, K.B., *Pakistan: The Formative Phase*, Oxford University Press, London, 1960.

22. Stephens, I., *Pakistan*, Penguin Books, Harmondsworth, 1964.

23. Wilcox, W.A., *Pakistan, the Consolidation of a Nation*, Columbia University Press, 1963.

24. Williams, L.F., Rushbrook, *The State of Pakistan*, Faber and Faber, 1962.

25. Gellner, E., 'A pendulum swing theory of Islam', in *Sociology of Religion*, Robertson R., (editor), Penguin Education, Harmondsworth, 1969.

26. Gellner, E., *Muslim Society*, Cambridge University Press, 1981.

27. Geertz, C., *Islam Observed*, Yale University Press, 1968 and 'Religion in Java: conflict and integration', in *Sociology of Religion*, Robertson, R., (editor), Penguin Education, Harmondsworth, 1969.

28. Chand, T., 'Dara Shikoh and the Upanishads', *Islamic Culture*, Vol. xvii, 1943, pp. 397-413; and Qanungo, K.R., *Dara Shukoh*, Calcutta, 1934 in addition to the literature on Aurangzeb contained in note 9. Dara Shikoh's contribution to Sufic thought is acknowledged by contemporary twentieth-century Sufi masters. See Lings, M., *What is Sufism?* Allen and Unwin, London, 1975, p. 99.

29. A study of the complexity of Mr. Bhutto's character within a socio-cultural context is awaited in spite of numerous biographies: Burki, S.J., *Pakistan under Bhutto, 1971-77*, Macmillan, London, 1980; Mody, P., *Zulfi my friend*, Thomson Press, Delhi, 1973; Mukerjee, D., *Zulfiqar Ali Bhutto*, Vikas, India, 1972; Schofield, V., *Bhutto: Trial and Execution*, Frank Cass, London, 1979; and Taseer, S., *Bhutto: A Political Biography*, Ithaca, London, 1980. There are many, sometimes contradictory, facets to his personality but for purposes of analysis we are concentrating on one and isolating it from the others. Thus is *B* highlighted and *C*—which Mr. Bhutto at times appeared to adhere to—moved to the background.

30. The song of Shah Baz Qalandar acknowledges the supremacy of Hazrat Ali the Prophet's son-in-law as 'number one among the great saints'—*Ali da pehla number*, and therefore establishes the Qalandar's impeccable spiritual lineage. The onomatopoeic refrain—*dama dam mast Qalandar*—is known to induce trance-like and ecstatic behaviour in believers.

31. Chand, op. cit., 1943.

32. For scathing ethnic contemporary references to Aurangzeb see Khushal Khan Khattak, the Pukhtun warrior-poet in Caroe, O., and Howell, E., *The Poems of Khushal Khan Khattak*, Oxford University Press, Karachi, 1963 and for a religious attack Shah Kalim-Allah Jahanabadi in Rizvi, S.A.A., *Shah Wali-Allah and his Times*, Marifat Publishing House, Canberra, ACT, Australia, 1980. Both ridiculed his austerity and condemned him as a hypocrite.

33. Spiro, M.E., 'Religion: problems of definition and explanation', in *Anthropological Approaches to the Study of Religion*, Banton, M., (editor), ASA monograph 3, Tavistock, London, 1973.

34. Aurangzeb's letters and notes reveal a man conscious of attempting to hold a difficult position with high moral courage and diligence. They also reveal a sensitive and often despairing man. I shall cite two examples to support my point. Aurangzeb bitterly commenting on his education is said to have taken his mentor to task thus: 'You taught me that the whole of *Franguistan* (Europe) was no more than some inconsiderable island, and the sovereigns of *Franguistan*—resembled our petty Rajas; and that Persia, Usbec, Kachguer, Tartary, Catay, Pegu, Siam, China, and Matchine, trembled at the name of the Kings of the Indies'. See Bernier, F., *Travels in the Mogul Empire*, Constable, A., (editor), London, 1891, pp. 155-61. In another example, he wrote across the petition of a Sunni noble who led the Mughal Army against the Marathas and who wished for advancement by abolishing the high post of a Shia, one of the 'accursed misbelievers': 'what connection have worldly affairs with religion? For you is your religion and for me is mine'. See Sarkar, J., *Anecdotes of Aurangzeb*, fourth edition, Calcutta, 1963, pp. 88-9.

35. Ahmad, op, cit., 1969, pp. 191-200.

36. Mr. Q. Aziz, Minister for Information at the Pakistan Embassy, London,

assured me that not a single hand has actually been amputated nor a single death caused by stoning for adultery, as punishment in Pakistan.

37. In his famous Presidential Address, 1930.

38. See note 7.

39. In times of crisis *C* leaders like Mr. Jinnah, have fallen back on Islamic themes: 'I say to every Muslim that Islam expects you, one and all, to do your duty'. See Saiyid, M.H., *Mohammad Ali Jinnah*, Sh. M. Ashraf, Lahore, 1953, p. 416. Although some Pakistanis believe 'there can be no doubt that Jinnah was a secularist and against theocracy', Munir, M., *From Jinnah to Zia*, Akbar Publishing House, Delhi, 1981, Mr. Jinnah's cultural identity with Muslims is established in his statements like: 'I shall never allow Muslims to become slaves of Hindus'. Sayeed, op. cit., p. 215.

40. When asked whether he was a Muslim by an interrogating British official after the 1857 uprisings Mirza Ghalib, probably Urdu's greatest poet, and author of significant Sufic verse, replied: 'only half. I don't eat pig but I do drink.' Ghalib was underlining in a light vein his rather personal and free interpretation of Islam.

41. Ahmed, A.S., *Millennium and Charisma among Pathans*, Routledge and Kegan Paul, London, 1976.

42. Tinker, H., *India and Pakistan*, Pall Mall Press, London, 1962, p. 206.

43. Mirza Ghalib, an eyewitness of the events of 1857 in Delhi wrote in a letter: '*Wallah ab sheher nahi hay camp hay chohwni hay na qila na sheher na bazaar na neher*—by God, there is no city, it is now a military camp; there is no fort (the Mughal Red Fort), no city (Delhi), no *bazaar*, no canals'. Ghalib, M., *Ghalib*, Ferozsons, 1973, p. 16.

44. Harrison, S., *In Afghanistan's Shadow*, Carnegie Endowment, New York, 1981; and Ahmed, A.S., 'Review of Harrison 1981', in *Journal of Asian Studies*, Berkeley, 1982.

45. It is said of his major work, *Ihya-ul-ulum*, 'If all the books of Islam were destroyed it would be but a slight loss if only the *Ihya* of Ghazzali were preserved'. See Al-Ghazzali, *The Alchemy of Happiness*, Field, C., (translator), Octagon Press, London, 1980, p. 13. See also Watt, W.M., *The Faith and Practice of Al-Ghazali*, London, 1953 and *The Muslim Intellectual: A Study of Al-Ghazali*, Edinburgh University Press, 1963.

46. Schimmel, A., *Mystical Dimensions of Islam*, University of North Carolina Press, Chapel Hill, 1975, p. 91.

2

The Islamization of The Kalash Kafirs

The history of the Kalash, so-called Kafirs, 'unbelievers', of Pakistan is the stuff of legend. Rudyard Kipling wrote a famous short story about them. It is widely believed they are descended from Alexander's troops. Campaigns have been fought and sieges laid, providing high drama in British India, in their land. The British left them alone but today the Kalash appear threatened by Islamization. They are caught between the Islamic *jihad,* holy war, in Afghanistan and Islamic revivalism in Pakistan. They are an exotic, lonely, tiny, island confronting a gigantic tidal wave of Islam.

There has been, perhaps, more speculation on, and fascination with the Kafirs, than with any other race in Central and South Asia. They lived in what was once called Kafiristan, the land of the Kafirs, in Afghanistan, and now live in the Chitral district of north Pakistan. The interest in the Kafirs began early.

Mahmud of Ghazni, who led the earliest Muslim invasions into India, in 1020 wished to convert the Kafirs to Islam. So did the dreaded Taimur the Lame. Babar, the founder of the Mughal Empire noted, with characteristic admiration, the quality of their wine in his autobiography.

Between 1895 to 1900, Amir Abdur Rahman, the Iron Amir of Afghanistan, converted the Afghan Kafirs to Islam by the sword. He renamed Kafiristan, their land, Nooristan, 'the land of light'. Kafir village names like Muldesh were replaced with Islamic ones, in this case, Islamabad. The Red

Kafirs, such as the Bashgalis, were distinguished from their kin living in Chitral who were called the Black Kafirs, Kalash — a popular distinction based on the colour of their dress: the *safed-posh,* wearers of white dress, and *sia-posh,* wearers of black dress.

The list of names of British empire-builders and scholar-administrators who were fascinated by them reads like a roll of honour of Empire. Starting with the first great scholar-administrator of the Frontier, Elphinstone, it goes on to Burnes, Raverty, Robertson, Bellew, Stein, and Morgenstierne. The first Europeans to enter Kafiristan were those attached to the Lockhart Mission of 1885-6. Robertson's voluminous *The Kafirs of the Hindu-Kush,* first published in 1896, and written after a year's stay among them, is still the most authoritative. Contemporary scholars like Doctor Schuyler Jones and Peter Parkes, continue to write of and visit them.

Many Victorian administrators had a low opinion of the Kafir. For Bruce, the Kafir was 'an unreclaimed savage' and for Colonel Durand, who administered them, 'the Kafir was a savage, pure and simple'. But for the majority, the Kafirs held a romantic spell.

Major Gordon reflected popular opinion, and two main themes in Victorian England when discussing Kafirs, in his letter to the *Times* on 5 February 1880. The two themes, their European origin and the threat of their extinction by Muslims, would remain dominant in featuring the Kalash. 'The Kafirs, love us and call us their European brethren . . . they being white like Europeans'. Besides, as W.W. Hunter was to note in the *Imperial Gazetteer of India* in 1885, 'they sat on chairs and used tables unlike other Indians'. The Major argued for a strong defensive pact with the Kafirs who had been 'shut out by the iron circle of their Mohamedan foes'. By 1913, it was announced that all Kafirs had been wiped out and were 'purely Musalman'. This alarm can be heard today. But it is perhaps a false alarm.

Scholars estimated, and population figures are little more, there were about 2,000 Kalash in 1955. About 20 years later, they had increased to almost 3,000. In 1984, there were about 4,000 Kalash. This demographic pattern appears consistent and reflects the generally high rate of reproduction in Pakistan which is about 3 per cent. As such, reports of the Kalash population dying out are incorrect. But there are other complex social and cultural problems.

The problem for the Kalash is not of their members leaving Kafiristan for Islam but that of Islam entering Kafiristan. There are presently about 4,000 Muslims living in their valleys, the highest number ever. Many of these, called *sheikhs,* have been converted from Kalash and like recent converts are fiercely orthodox. But many are settlers who have acquired property either through sale or swindle—valuable walnut trees mortgaged for two rupees or half an acre of land for fifty.

More than ten mosques are now situated in Kafiristan. Loudspeakers proclaim the greatness of Allah, the Beneficient, the Merciful, five times daily. The largest mosque in Bumboret holds a hundred worshippers. It was built with a donation, recorded on stone, by a zealous visitor from the Punjab. Its loudspeakers reverberate in the valley. All transport and most of the hotels are owned by Muslims.

Why does a Kalash become a Muslim? Sometimes to escape a ruinous debt, sometimes to gain employment, sometimes, as in the cases of many women, to find spouses and through them a higher standard of living. But rarely does he become a Muslim by physical force. The Muslim explanation is that by accepting Islam, the Kafir learns to lead a cleaner, more moral, and better physical life in this world besides escaping from the threat of eternal damnation in the next.

According to a folk tale, the Kalash believe they are descended from a son and daughter of Adam and Eve. When mankind was being settled they were sent to a legendary land, Tsiam. But they yearned for their own land. They objected and were returned to Kafiristan which God had reserved for himself because of its beauty. In their songs, they still sing of the Tsiam they abandoned.

The Kafirs are an ancient race. Professor Morgenstierne in 1929 was given a genealogical charter by a religious leader which traced ascendants to 54 generations, three to four centuries before Islam. They have memories of having ruled vast tracts in this area.

The Kalash live in three high valleys, difficult of access, Bumboret, Birir, and Rumboor, jointly called Kafiristan. They are part of Chitral, the northern-most district of Pakistan. Chitral is one of the most inaccessible districts of Pakistan. For about six months the Lowari Pass, over 10,000 feet, over which passes the only road to the rest of Pakistan, is closed. This inaccessibility has reinforced the isolation of Kafiristan.

Kalash religion, customs, and social life differ radically from that of their Islamic neighbours who surround them on all sides. Wine festivals, blood sacrifices, wooden effigies, sexually promiscuous behaviour during certain rites, and communal dancing are anathema to Muslims. Kipling's *'The man who would be king'* contains a garbled version of the *bodalak* institution which centred on the rite of selecting the fittest male of the tribe, feeding and caring for him, and then allowing him to cohabit for a brief period with any number of women to improve the stock. Kipling was apparently inspired by the supposed travels of Gardner in Kafiristan, and his information that in 1770, two Europeans lived among and were eventually killed by the Kafirs. Appropriately, Sean Connery and Michael Caine played the two adventurers in the film.

In their black ankle-length dresses, and a head dress with cowrie-shells on it, the Kalash women remain distinct. However, the men have begun to wear clothes worn by their Muslim neighbours. The local Kalash have also adopted Muslim names—Saifullah Jan and Abdul Khaliq. Their speech, too, is punctuated by modern Urdu and Persian idioms. Many men are only to be distinguished by the feathers or ornaments they wear in their caps. These were once a symbol of their traditional animosity with the Muslims. Traditionally, the right to wear a feather was conferred by the tribe on those who killed a Muslim.

In the early seventies, the Prime Minister of Pakistan, Mr. Zulfikar Ali Bhutto, visited Bumboret and was enchanted by the Kalash for which they still honour his memory. He expressed positive discrimination towards the Kalash, much to the chagrin of the *sheikhs*. He wished to preserve them and their culture. A jeepable road, the first, to be built in to Bumboret, was ordered by him. This brought a flood of visitors. The density of visitors to native population is probably among the highest in the world including the obligatory Japanese anthropologist and Cambridge female undergraduates in Kalash dresses, gone quite native.

The material life of the Kalash is extremely poor. Hygiene, education, balanced diet, and medical facilities are almost absent. There is no electricity in the valleys. The average Kalash looks far older than his or her years. Added to this are the formidable social, and psychological pressures resulting from being viewed as 'dirty' non-believers, by aggressive and powerful neighbours. They now speak of their festivals and customs with ambiguity—racial pride clashing with feeling of self-contempt. The *bodalak* institution is all but dead, the wooden effigies that guarded Kalash graves stolen, sold or destroyed, the wine festivals increasingly rare.

However, the recent media attention and sympathy of foreigners have combined with the sometimes crude, local, proselytizing efforts to spark a reaction among the Kalash. Kalash elders and leaders have mobilized their people to resist conversion to Islam and revive pride in their own customs and culture. Too much change has already taken place, they say, and cite dress, name, and customs. 'By the grace of Allah Almighty', said Saifullah, the Kalash, to me, unaware of the irony and supporting the very point he wished to reject, 'we are now resisting conversion to Islam and take pride in our culture'. In the last year or two, this campaign has effectively brought to a halt any further conversions, he claims.

Reports of the Kalash ceasing to be Kafirs by the end of the century are exaggerated. But what will become of the Kalash? Will they become part Muslim, remain part Kafirs?

Remain part myth, part real? Will they continue to reflect
the insecurity of a small threatened minority in a turbulent
part of the world?

In its commitment to Islamization, the Government of
Pakistan has not neglected its minorities. A Kalash Foundation
has been set up to assist the Kalash. This is a step in the right
direction. The Government of Pakistan, with about 90 million
Muslims in its fold, is like an elephant to the eggshell of the
4,000 Kalash and may well afford to tread softly in their
valleys. Too much pressure will simply crush them and too
little allow the locals to do the same. The Kafirs have for a
thousand years seen one, the aggressive, face of Islam.
Conquerors have used the sword, priests hurled threats. But
there are other faces of Islam, too. These are represented by
Sufi masters and sages, gentle and wise, believing in *sulh-i-kul,*
peace with all, who preferred to live further south, across the
river Indus, where greater numbers awaited conversion. For
them, of the 99 great names and attributes of Allah, the two
greatest are — the Beneficient and the Merciful. They are also
the most used. Perhaps, their application by Muslims would
be the most humane answer to the Kalash problem.

3

Mor and *Tor*:
Binary and Opposing Models of
Pukhtun Femalehood

This chapter briefly outlines the position of women in Pukhtun tribal society. The data are derived from fieldwork in the North-West Frontier Province of Pakistan among the Mohmand clans living in the Mohmand Agency in the Tribal Areas (where the ordinary criminal, civil, and revenue laws of the land do not apply) and in Peshawar District (subject to the laws of the land) in 1975-6. The former are referred to as Tribal Area Mohmands, TAM, and the latter as Settled Area Mohmands, SAM.

Pukhtuns constitute 90 per cent to 95 per cent of the total population of the Tribal Areas of the North-West Frontier Province. It is a man's world. The direct laudatory equivalent to *Pukhto* is *saritob*, 'manhood' or 'honour'. Descent is reckoned through male ascendants; residence after marriage is virilocal, preferred marriages are to patrilateral parallel cousins. The Pukhtun's honour is tied to that of his women who exist to serve him and be loyal to his cause. Under Pukhtun custom (*riwaj*), women inherit no land. However deviant from the ideal type, Pukhtuns will not compromise their concept of women: until recently the Bela Mohmandan SAM elders refused to accept a girls' primary school in their village. Ideal women learn only to run a household. Paradoxically the most fanatic supporters of *Pukhtunwali,* the Code of the Pukhtuns, appear to be women. In this couplet a woman exhorts her male to uphold *Pukhtunwali* at the cost of his life and her happiness:

Go to war and become a martyr and then
I shall spread out my best shawl upon your shrine.

(*Enevoldsen*: 63)[1]

Such female literary emotions are translated into fierce inter-
necine conflicts.

Ideally women are conceptualized as forming two opposite
and polar models. *Mor*, the mother, on the one hand, with
emotive echoes from the common saying of the Prophet of
Islam that heaven lies beneath the feet of the mother. On the
other hand, where her chastity has been compromised and
the honour of her close agnatic kin — father, husband or
brothers — is at stake, she is considered in a state of *tor*,
literally black. Colour symbolism is a universal tribal
phenomenon[2] and among the Pukhtuns black symbolizes the
colour of death, evil, and negativity while white symbolizes
purity and goodness. Empirically, *tor* cases almost always
approximate to the ideal type model where both actors, but
especially the woman, are killed by the closest male kin, as
the two case-studies below show. However, the actual *mor*
model deviates considerably from the ideal. Life for women
is physically hard and monotonous, as is shown by the prototype daily timetables we recorded for Mohmand women.
Women cook meals, clean the house, collect water, feed and
milk animals, besides performing other normal duties such as
caring for children etc., and they also help in harvesting and
threshing crops. We recorded over a fortnight the detailed
daily movements of certain TAM and SAM families stratified
by lineage, occupation, and status, and selected at random
(Chart 3.1). Clearly women may be idealized as *mor* or
mother, implying high status and position in society, but
their daily lot is a hard and exhausting one.

Perhaps their lot is best summed up in the proverb which
places them either in the house (*kor*) or the grave (*gor*): 'For
a woman either the house or the grave'.[3] Men admit in private
that the life of a woman is hard: 'the lot of women is miser-
able, they are helpless'—(*khazay ajaz qam day, be wasa de*).

Women are excluded from traditional and central prestige-
conferring Pukhtun institutions such as the council of elders

(*jirga*); the village guest rooms (*hujra*); the war party (*lakhkar*); or the sectional clan chieftanship (*maliki*). They are even excluded from certain rights accorded to them by Islam: for instance, they are given in marriage without their consent, they cannot claim any form of divorce compensation (*haq mehr*); there is no written marriage contract, they cannot own or inherit any land or, in any case, and under any conditions, divorce their spouse. 'One who has divorced his woman' (*zantalaq*) is a term of abuse. A divorced woman would threaten the rigid norms of chastity and the woman risks the label of *tor* and therefore would be liable to be killed. There

Chart 3.1: A Typical Day for Women from Different Social Categories

Time	Mrs. A (senior lineage)	Mrs. B (junior lineage)	Mrs. C (craftsmen)
*sahar** 6-8 a.m.	5.30. pray; make tea; wash dishes; sweep house and cattle shed (*ghojal*); feed cattle; chop wood; milk goats	5.30. pray; warm water for ablution; make tea; clean *ghojal*; chop wood; milk goats, feed buffaloes	5 a.m. pray; warm water; milk goat for tea; make tea; chop wood; clean *ghojal*; feed cattle, send them out
*dodai*** 11-1 p.m.	Water from village well; cook lunch	Tend to old mother-in-law; wash clothes; cook lunch	Water from well; put bed and quilts in sun to kill bed bugs; beat quilts and beds; cook lunch
*maspakhin** 1-4 p.m.	2-3 wash family clothes; make tea; knead flour	Daughter visits as fought with in-laws; accompany her to patch up; make tea	Make tea; knead flour; bring in beds
*mazigar** 4-6 p.m.	Cook dinner; milk goats	Knead flour; milk goats; cook dinner	Knead flour; cook dinner
*makham** 6-7 p.m.	Dinner	Tend to cattle; dinner	Bring in and pen animals; dinner
*maskhotan** 7 p.m.	Make beds for children; listen to *Pukhto* programme on radio; 9.30 p.m. sleep	Warm sand (*takor*) to warm bed for mother-in-law; sleep 8 p.m.	Pray; sleep by 9 p.m.

  * vernacular terms for the 'divisions of the day'.
** vernacular term for 'meal'.

was not a single example of a Pukhtun divorced woman in our field work area.

Chastity and seclusion of women are two laws rigidly observed by society. The penalty for deviance is extreme. They are secluded from social life. They rarely, if ever, go to the market. Men shop and provide household necessities. Women usually visit their own lineages and are acutely aware of the principle of unilineal descent in society and repeat: 'we are descended from one ancestor' (*mong the yaw baba awlad you*). If women frequent a path to the well, it becomes 'private' or 'women's path' (*de zanana lar da*). Men are supposed to avoid using it especially during the hours women use it. Women congregate at the well to gossip and exchange notes. *Mazigaray* is the word used to describe women going to the well to collect water and sitting down for gossip.

The following are two *tor* cases illustrating its operative principles in society. The first took place in the Tribal Areas and the second in the Settled Area. The severity of the first case contrasts with the second case in which the male escapes after payment of 'shame compensation' (*uzar*).

A Pukhtun married couple D and E, arrive at Malik, A's village, as clients (*hamsaya*) seeking political refuge from agnatic rivalry (*tarboorwali*). B, A's son, begins a quiet affair with E. D reports the matter to A who arranges a feast, at the end of which he asks all present to pray. He then pulls out his revolver and empties six shots into his son B. *Pukhto* has been done. After the forty days of Islamic mourning for his son's death A calls D and gives him the same revolver and asks him to also do *Pukhto* by shooting his own wife E. D

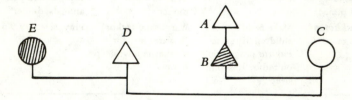

Figure 3.1: *Tor* Case One (TAM)

shoots *E. A* then declares in public that as of now *D* is his legal son and marries him to his dead son's wife *C.*

D, engaged to *B,* was picking maize in the field when *E,* a young cousin, chanced on her and while he talked to her *B* happened along and accused them of being *tor. B* complained to *A* who, with his son *C,* shot his daughter *D. E* ran away from the area and went into hiding. The elders arranged *uzar* worth rupees 1,500 so as not to split the group. *E* was later allowed to return.

The family is highly conscious that 'a female belongs to another—(her husband)'—(*khazay kho pradai de*), and is therefore a 'temporary visitor' in the home. Patriarchs rarely remember the names or the numbers of female descendants from married daughters, they simply do not exist or count in the social universe. Even their names are 'lost' and are 'anonymous', they are referred to as 'house' (*kor*), or 'family' (*bal bach*), or simply 'woman' (*khaza*). Once married, they maintain no connection with their natal kin and are tradition-bound to defend and uphold their husband's honour even to the extent of killing their own male siblings.[4]

Finally, women are literally 'sold' for a straight 'bride-price' ranging from ten to twenty thousand rupees which the father normally keeps. There is, however, a tendency to divert some of the 'bride-price' into making clothes, furniture, or jewellery for the bride especially among groups who are in contact with the more Settled Areas of the Province. The internal structure of the family presupposes from the first the existence of social rules regulating forms of marriage, filiation, and

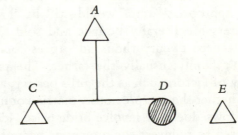

Figure 3.2: *Tor* Case Two (SAM)

residence which are required for the legitimate existence of
any family and which determine some aspects of the
'developmental cycle'.[5] Marriage is strongly endogamous and
the preferred form is to the patrilateral parallel cousins. As
Barth points out, with reference to Swat Pukhtun[6] marriage
it is possible to list six characteristics of the rites: (a) food
and services are reciprocated; (b) ceremonies are public and
well attended; (c) the scale of the ceremonies is commensurate
with wealth and rank; (d) there is a moral compulsion to
attend; (e) those who dodge this expectation advertise their
enmity; and (f) the ceremonies give men a chance to establish
political ties.[7] Barth is also correct in saying that marriage is
seen as the most significant rite in society as, for instance,
funerals are among the Giriama.[8] The most popular season
for marriages is spring when the weather is pleasant and,
more importantly, when money from the sale of crops has
come in. Marriages never take place in the month of *Rabi-ul-
Awal*, in which the Prophet died, in *Moharram*, in which his
grandsons were martyred, or in *Ramazan*, the month of fasting.

The following three customs, embodying *Pukhto* concepts
and illustrating the strength of the 'native model' where they
clash with Islamic ones, are tacitly maintained although widely
condemned. Firstly, the un-Islamic custom which is condemned by older men (*mashar*), and by younger men (*kashar*),
alike, and is slowly but steadily losing hold, is that of 'money
for the head' (*sar paisey*) or bride-price for the girl. Anthropologists working in Africa suggested 'bride-wealth' as an
alternative term to bride-price as the latter, crudely put,
implies buying and selling. However, in the Tribal Areas the
more appropriate term would still be 'bride-price' because
daughters are literally bought and sold. The bride's father
takes ten to twenty thousand rupees for the girl from the
groom's family, usually the father. The price depends on a
variety of factors such as the girl's beauty, age, lineage, status,
and whether she was previously married or not. The remarriage
of widows does not involve bride-price. Ideally the father is
supposed to re-invest the money as part of the dowry but he

rarely does so. Bride-prices were low a century ago and 'a man wanting a hard-working, useful wife could easily procure an Afridi or Orakzai woman for a sum varying from rupees 150 to 200'.[9]

Cash and material items flow from the groom's to the bride's family in far larger sums than the amount she brings as her dowry, unlike in other societies on the subcontinent, where dowry consists of jewellery, furniture, and cash.[10] In marriage, bride-price may often be paid in instalments after the marriage (nikah) if the person is not well off. Society considers keeping a daughter at home after she is 15 or 16 a sign of disgrace. Among the Musa Khel, the Upper Mohmands, no man or woman over 25 is single.[11] However, poverty is an impediment to marriage. Zaidullah of the junior lineage in SAM, has two daughters both over 21, but as he is very poor no one is prepared to marry them or even put a minimal 'cost' on them in the form of bride-price. On the other hand Hamesh Gul, senior lineage, also has an unmarried daughter of about the same age but he will not marry her off to 'anyone' as he feels, being a member of the senior lineage, that he has not found a suitor of her status. Meraj Gul, 30 years old, a Do Khel of the junior lineage and the son of Khairaz Gul who is blind, poor, and about 70 years old, cannot find a bride as he has no money. No father is prepared to give away his daughter 'free' to him.

A TAM elder related an anecdote which illustrates why bride-price (sar paisey) is expected and taken by Mohmands. A father married his daughter 'free' and when the bridal party was returning home a stream had to be crossed. The husband made his new bride wade across it. The girl was furious and rebuked the groom saying he had no respect for her. The husband agreed. He said, 'You were given free to me. You cost me nothing'. So she returned home promptly to her father who then charged a bride-price. This time the husband arranged for her to be carried in a litter (dolai) over the stream.

Secondly, Pukhto can literally mean 'word' of honour. Most TAM marriages, highly endogamous to lineage in any case, result from mothers 'booking' a girl at birth; the 'word' is given and accepted as such by the community. The 'booking' by the boy's mother of a new-born girl is called *niwaka* and is tantamount to the formal engagement (*koidan*) often and not unnaturally of little importance in tribal society. Henceforth, the girl is considered engaged and as good as married to the boy. Violation of this verbal and informal agreement involves the entire revenge and *tor* sequence *as if* the girl were actually married. This explains why the fiancé in some of the *tor* cases we recorded took it on himself to take revenge; his fiancée was conceptualized as his wife by both him and the community. Her elopement or abduction meant dishonour for him.

The simplicity of ritual in the Tribal Areas based on *nang*, (honour) contrasts with those societies in the Settled Areas based on *qalang* (rents and taxes)[12] where marriage functions pass through complex stages involving ritual and expenditure.[13] For instance, the engagement in *nang* is an informal commitment often just the 'word', but in *qalang* it is an elaborate ceremony.[14]

Thirdly, the agreed rights of a woman under Islamic Law in the event of divorce, *haq mehr*, are never mentioned by either party, let alone claimed. Another deviance from Islamic tradition is that the formal marriage ceremony, the *nikah* is performed after the bride is brought from her natal home to the groom's house, which implicitly reflects the lower status of the 'girl-giver' and explicitly reflects the general status of women. Once at the groom's house the bride is in no position to refuse consent to the marriage. Almost all Mohmands are so married, *mashar* and *kashar*. General illiteracy reinforces ignorance of female rights. *Haq mehr* would never be given either in TAM or SAM, as divorce involves the honour of a Pukhtun, and is theoretically impossible in Pukhtun society. Although a woman has the right to divorce her husband under Islamic Law, this is a social impossibility among Pukhtuns. If she is divorced legally and married to another man she would be considered as having become *tor* and both would run the risk of being shot; the question of rights in divorce cases, therefore, remains hypothetical. As already mentioned, to our knowledge, no case has ever been recorded of a Pukhtun divorce. No Pukhtun, supremely conscious as he is of his honour being tied to that of his women, would divorce his wife.

A Pukhtun may remarry for a variety of reasons but mainly if his wife is barren, although the incidence of polygamy is low among the Mohmands being 0.4 per cent in our entire field work area. Of the total TAM males 0.6 per cent and of the SAM males 0.2 per cent were polygamous with two or, in very rare cases, more living wives. We may conclude that Mohmand society is largely monogamous.

It has been shown[15] that endogamy is more prevalent among Muslim tribal societies than among non-tribals. Endo-gamous family marriages of tribals were as high as 71 per cent and contrasted with 37 per cent for non-tribal families, while non-tribal village endogamy was 78 per cent, almost as high as for tribal village endogamy, 80 per cent.[16] These figures illuminate the significance of the highly endogamous nature of the Mohmand where marriages are entirely endogamous to the clan. Barth makes a valid point that among tribal groups there is a political emphasis in contracting marriages and in the non-tribal areas there is an economic emphasis on marriage. However, our own data does not testify to this as, in fact, both TAM and SAM, in spite of the latter's encapsulated condition and dependence on agriculture, remain highly endogamous. TAM marriages may emphasize political alliances that cover a wider geographical and genealogical span, but, they are nonetheless highly endogamous.

Our findings corroborate those for the Swat Pukhtuns. 'In contrast to what is found in some other lineage-based societies in the Middle East,[17] marriages are rarely sought with close agnatic collaterals. Several Pukhtun chiefs volunteered reasons for this. 'Marriage with the father's brother's daughter, they said, is known as a device for preventing conflict between agnatic cousins, but is never very successful . . . It is better to use the marriage of daughters and sisters to establish contacts or reaffirm alliances with persons of similar political interests to one's own; then one will be strong in the inevitable conflicts with close agnates'.[18] However, it is important to point out that Pukhtun girls are seldom, if ever, 'given' in such marriages although non-Pukhtun women are 'taken' in marriage into the Pukhtun group.

The following are two examples of typical Mohmand marriages and expenditures incurred (Table 3.1). Fanzoon's (senior lineage) future father-in-law, Sobat, took rupees 2,000 for the girl but spent most of it on her future domestic needs such as crockery, quilts, etc. Arabistan (service group) paid no *sar paisey* but it was understood that he would be compensating by excessive expenditure on gold, furniture etc., for the girl, as in theory the *sar paisey* is to be spent by the father on the girl's material needs in her future home. Engagement (*koidan*) expenditure has been included in the list. *Koidan* is traditionally a simple and informal affair. Usually clothes given would include six or eight unstitched suits of clothing (*kames-partog*), vests, socks, slippers, mirror, combs, soap, bangles, towels, cots, quilts, a tin box, and perhaps a cupboard. Nowadays cosmetics like lipstick and

Table 3.1: **Marriage Expenditure** (in rupees)

	Fanzoon (senior lineage)		Arabistan (barber-service group)	
1. *Sar paisey* (bride-price)		2,000		
2. Groom provides	4 *tolas* gold	2,460	5 *tolas* gold	3,355
	clothes, etc.	1,000	clothes, etc.	3,500
3. Food, *dodai*		1,185		3,680
4. Extras	relatives and occupational groups	200		1,200
5. Transport				560
Total		6,845		12,295

powder may also be expected; extras would be a standard meal of rice. If the groom is poor, as in Fanzoon's case, rice would be of low quality, but if he is better off as in Arabistan's case, then better rice cooked in vegetable oil is served. Chicken and meat are cooked by senior Maliks but few people can afford such items. There is no custom of serving sweetmeats or fruit following the simple meal of rice and vegetable oil. Guests may number between 1,500 to 2,000 and take turns to eat in groups at the groom's house.

The examples illustrate two points, one social and the other economic: marriages, like the other social rites of all groups, follow an identical pattern and, secondly, the average economic standard of the occupational groups *vis-a-vis* Pukhtun groups is reflected in the comparative expenditures above. Although this should not be taken as an absolute comparison, the barber's expenditure is almost double that of a member of the senior lineage. Haji Gul, the father of Arabistan, has recently returned from employment in Iran and is said to have brought back some 40,000 rupees.

The generalized and traditional movement of connubial investments is depicted graphically in Figure 3.3 and the numbers relate to items in Table 3.1: bride-price (1) and

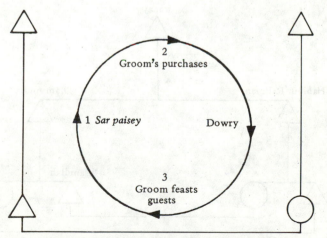

Figure 3.3: Pattern of Marriage Expenditure

groom's purchases (2) which may be utilized as 'dowry' by the girl's father. In TAM the father usually keeps almost the entire *sar paisey* and sends his daughter with very little to her future home. Expenditure is almost entirely borne by the groom's family. Of all the *rites de passage* marriage is the most expensive and elaborate. Birth, circumcision, and death involve a certain amount of expenditure on food cooked for guests and payments made to members of occupational groups, but come nowhere near marriage expenditure: average expenditure for birth and circumcision amount to between rupees 500 to rupees 1,000 and death to about rupees 1,000 to 1,500. Marriage is the best illustration of Veblen's 'conspicuous consumption' and show of status among the Mohmand. Needless to say, economic and social strength and the desire to display them determine the quality of the feast and the quantity of guests involved in the rites and vary from individual to individual.

Two typical examples of exchange (*badal*) marriages from the senior lineage are given here. The first is the most common and typical example of a simple *badal* marriage where two brothers exchange sons and daughters. No *sar paisey* or other

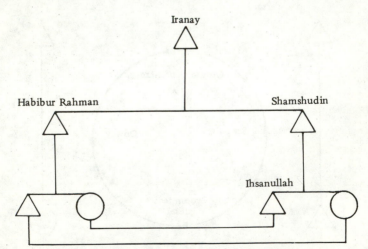

Figure 3.4.a: Exchange *(Badal)* Marriages

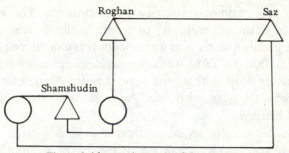

Figure 3.4.b: Exchange *(Badal)* Marriages

elaborate costs are involved. As Ihsanullah, son of Shamshudin, the elder of the SAM village, was marrying his father's brother's daughter (Figure 3.4.a) and as part of a *badal* marriage, there was no bride-price; however, each father still spent about rupees 7,000 to 8,000 for the food for guests, crockery, cots, quilts, etc. *Badal* marriages, like Ihsanullah's, usually take place on the same day.

Not all *badal* marriages are straightforward brother-sister exchanges; some involve more complex relationships. For instance, Saz marries Shamshudin's sister and Shamshudin, in exchange, marries Saz's brother's daughter (Figure 3.4.b). These intermarriages can be acutely awkward and complicate matters in intense cases of agnatic rivalry.

Levirate is more common in TAM than SAM and one of the only two examples of it in SAM was when Dawai Khan married the wife, who had already two little daughters, of his father's dead brother Munawar Khan (Figure 3.5). Such a

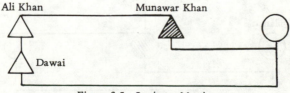

Figure 3.5: Levirate Marriage

marriage is considered socially homogamous. The *nikah* is performed without ceremony or guests in the evening and the marriage passes quietly and unnoticed. It is considered entirely a family affair. In TAM levirate marriages are more common. For instance Haji Abbas, the son of Sultan Jan, married his dead brother's wife who had two children from her first husband Karim.

Another example which indicates deviance from *Pukhto* endogamy and also hypogamy as it meant the woman 'leaving' the lineage geographically and genealogically for a home in Peshawar is the marriage of the wife of Hussain's dead brother to a man from Peshawar. The community disapproved and felt she should have married Hussain or another agnate.

An example of sororate marriage in SAM involved Shamshudin's first cousin, Saida Jan who married his dead wife's sister, both patrilateral parallel cousins. Another instance of sororate marriage is taken from TAM involving Shahmat of the senior lineage (Figure 3.6).

Men in formal and informal interviews were aware of such deviances from Islamic customs and condemned such practices. Nonetheless they admitted that they were helpless to change them as 'this was Pukhto custom — *riwaj*'. In an apt categorization various TAM elders described women as *khidmatgaray*, 'those who serve' a term often used for the non-Mohmand occupational group (*qasabgar*), like carpenters and barbers.

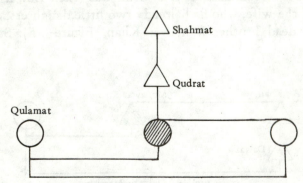

Figure 3.6: Sororate Marriage

The following two cases of deviance in marriage and inheritance are both from SAM: Shahtoota, now 60 years old, was left a widow when her husband died 30 years ago, leaving a son and daughter as babies. He had written the house in which she is now living in her name. She is one example of an unmarried widow. The norm is to 'remarry' the widow to a brother or father's brother's son, an arrangement that simultaneously satisfies the law of honour and ensures that property remains within the family. In another example, a woman inherited land from her dead husband's property. Both these examples are seen as 'deviances' from tradition and would not have been possible in TAM where Pukhtun laws are still supreme. Empirically and on the strength of the examples cited earlier women are crammed into the interstices of tribal structure with little apparent scope for roles of social importance. However, this is not entirely a correct picture.

Many women exert considerable influence on, and even dominate, their men. In theory women stand in low status but in practice they are often close and valued companions, directly affecting the lives of their men. Towards the end of our field work we saw how Hussain Khan, about 80 years old, otherwise tough and invulnerable, was a broken man when his wife died. For days on end he would not eat and would cry like a child at the slightest provocation. Sitting in the *hujra* he would repeat his life was 'over' and those around him, representing various lineages and groups, would agree that the late Mrs. Hussain was like a mother to all of them. The cause of her death heightened the sense of tragedy. Hussain's son had brought pesticides for the sugar-cane crop from the Agricultural Department and his mother, thinking it was medicine for her as she was ill at the time, drank it and died within an hour. The village elders rushed her to the dispensary in Michni and then hoped to save her life by taking her to the hospital in Peshawar, but she died in the bus. Hussain Khan was inconsolable. He constantly said, 'I'm ruined' (*gharak shom*), and that until this time at 80 he could work 'harder and better' than his sons and grandsons, but

now no longer had the willpower to carry on. He said he had
married his wife, who was 15 years younger than himself,
some 50 years ago and she was like a friend, advisor, and
comrade to him. In a similar situation, and again during our
field work, Shahmat's wife, an old and trusted companion,
died in the Tribal Areas in 1976. Shahmat suddenly seemed
to have lost the will to live and died within two weeks of her
death.

It is clear from various case-studies that we recorded that
women play an important part in upholding, interpreting,
and perpetuating the two key concepts of the Code of the
Pukhtuns (*Pukhtunwali*): agnatic rivalry, (*tarboorwali*), and
chastity of women (*tor*). It is the taunting sarcastic comments
(*peghor*) by women at the well in the afternoon in what is
called 'You said, I said' (*taa wayl ma wayl*) that triggers and
perpetuates enmities which often result in death. In a well-
known folk song a mother exhorts her son to live up to
Pukhtunwali:

> If you are not brave what are you then?
> You who sucked the breasts of a true Pukhtun mother.
> (*Enevoldsen*: 61)[19]

In various examples women have attempted to live up to
expected normative Pukhtun behaviour to the extent of
helping to commit premeditated murder of their own male
siblings in order to take revenge for agnatic killings.

The interesting question that poses itself is why women, a
group so obviously suppressed, are among the most fanatical
supporters of the Pukhtun ideology? From a Marxist view-
point it raises interesting theoretical questions. Here is an
obviously oppressed group which instead of shaking off the
shackles of bondage is in the forefront of preserving what
may be seen justifiably, through subjective criteria, as an
oppressive ideology. Perhaps the answer lies partly in their
insecurity. If they are to maintain their security and respect
in society they must then live up to the ideal concept of the
Pukhtun woman, a concept conceived by and for men. Her
main role in life appears to be to serve her husband and is

summed up in a famous proverb: 'Husband is another name for God'.[20] *Mor* and *Tor* the binary and opposing models of Pukhtun femalehood, conceptualize two forms of oppression from which there is no escape.

Finally, and with the methodology of the social sciences in mind, a focus on women may help the traditional literature to prevent what has been termed elsewhere as a 'synecdochic' approach to the subject[21] and, by correcting the imbalance, provide us with a polychromic and, as far as possible, accurate picture of social structures, groups, and systems.

NOTES

1. Enevoldsen, J., *Sound the bells, O moon, rise and shine,* University Book Agency, Peshawar, n.d., p. 63.

2. Turner, B.S., *Weber and Islam: A critical study,* Routledge and Kegan Paul, London, 1974.

3. Ahmed, A.S., *Mataloona: Pukhto proverbs,* Oxford University Press, Karachi, 1975.

4. Ahmed, A.S., *Pukhtun Economy and Society,* Routledge and Kegan Paul, London, 1980.

5. Fortes, M., 'Introduction', in *The developmental cycle in domestic groups,* Goody, J.R., (editor), Cambridge University Press, 1958; and Goody, J.R., *Domestic groups,* Reading, Massachusetts, Addison Wesley, 1972, pp. 22-8.

6. I agree with the reviewers of my previous book (op. cit., 1976) who criticized me in otherwise favourable reviews for using the term Pathan instead of Pukhtun or Pashtun. The word Pathan does not exist among Pukhto speakers and the Pukhtuns; it is an Anglo-Indian corruption. Therefore, I use the correct term in this study.

7. Barth, F., *Political Leadership among Swat Pathans,* Athlone Press, London, 1972.

8. Parkin, D.J., *Palms, wine and witnesses,* Inter-text Books, Aylesbury, Bucks, 1972.

9. *Gazetteer 1883-4, Kohat District,* Punjab Government, Calcutta, p. 63.

10. Goody, J.R., and Tambiah, S.J., *Bridewealth and Dowry,* Cambridge University Press, 1973; Lewis, O., *Village Life in Northern India: Studies in a Delhi Village,* University of Illinois Press, Urbana, 1958; and Mayer, A.C., *Caste and kinship in Central India,* Routledge and Kegan Paul, London, 1970.

11. Mohmand, J.S., *Social Organization of Musa Khel Mohmands,* M.A.thesis, University of Punjab, Pakistan, 1966.

12. Ahmed, op. cit., 1976.

13. Barth, op. cit., 1972, pp. 38-9.

14. Ibid., p. 38.

15. Barth, F., *Principles of Social Organization in Southern Kurdistan,* Universitets Etnografiske Museum Bulletin, No. 7, Oslo, 1953, Table III, p. 68.

16. Ibid.

17. Ibid.

18. Barth, op. cit., 1972, p. 40.

19. Enevoldsen, op. cit., n.d., p. 61.

20. Ahmed, op. cit., 1975, p. 32.

21. Ahmed, op. cit., 1976.

4
Death in Islam:
The Hawkes Bay Case

In this chapter I have examined the relationship between attitudes to death and the social order through a recent case-study from Pakistan — the Hawkes Bay case. Various social factors which may help to explain the incident are discussed, including tensions arising from changing contemporary values, local attitudes to leadership, and the kinship connections of the participants. The case also raises important issues about concepts of death, sacrifice, and martyrdom among Shia and Sunni Muslims, and shows how ideas about the status of the individual in the afterworld may effect social behaviour in this one. The anthropological literature on the subject is not extensive and information on Muslim societies is particularly scarce.[1]

In late February, 1983, 38 Shia Muslims entered the Arabian Sea at Hawkes Bay in Karachi in response to revelations received by one of their number. The women and children in the group, about half the number, had been placed in six large trunks. The leader of the group, Sayyed Willayat Hussain Shah, pointing his religious banner at the waves, led the procession. Willayat Shah believed that a path would open in the sea which would lead him to Basra, from where the party would proceed to Karbala, the holy city in Iraq. A few hours later, almost half the party had lost their lives and the survivors emerged in varying stages of exhaustion and consciousness.

Pakistan was astonished and agog at the incident. Religious leaders, intellectuals, and newspapers discussed the event threadbare.[2] The discussions revealed almost as much about those participating in them as they did about the incident. Some intellectuals saw the episode as evidence of 'insanity'[3] and the leaders of the group were described as 'mentally unbalanced individuals with twisted and deviant personalities, the source of death and destruction'.[4] Sunnis dismissed the matter as yet another Shia aberration from orthodox Islam. The Shias, on the other hand, pointed to the event as a confirmation of their faith.[5] Only the Shias, they argued, were capable of such extreme devotion, of such a sacrifice. It was, undoubtedly, a case rooted in Shia mythology, which pre-conditioned the community to respond to, and enact, the drama. The Shia in our case lived in Chakwal Tehsil, in Punjab.[6]

Chakwal Tehsil

Willayat Shah's family lived in a small village, Rehna Sayyedan, about 10 miles from Chakwal Tehsil in District Jhelum. Located on the main Grand Trunk Road, Jhelum is about 70 miles from Chakwal Tehsil. A population of about 250,000 live there. Chakwal and Jhelum are rainfed agricultural areas, unlike the canal colonies in Punjab — Lyallpur, now Faisalabad, and Sahiwal, with rich irrigated lands. The population of the village itself is about 2,000 consisting primarily of the Sayyeds — the upper, and Arain — the lower social group. The latter are challenging the authority of the former through new channels of employment, hard work, and frugality.[7] The village is somewhat isolated from the rest of Pakistan. Electricity has only recently arrived and the road to Chakwal Tehsil is not yet metalled. This is one of the hottest areas in the country. Winters are short and the rainfall is unreliable. Poor harvests have pushed people off the land to look for employment outside Chakwal Tehsil. Many have joined the armed services — the district is a rich recruiting ground for the Pakistan Army. From the sixties, the Arab states offered opportunities for employment. Willayat Shah, after his service as a junior officer in the Pakistan Air Force, left to work in Saudi Arabia. He returned to Pakistan in 1981 after a stay of four years.

Rehna Sayyedan is self-consciously religious. Its very name announces a holy lineage, that of the Sayyeds, the descendants of the Holy Prophet, and means 'the abode of the Sayyeds'. Many of the Shia actors in the drama bear names derived from members of the Holy Prophet's family: Abbass and Hussain for men, and Fatima for women. But there is tension in the area between Shia and Sunni, a tension made more acute by the fact that their members are equally balanced. The economic subordination of the Sunni by the Shia reinforces the tension. Conflict between Shia and Sunni easily converts into a conflict between landlord and tenant. This opposition also runs through the local administration. The local government councillor, for example, is Sunni but the village headman (*lambardar*) is Shia. Even families are divided along Shia-Sunni lines. Where individuals have changed affiliation, relationships have been severely strained. There are, as is shown in Figure 4.1, at least, four known cases of Sunni affiliation closely related to the main actor in the drama, Naseem Fatima. The tension is exacerbated by the current emphasis on Sunni forms of religion by the Government of Pakistan. The Shias, about 20 per cent of Pakistan's 90 million people, resent this emphasis. The Jamaat-e-Islami, the major orthodox Sunni political party of Pakistan, is active in the area. In the background, is the larger ideological tension between the Shias and Sunnis in Pakistan. From 1980 onwards, this tension became severe and erupted into clashes between the two, especially in Karachi. And, beyond the south-western borders of Pakistan, a vigorous Shia revivalism in Iran, has unsettled neighbouring Sunni states allied to Pakistan—like Saudi Arabia.

Willayat Shah was living in Saudi Arabia when Imam Khomeini returned to Iran at the head of his revolution in 1979. Being a devout Shia, he would have been inspired by the message and success of the Imam, but Saudi Arabia was no place to express his rekindled Shia enthusiasm.[8] He would, however, have been dreaming around the themes of the revolution: sacrifice, death, change, and martyrdom. His first act on returning home was to begin the construction of a mosque.

The Hawkes Bay Case

On 18 February 1981, Willayat Shah had been engrossed in supervising the construction of the mosque. Late that evening, Naseem Fatima, his eldest child, entered his bedroom and announced she had been visited by a revelation—*basharat*. She had heard the voice of a lady speaking to her through the walls of the house. The apprehensive father suggested she identify the voice. For the first few days, the voice was identified as that of Bibi Roqayya, close kin of Imam Hussain, the grandson of the Holy Prophet, buried in Karbala.

Some hand-prints next appeared on the wall of Willayat Shah's bedroom. They were made with henna mixed with clay. A hand-print has highly emotive significance among the Shia Muslims. It is symbolic of the five holiest people in Islam: the Holy Prophet, his daughter, Hazrat Fatima, his son-in-law, Hazrat Ali, and his grandsons, Hazrat Hassan and Hazrat Imam Hussain. The news of the hand-prints spread like wild fire in the area. The impact on the village was electric. It was described thus by an informant: 'for the next fifteen days or so the usual business of life came to a halt. People gave up their work, women even stopped cooking meals. Everyone gathered in the house of Willayat Hussain to see the print, to touch it, to pray, and to participate in the mourning (*azadari*) which was constantly going on'.[9] The *azadari*, a recitation of devotional hymns and poems in honour of, in particular, Hazrat Hussain, was a direct consequence of the hand-prints. It created a highly charged and contagious atmosphere among the participants.

Sunnis, however, were cynical about the whole affair. They would remain adamant opponents of Naseem's miracles (*maujza*). Opinion was divided among the Shia Muslims. Established families like the Sayyeds scoffed at Naseem and her miracles and, at first, both Willayat Shah and his daughter had their doubts. As if to dispel these doubts Imam Mahdi, or Imam-e-Ghaib, the twelfth Imam, himself appeared in the dreams of Naseem. Earlier, Bibi Roqayya had announced that the Imam rather than she would communicate with Naseem. The Imam wore white clothes and was of pleasing appearance.[10] All doubts in her mind were now dispelled and he addressed her as *Bibi Pak* — pure lady.

.The Imam, with whom she now communicated directly, began to deliver explicit orders (*amar*). One commanded the expulsion of the carpenter who was working for Willayat in his house[11] and who had overcharged him by a thousand rupees, in connivance with the contractor. He was ordered never to work at a Sayyed's house again, or both would be losers in the transaction. To compensate Willayat, the Imam placed five hundred rupees in a copy of the Holy Quran and ordered the carpenter to pay the remaining five hundred. The orders increased in frequency. They soon included matters of property and marriage. The family, at least, no longer doubted the miracles. They obeyed the divine orders without question. During the revelations, Naseem would demand complete privacy in her room. Her condition would change. She would quiver and tremble. Noises would sound in her head beforehand and the trauma of the revelations often caused her to faint afterwards. The orders would come to her on the days the Imams died or were made martyrs. 'The Imam', according to her father, 'had captured her mind and heart'.[12]

Local Shia religious leaders and lecturers (*zakirs*) acknowledged Naseem and visited her regularly. Of the three most regular visitors one, Sakhawat Hussain Jaffery, was particularly favoured. Naseem claimed that she had been especially ordered by the Imam to single him out. They were often alone for long periods. Naseem began to organize *azadari* regularly. These meetings were charged with emotion and created devout ecstasy in the participants. They were held next to the local primary school. Many people attended, with such noisy devotion, that the school had to close down. Naseem now completely dominated the life of the village. Before moving to the next phase of the case, let us pause to examine the effect of the revelations on some of the main actors in the drama.

Naseem was a shy, pleasant looking girl, with an innocent expression on her face, who had a history of fits. There was talk of getting her married. Although she had only studied up to class five, her teachers recall her passionate interest in religion, especially in the lives of the Imams. She had a pleasing voice when reciting *nauhas* or poems about Karbala, many of which she composed herself. After her revelations there was a perceptible change in Naseem. She began to gain weight, wear costly dresses, and perfumes. She became noticeably gregarious and confident. In a remarkable gesture of independence, especially so for a Sayyed girl in the area, she abandoned the *parda* or veil. According to Shia belief, any believer may become the vehicle for divine communication. Naseem turned to the dominant person in her life, her father, upon receiving communications and he interpreted them in his own light.

Willayat Shah, about fifty, strong and domineering, now reasserted himself in village affairs after an absence of years. His daughter's religious experience had begun soon after his retirement from Arabia. He had an older brother to whom, because of the traditional structure of rural society, he was subordinate. His period in Saudi Arabia had enhanced his economic, but not his social position. Because of the miracles and revelations of his daughter, however, he gained a dominant position in the social life of the area. Sardar Bibi, Naseem's mother, was dominated by her husband and daughter and identified wholly with the latter. She was said to have been a Sunni before her marriage and this created an underlying tension in the family. In an expression of loyalty to her husband, she severed relations with her parents and brothers because they disapproved of her conversion. She obeyed her daughter's revelations blindly.

Another actor in the drama was Sakhawat Jaffery, a *zakir* of Chakwal Tehsil. He was not a Sayyed and his father was said to be a butcher. He had thus risen in the social order. Willayat Shah rewarded him for his loyalty with gifts — refrigerators, televisions, fans, etc. When he needed money for a new business he was presented with about 20,000 rupees. With this sum, he opened a small shop selling general goods. He was given such gifts on the specific orders of the Imam to Naseem. In turn, he was the only one of the three *zakirs* who personally testified to the authenticity of the miracles of Naseem. Naseem was regularly visited by Sakhawat Jaffery and she reciprocated. In a gesture of affection, contravening social custom, Naseem named Sakhawat's male child, a few months old, Rizwan Abbass. Such names, deriving from the Holy Prophet's family, were traditionally reserved for Sayyeds.

Most people were cynical about the relationship between Naseem and the *zakir*. Sakhawat's own wife, who had complete faith in Naseem, said people had spread 'dirty talk' (*gandi batey*) about Naseem and her husband.[13] In spite of his belief in the revelations, Sakhawat Jaffery did not join the pilgrimage to Hawkes Bay. He had recently opened his shop and explained that abrupt departure would ensure its failure. Naseem was understanding: 'this is not a trip for *zakirs*. We want to see you prosper'.[14]

After the visions, Naseem's followers bestowed on her the title already used by the Imam, *Pak Bibi,* or pure lady. The transformation in her appearance and character was now complete. She radiated confidence. Her following spread outside the village. In particular, she developed an attachment with the people of a neighbouring village, Mureed, who were recently converted Muslims — *sheikhs,* and who whole-heartedly believed in her. Most of them were *kammis,* belonging to such occupational groups as barbers and cobblers. Naseem, as a Sayyed, represented for them the house of the Prophet while her father, being relatively well off, was a potential source of financial support. Seventeen of the villagers of Mureed would follow her to Hawkes Bay.

The normal life of the village was disrupted by the affair. The Shia Muslims, in particular, 'whole-heartedly accepted the phenomenon' but, not unnaturally, 'the regular routine life of the village was paralysed'. In particular, 'women stopped doing their household jobs'.[15] Some placed obstacles in Naseem's path, teasing her family members, especially children on their way to school, and dumping rubbish in front of her house. The Sayyeds who did not believe in her ill-treated her followers from Mureed.

Meanwhile, a series of miracles was taking place which riveted society. Blood was found on the floor of Willayat Shah's bedroom. Naseem declared this to be the blood of Hazrat Ali Asghar, the male child of Hazrat Hussain, martyred at Karbala. On another occasion, visitors were locked in a room and told that angels would bear down a flag from heaven. When the door was opened, indeed, there was a flag. On one occasion four children disappeared, to appear again later. But the greatest miracle of all remained Naseem's constant communication with the Imam. Supplicants would pray in front of Naseem's room, expressing their demands in a loud voice. The Imam would be consulted not only on profound matters but also on trivial ones, such as whether a guest should be given tea or food. Naseem, who received many of her orders during fainting fits, would then convey a reply on behalf of the Imam.

There came a time, however, when Naseem's authority was disputed. Doubts arose first from the failure of certain of her predictions and, second, from the public refusal of her kin to redistribute their property according to her orders. Naseem had been making extravagant predictions regarding illness, birth, and death. Some of these came true, others did not. In one particular case, she predicted the death of a certain person within a specified period. He did not die. In another case, the elder brother of Willayat was asked to surrender his house for religious purposes which he refused to do. A cousin also refused when asked to hand over his property to Willayat. In yet another case Naseem, perhaps compensating for a Sunni mother in a Shia household, ordered the engagement of her cousin to a non-Shia to be broken – it was not.

Naseem and Willayat responded to such rebellion with fierce denunciation. The rebels were branded as *murtid,* those who have renounced Islam and are, therefore, outside the pale. Their relatives were forbidden to have any contact with them. In some cases, parents were asked not to see their children and vice versa. While taking firm measures against those who did not believe, the followers were charged with renewed activity, calculated to reinforce group cohesiveness. The frequency of religious meetings increased as did visits to shrines. Participation was limited to believers.

Naseem's physical condition now began to correspond with the revelations – she lost weight and her colour became dark when she was not receiving them, she glowed with health when she was. People freely equated her physical appearance with her spiritual condition. She lost *noor,* divine luminosity, in her periods of despondency, and regained it when receiving revelations. For her believers, it was literally a question of light and darkness. But the crisis in Naseem was reaching its peak; so was the tension in the community.

Exactly, two years after the first communication began, Naseem asked her father a question on behalf of the Imam: would the believers plunge into the sea as an expression of their faith? The question was not figurative. The Imam meant it literally. The believers were expected to walk into the sea from where they would be miraculously transported to Karbala in Iraq without worldly means. Naseem promised that even the 124,000 prophets recognized by Muslims would be amazed at the sacrifice.[16]

Those who believed in the miracles immediately agreed to the proposition. Willayat was the first to agree: he would lead the party.[17] There was no debate, no vacillation. They would walk into the sea at Karachi, and their faith would take them to the holy city of Karbala. Since the revelations began, Willayat had spent about half a million rupees and had disposed of almost all his property. He now quickly disposed of what remained to pay for the pilgrimage. The party consisted of 42 people, whose ages ranged from 80 years to 4 months. Seventeen of them were from Mureed and most of the remaining were related (Figure 4.1). Willayat, his brother and cousin, distributed all their belongings, retaining one pair of black clothes, symbolic of mourning, only. They hired trucks to take them to Karachi. With them were six large wooden and tin trunks. They also took with them the Shia symbols of martyrdom at Karbala: *alam* (flag), *taboot* (picture of the mourning procession), *jhola* (swing), and *shabi* (picture of the holy images).

Stopping over at shrines for prayers in Lahore and Multan, they arrived in Karachi on the third day. Karachi was in the throes of anti-government demonstrations and the police had imposed a curfew. The tension in the city directly reflected the conflict between Shia and Sunni Muslims in Pakistan. In spite of this, the party was not stopped as they made their way to Hawkes Bay. For them this was another miracle.[18] At Hawkes Bay, the party offered two prayers, *nafil*, and read ten *surahs* from the Holy Quran, including *al-Qadr*, an early Meccan *surah*, which states 'the Night of Destiny is better than a thousand months'.[19] The verse was well chosen—for the party, it was, indeed, the night of destiny.

The Imam then issued final instructions to Naseem. The women and children were to be locked in the six trunks, and

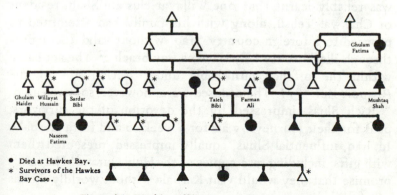

Figure 4.1: Kinship Affiliations of Naseem Fatima

the virgin girls were to sit with her in one of them. Willayat was asked to hold the *taboot* along with three other men. Willayat's cousin, Mushtaq, was appointed chief (*salar*) of the party. He was ordered to lock the trunks, push them into the sea, and throw away the keys. He would then walk into the water with an *alam*.

At this stage four young people from Mureed, two men and two girls, became frightened. This fear, too, 'was put in their hearts by the Imam'.[20] Naseem, therefore, willingly exempted them from the journey. The remaining 38 entered the sea. Mothers saw children, and children saw old parents, descending into the dark waters. But there 'were no *ah* (cries) or *ansoo* (tears)'.[21] Those in five out of the six trunks died. One of the trunks was shattered by the waves and its passengers survived. Those on foot also survived; they were thrown back on to the beach by the waves. The operation which had begun in the late hours of the night was over by early morning when the police and the press reached Hawkes Bay. The survivors were in high spirits—there was neither regret nor remorse among them. Only a divine calm, a deep ecstasy.

The Karachi police in a display of bureaucratic zeal arrested the survivors. They were charged with attempting to leave the country without visas. The official version read: 'The Incharge, FIA Passport Cell, in an application filed in the court said, it was reliably learnt that one Willayat Hussain Shah, resident of Chakwal Tehsil, along with his family had attempted to proceed to a foreign country 'Iraq' without valid documents through illegal route i.e., Hawkes Bay beach'.[22] The act came within the offence punishable under section 3/4 of the *Passport Act 1974*. The accused were, however, soon released.

Rich Shias, impressed by the devotion of the survivors, paid for their journey by air for a week to and from Karbala. In Iraq, influential Shias, equally impressed, presented them with gifts, including rare copies of the Holy Quran.[23] Naseem's promise that they would visit Karbala without worldly means was fulfilled.

Social Change, Leadership, and Kinship in Chakwal Society

In an attempt to find a sociological explanation of the Hawkes Bay case, I shall begin by putting forward a thesis based on the *Dubai chalo*, 'let us go to Dubai', theme in Pakistan society.[24] Briefly, the thesis suggests that Pakistani workers, returning from Arab lands with their pockets full of money, are no longer prepared to accept the *status quo* of the social order from which they had escaped. The returnees demand more social status and authority in society. In their own eyes, they have earned the right to be respected by their long and usually hard periods abroad. But they may have little idea how exactly to go about changing society, or even whether they wish to move it 'forward' or back to older, more traditional, ways. Their new social confidence, backed by economic wealth and combined with frustration at the slow pace of change, may result in tension and dramatic developments of which the Hawkes Bay case is an example.

Consider Willayat Shah. Belonging to the junior lineage of a Shia family and with a Sunni wife, he escaped to Arabia determined, it may be assumed, to make good on his return. After four hard years there, he returned with considerable wealth, but society had remained the same and there was no perceptible change in his social position. Willayat's immediate family were acutely aware of his predicament. His closest child and eldest daughter, fully grown and intelligent, and herself under pressure to get married, responded to the crisis in their lives with a series of dramatic, divine pronouncements. In her case, social crisis had triggered psychological reactions. The revelations were calculated to disturb the social equations of the village forever. Naseem dominated not only the social but also, and more importantly for the family, the religious life of the area. Willayat Shah had finally arrived. Both he and Naseem now reached out towards the better, truer world that, for Muslims, lies beyond death. Through their deaths they would gain an ascendancy which would be final and unassailable. They would triumph through the Shia themes of death, martyrdom, and sacrifice.

For the actors in our case, society provided the stress but failed to suggest cures. We know that at least four individuals closely related to the key actor, Naseem, suffered from tension due to mixed loyalties in the Shia-Sunni line up: her grandmother, her mother, her uncle, and her aunt's husband were rumoured to have been Sunni in the past. It was known that her grandmother's family were Sunni. By assuming the role of Shia medium, Naseem was socially compensating for the Sunni connections in her family. Under such complex pressures, religion is the most convenient straw to clutch. The stress thus assumes a form of illness, but the illness is both mental and physical and 'in its expression culturally patterned'.[25] One must look for cultural acts and symbolic forms which have local significance, including sacrifice and martyrdom. This case is certainly patterned by the religious sociology of Chakwal Tehsil.

Willayat Shah compared the sacrifice of his family to that of Karbala because 'he and his group had been assigned a duty to save the religion and the faith'.[26] In an interview given to Tariq Aziz, on Pakistan Television, he explained why Karachi was selected. He could have died in a pond in the village, he said. But the world would not have known of their faith. The prediction of his daughter had indeed come true. The world was amazed at the miracle of Hawkes Bay and people would talk of them as martyrs forever. Throughout the interviews he remained proud and unrepentant. His perception of those hours at Hawkes Bay are revealing. He 'insisted that he had been walking on the sea all the while like a truck driving on flat road'.[27] He felt no fear, no regret. Most significantly, he remained convinced that the revelations would continue, even after the death of Naseem, through a male member of the family.[28] Willayat's wife, Sardar Bibi, reacted with a fervour equal to that of her husband. 'If the Imam tells us to sacrifice this baby too', she said, pointing to an infant she was feeding during an interview, 'I'll do it'.[29]

Willayat's eldest sister, Taleh Bibi, divorced and living with her brother, lost one daughter in the incident. She herself survived because she was in the trunk that did not sink. She, too, believes the miracle will continue through a male member of their family. In relation to the Islamic concept of death, it is significant that she had mixed feelings about her own survival. Although relieved to be alive, and although she gives this as another proof of the miracle, she is nonetheless envious of those who died and thereby gained paradise.

Was the psychological condition of Naseem cause or effect of her religious experience? We know that her peculiarities of temperament became acceptable after the revelations. Her fits, her rapture, her ecstasy, now made sense. She was touched by the divine. Even her acts defying tradition in Chakwal Tehsil — such as abandoning the veil or being alone with a man — expressed her transcendent independence. Examples of trance, spirit possession, and ecstatic behaviour have been recorded among Muslim groups from the Turkmen[30] to the Baluch.[31] It is commonplace that highly gifted but disturbed individuals adapt religious idioms to consolidate their social position or to dominate their social environment. Women have heard voices before, all over the world. Joan of Arc's voices advised her to lead her nation into fighting the English. Naseem's urged her to lead her followers into the sea. In order to understand the motives of those involved in this case, we need to combine an appreciation of religious mythology with an examination of certain sociological factors. There was more than just *jazba* (ecstasy,) at work in Chakwal Tehsil. What did the followers think was awaiting them at Karachi?

Both local leadership and kinship helped to determine who would be on the beach that night. The importance of a leader in an Islamic community, Shia or Sunni, is critical. The group is judged by its leadership.[32] In different ways Willayat, Naseem, and Sakhawat Jaffery played leading parts in the drama, but we look in vain for a Savanarola figure in either Willayat or Sakhawat. Leadership was by consensus. They were all agreed upon Naseem's special role in the drama. She led, as much as she was led by, her father and the *zakir*. The followers were responding not to one leader in their immediate community but to the concept of leadership in Shia society. They were responding to symbols centuries old and emotions perennially kept alive in Shia society. What is significant is the lack of ambivalence in the majority of the followers. Even the call for the ultimate sacrifice evoked an unequivocal response among most of them. Asad's interesting question, 'how does power create religion?'[33] may, therefore, be turned around. The Hawkes Bay case provides an interesting example of how religion may create power.

Willayat Shah was a forceful person who mobilized public opinion behind his daughter. The zakirs, especially Sakhawat Jaffery, supported him and he, in turn, assisted Sakhawat Jaffery financially. Apart from assisting the zakirs, Willayat also paid sums to a variety of other people. Among the bene-ficiaries were members of the traditionally lower social class, mostly artisans, barbers, and blacksmiths. The seventeen people from Mureed who were prepared to walk into the sea were from this class. In fact, four of this group backed out at the last minute and although thirteen entered the sea, only three of them died. The people of Mureed were recent converts to Islam and, like all converts, they were eager to exhibit their religious fervour. They looked to Willayat Shah for religious and financial support. For them, he was both a Sayyed and a man of means, and they were enraptured by his daughter. Through him and his daughter, they found access to a higher social level.

Whatever the levelling effect of religion, and the loyalties it created, the Sayyeds rarely allowed their genealogy to be forgotten : the rural Punjab class structure was recognizable despite the experience at Hawkes Bay. Even in death, class distinctions remained—three of the four men who held the taboot as they stepped into the waters were Sayyeds, and the non-Sayyed was swept into the sea. Later, with a strange twist of logic, Willayat explained this by suggesting that his faith was weak.[34] His faith was weak because he was not a Sayyed, while the three Sayyeds who survived did so, because, their intentions were pure. And yet, he also argued that those Sayyeds who died did so, because, of their purity. Sayyeds, obviously, won whether the coin landed heads or tails. The Sayyeds, of course, provided Willayat's main support and many of them were his relatives. Of those who walked into the sea, twenty-five, were related (Figure 4.1). For these, Willayat was the elder of the family — father to one, brother to another, and an uncle to others. Of the eighteen who died, fifteen were his near relatives, while ten of his kin survived. Religious loyalty was, here, clearly buttressed by ties of kinship.

There was, however, structural resistance to Naseem and her revelations. The Sunni dismissed them out of hand and even the Shia were not unanimous in supporting her. The Sayyeds, senior in the Shia hierarchy, ill-treated Naseem's followers, especially the poorer ones, teased her family, and even dumped rubbish on her doorstep. The older, more established, Shia lineages felt threatened by the emergence of Naseem since she challenged their authority. Willayat's own brother, Ghulam Haider, suspected of having Sunni affiliation, kept away from the entire affair. The *zakir*, himself a close confidant and beneficiary of Naseem, but worldly wise, chose not to accompany the party on some pretext. And at the last moment, by the sea, four followers backed out. But, although there was opposition and resistance at every stage, thirty-eight people were prepared to sacrifice their lives on the basis of Naseem's commands and revelations. The explanation for their behaviour partly lies, as stated earlier, in the forces of social change, leadership, and kinship in Chakwal society. But there are also other, more ideological and mythological dimensions to consider.

Death, Sects and Women in Muslim Society

There is no substantial difference between the core theological beliefs of Shia and Sunni. Both believe in the central and

Omnipotent position of Allah and both accept the supremacy of the Holy Prophet as the messenger of Allah. The Holy Quran is revered by both as the divine message of Allah, and its arguments relating to notions of death and the afterworld are accepted by both. Discussion of death is indeed central to the Holy Quran, which has many verses on the theme that 'every soul must taste of death'.

Death in Muslim society is seen as part of a natural, pre-ordained, immutable order, as directly linked to the actions of the living and, as part of a continuing process in the destiny of the individual. Humans 'transfer' from this to the next world (the word for death in Urdu and Arabic, *inteqal*, derives from the Arabic *muntaqil* to 'transfer'). It becomes, therefore, a means to an end, 'the beginning of a journey'.[35] The Holy Quran warns 'unto Him you shall be made to return'.[36] On hearing of someone's death, a Muslim utters the words: 'from God we come, to God we shall go'. For Muslims, there is no escaping the consequences of death.[37]

In Islam—both Shia and Sunni, life and death are conceptualized as binary opposites. *Al-akhira,* the end, is the moment of truth, determining the future of a person. The individual is alone in that hour; all ties including those with parents and family are repudiated.[38] At that time, all veils between man and 'the objective moral reality will be rent'.[39] *Al-akhira* is opposed to *al-dunya,* the here and now, which may mean base pursuits. Indeed, *Alam-e-Uqba,* a popular book in Urdu on death in Islam, has sections called 'Your death is better than your living'.[40] Given the awesome facts of *al-akhira,* human beings must prepare for it in this life. Together, *al-akhira* and *dunya* are a unitary whole, the latter determining the nature of the former. Life after death is explicit in Islam and central to its theology. In a general sense, this partly explains the attitudes to death shown both in the traditional religious war, *jihad,* and in contemporary events in the Muslim world. Those who killed President Sadaat in Cairo and awaited death, like Lieutenant Islambuli, calmly, during the trials and those who died following Imam Khomeini's call in Iran, first against the Shah and later against the Iraqis, believed they were dying for a just, and Islamic, cause. Matters are complicated when *jihad* is freely translated as a struggle against any enemy, including Muslims.[41] But the problems between Shia and Sunni lie in this world and are rooted in the history, not theology, of Islam.

Islamic history, Shias maintain, began to go wrong when Hazrat Ali, married to Hazrat Fatima, daughter of the Prophet, was not made the first caliph after the death of his father-in-law. To make matters worse, Hazrat Ali was assassinated. Hazrat Ali's two sons, Hazrat Hassan and Hazrat Hussain, following in their father's footsteps, opposed tyranny and upheld the puritan principles of Islam. Both were also martyred. Hazrat Hussain was martyred, facing impossible odds on a battlefield, with his family and followers, at Karbala. Among those killed at Karbala, was Hazrat Hussain's six month old son, Hazrat Ali Asghar (who appeared to Naseem in Chakwal Tehsil). The Prophet, Hazrat Fatima, Ali, Hassan and Hussain are the five key figures for Shia theology and history. These are the *panj tan pak,* 'the pure five', of Shias in Pakistan, including those in Chakwal Tehsil. Since three of them were martyred in the cause of Islam, death, martyrdom, tears, and sacrifice form the central core of Shia mythology.[42] Members of the Shia community are expected to respond with fervour (*jazba*) to a call for sacrifice by the leadership. A sense of sectarian uniqueness, of group loyalty, faith in the leadership, readiness for sacrifice, devout ecstasy during divine ritual, characterize the community. It has been called 'the Karbala paradigm'[43] and would have been exhibited in Chakwal Tehsil.

In Pakistan today, where about 20 per cent of the 90 million population are Shias, Shia-Sunni differences can degenerate into conflict. This is especially so during *Moharram,* the ten days of Shia mourning for the events at Karbala. During this period Shias mourn, flagellate themselves, organize processions symbolic of Karbala, and recite moving poems of the tragedy at Karbala which reduce those present to tears and quivering rapture. Conflict with Sunnis is often sparked

as a result of overzealous Shias abusing figures respected by
Sunnis, such as Hazrat Umar. It was one such riot which had
paralysed Karachi when the party from Chakwal Tehsil arrived
there on its way to the Arabian Sea. Chakwal society itself is
riven with Shia and Sunni opposition which has a long and
bitter history. Local politics, marriages, and economics are
based on this opposition. Sectarian tension and loyalties also
divide families. Some of Willayat's own nearest kin were either
secret Sunnis or suspected of being sympathizers. These
divided loyalties must have led to severe tension both, for
him, and his daughter.

An appreciation of the five central figures of the Shias also
helps us to understand the role of women in that community.
The position of Hazrat Fatima is central. Her popularity
among the Shia in Chakwal Tehsil may be judged by the fact
that seven women in Willayat Shah's family carry her name.
Two of these are called Ghulam Fatima, or slave of Fatima.
Always a great favourite of her father, Hazrat Fatima provides
the link between her father and husband and between her
sons and their grandfather. The Sayyeds, those claiming
descent from the Prophet, do so through Hazrat Fatima. So
do the twelve Imams, revered by the Shia. In addition,
Fatima's mother and the Prophet's first wife, Hazrat Khadijah,
is also an object of reverence. Two other women feature in
Shia mythology, but neither is a popular figure. They are
Hazrat Ayesha and Hazrat Hafsa, both wives of the Prophet.
The reason for their unpopularity is linked to the question of
Hazrat Ali's succession. Ayesha was the daughter of Abu
Bakar and Hafsa of Umar, the two who preceded Ali as caliph.
Ayesha is singled out as she opposed Ali actively after her
husband's death.

Thus, one of the five revered figures of the Shia is a
woman. Among the Sunnis a similar listing—of the Prophet
and the first four righteous caliphs—consists entirely of
males. In other matters, too, Shia women are better off than
Sunnis. Shia women, for example, often inherit shares equal
to that inherited by male kin, whereas among educated Sunni,

women receive, at best, one half of what a male inherits. In the rural areas, they seldom inherit at all. Shia women also play a leading role in ritual. The organization of *marsyas* and *azadari*, the enactment of the death drama of Karbala, all involve the active participation of women.

Of the 18 people who died at Hawkes Bay, 10 were women, a notably large number in view of the fact that only 16 of the 42 who set out on the pilgrimage were women. Willayat Shah lost both his mother and daughter. It may be argued that the women were unequivocally committed to sacrifice. By locking themselves in trunks they had sealed their own fates. For them there was no coming back from the waves. Their sense of sacrifice and passion for the cause were supreme.

The attitudes of the two communities to the Hawkes Bay incident reveal their ideological positions. Sunnis, as we saw above, condemned the entire episode as 'bizarre' and dismissed it as 'insanity'. This, they argued, was mumbo-jumbo and quackery, and not in keeping with the logic and rationality which is Islam. For Shias all the ingredients of high devotion were amply displayed. Through it, they felt they had once again established their superior love for Islam. Here there was sacrifice, persecution, death, and martyrdom—the Shia paradigm. Educated Shia, who found it awkward to explain the Hawkes Bay case, nonetheless, applauded the *jazba* of the group. As one journalist concluded his report: 'there are millions who don't have the slightest doubt that they have demonstrated the highest degree of sacrifice by answering the call and order of the hidden Imam'[44] The idea of sacrificing life and property for Allah exists both in Shia and Sunni Islam and is supported in the Holy Quran. Sacrifice and its symbolism are part of Islamic religious culture. Ibrahim's willingness to sacrifice his son Ismail, for example, is celebrated annually throughout the Muslim world at *Eid-ul-Azha*. But for the Shias, sacrifice holds a central place in social behaviour and sectarian mythology. Here, it is necessary to distinguish between suicide—throwing away life given by God, and sacrifice—or dedication of that life to God. Suicide is a punishable offence in Islam.[45] Sunnis, therefore, seeing the deaths at Hawkes Bay as suicide, disapproved. They saw the episode as a throwing away of valuable lives, whereas Shias saw it as a sacrifice which would confirm their devotion. Willayat Shah was convinced his mission was divine and that he had proved this through a dramatic act of sacrifice. Reward, he was certain, would be paradise in the afterworld.[46] In interviews after the event, he expressed his wish to be martyred, (*shaheed*). There was no remorse; there was only *jazba*. To a remarkable degree Shia tradition, and the practice of death and sacrifice, coincided in this case. For the Shia in Chakwal Tehsil, text and practice were one.

Suffering thus became as much an expression of faith as of social solidarity. 'As a religious problem, the problem of suffering is, paradoxically, not how to avoid suffering but how to suffer, how to make of physical pain, personal loss, worldly defeat, or the helpless contemplation of others' agony something bearable, supportable—something, as we say, sufferable'.[47] Suffering, martyrdom, and death, the Karbala paradigm, create an emotionally receptive social environment for sacrifice. Death in our case, therefore, became a cementing, a defining, a status-bestowing act for the community. It consolidated the living as it hallowed the memory of the dead.

NOTES

1. See for example, Banton, M., (editor), in *Anthropological Approaches to the Study of Religion*, ASA Monograph 3, London, 1973; Bloch, M., and Parry, J., (editors), *Death and the Regeneration of Life,* Cambridge University Press, New York, 1982; Evans-Pritchard, E.E., *Witchcraft, Oracles and Magic Among the Azande,* Oxford Clarendon Press, 1937 and *Theories of Primitive Religion,* Oxford Clarendon Press, 1965; Douglas, M., (editor), *Witchcraft, Confessions and Accusations,* ASA Monograph 9, London, 1970; Geertz, C., 'Religion as a Cultural System' in *Anthropological Approaches to the Study of Religion*, Banton, M., (editor), ASA Monograph 3, London, 1973; Keyes, C.F., 'From death to rebirth; Northern Thai Conceptions of Immortality', paper presented to the Annual Meeting of the Association for Asia Studies, 1981 and 'The Interpretative basis of Depression', in *Culture and Depression,* Kleinman, A., and Good, B.J., (editors), forthcoming; Lewis, I.M., *Ecstatic Religion, an Anthropological Study of Spirit*

Possession and Shamanism, Penguin Books, 1971; Werbner, R.P., (editor), *Regional Cults,* ASA Monograph 16, Tavistock, London, 1977; and Winter, E.R., 'Territorial Groupings and Religion among the Iraqw', in *Anthropological Approaches to the Study of Religion,* Banton, M., (editor), ASA Monograph 3, London, 1973.

2. A committee was set up by Dr. M. Afzal, the Minister of Education, to examine the problem. It was chaired by Dr. Z.A. Ansari and included some of Pakistan's most eminent psychiatrists and psychologists. I represented the social scientists. See Pervez, S., *Hawkes Bay Incident: A Psycho-Social Case-study,* National Institute of Psychology, Islamabad, 1983.

3. Salahuddin, G., 'A Glimpse of our Insanity?' *The Herald,* Karachi, March 1983.

4. Irfani, S., 'From Jonestown to Hawkes Bay', *The Muslim,* March 1983.

5. Jaffery, S., 'Why didn't God take us too?' *The Herald,* Karachi, March 1983; and Yusufzai, R., 'Psychiatrists Views of Two Recent Episodes', *The Muslim,* 18 March 1983.

6. The organization of Punjab society into agricultural-peasant groups defined by ethnicity and occupation, is well-documented. See, Ahmed, op. cit., 1984, cited in chapter 1; Ahmad, S., 'Peasant Classes in Pakistan', in *Imperialism and Revolution in South Asia,* Gough, K., and Sharma, H.P., (editors), Monthly Review Press, New York, 1973 and *Class and Power in a Punjabi Village,* Monthly Review Press, New York, 1977; Alavi, H., 'Kinship in West Punjab Villages', *Contributions to Indian Sociology,* NS 6, 1972, pp. 1-27 and 'Peasant Classes and Primordial Loyalties', *Journal of Peasant Studies,* Vol. I, 1973, pp. 23-62; Balneaves, E., *Waterless Moon,* Lutherworth Press, London, 1955; Darling, M.L., *The Punjab Peasant in Prosperity and Debt,* Oxford University Press, London, 1925 and *Rusticus Loquitor,* or *The Old Light and the New in the Punjab Village,* Oxford University Press, London, 1930 and *Wisdom and Waste in the Punjab Village,* Oxford University Press, London, 1934; and Eglar, Z., *A Punjabi Village in Pakistan,* Columbia University Press, New York, 1960; Ibbetson, D.C.J., *Outlines of Punjab Ethnography, Extracts from the Punjab Census Report of 1881, Treating of Religion, Language and Caste,* Government Printing, Calcutta, 1883; and Pettigrew, J., *Robber Noblemen,* Routledge and Kegan Paul, London, 1975.

7. Ahmed, A.S., 'Zia's victory in the field: the Arain work ethic that keeps a President in Power', *The Guardian,* London, 1984.

8. Ahmed, A.S., 'Saudi Arabia: Islam, Ethnicity and the State', forthcoming paper.

9. Pervez, S., *Hawkes Bay Incident: A Psycho-Social Case-study,* National Institute of Psychology, Islamabad, 1983.

10. Ansari, Z.A., and *et al,* 'Urdu Notes for Study', based on interviews conducted by National Institute of Psychology, Islamabad, 1983, p. 6.

11. Ibid., p. 7.

12. Ibid., p. 8.

13. Ibid., p. 4.

14. Ibid.

15. Jaffery, op. cit., 1983.

16. Ansari, op. cit., 1983, p. 3.

17. Ibid.

18. Ibid.

19. Asad, M., *The Message of the Quran,* translated and explained, Dar-ul-andalus, Gibraltar, 1980; and the Holy Quran, 112:3.

20. Ansari, op. cit., 1983, p. 3.

21. Ibid., p. 4.

22. *Dawn,* March 1983.

23. Ansari, op. cit., 1983, p. 6.

24. Ahmed, A.S., *Dubai Chalo:* Problems in the Ethnic Encounter between Middle Eastern and South Asian Muslim Societies', *Asian Affairs,* Vol. XV, Part III, 1984, pp. 262-76.

25. Fox, R., *Encounter with Anthropology,* Penguin Books, 1973.

26. Pervez, op. cit., 1983, p. 22.

27. Irfani, op. cit., 1983.
28. Ansari, op. cit., 1983, p. 4.
29. Jaffery, op. cit., 1983, p. 27.
30. Basilov, V.N., 'Honour Groups in Traditional Turkmenian Society', in *Islam in Tribal Societies: From the Atlas to the Indus,* Ahmed, A.S., and Hart; D., (editors), Routledge and Kegan Paul, London, 1984.
31. Bray, D., *The Life History of a Brahui,* Royal Book Company, Karachi, 1977.
32. The Holy Quran, 5:109 and 7: 6-7.
33. Asad, T., 'Anthropological Conception of Religion: Reflections on Geertz', *MAN,* N.S., Vol. 18, No. 2, 1983.
34. Pervez, op. cit., 1983, p. 37.
35. Abd al-Qadir, As-Sufi 'Death, the Beginning of a Journey', in *Islamic Book of the Dead: A collection of Hadiths on the Fire and the Garden,* Abd ar-Rahim ibn Ahmad al-Qadir (editor), Diwan Press, England, 1977.
36. The Holy Quran, *al-Ankabut* : 21.
37. Muslim, Imam, *Sahih Muslim,* Ah. H., Siddiqi, (translator), Sh. M. Ashraf, Lahore, 1981.
38. The Holy Quran, 82:19.
39. Rahman, F., *Major Themes of the Quran,* Bibliotheca Islamica, 1980.
40. Sialkoti, Maulana, M.S., *Alam-e-Uqba,* Nomani Kutub Khana, Lahore, n.d. See also Saeed, M.A., *What happens after Death?* Khan, M.H., (translator), Dini Book Depot, Urdu Bazar, Delhi, 1982. In another popular book the author promises the reader, in the sub-title, 'glimpses of life beyond the grave'. One section in the book is entitled 'the depth of hell: if a stone is thrown into hell it will take seventy years to reach its bottom', (Islam, K.M., *The Spectacle of Death,* Tablighi Kutub Khana, Lahore, 1976, p. 284). For discussion of *djahannam,* the Muslim hell, see Gibb, H.A.R., and Kramers, J.H., *Shorter Encyclopaedia of Islam,* South Asian Publishers, Karachi, 1981. Maulana Maudoodi discusses the importance of death, the after-life and its relationship to man's life on earth, in a dispassionate analysis of Islamic society, Maudoodi, M., Abu ala, *Islami Tehzib Our Os Key Osool-o-Mobadi,* Islamic Publications, Shah Alam Market, Lahore, 1968. See also chapter six, 'Eschatology', in Rahman, op. cit., 1980.
41. Ahmed, A.S., *Religion and Politics in Muslim Society: Order and Conflict in Pakistan,* Cambridge University Press, New York, 1983.
42. Algar, H., *Religion and State in Iran 1785-1906,* University of California Press, Berkeley, 1969; Fischer, M.J.M., *Iran: From Religious dispute to Revolution,* Harvard University Press, Cambridge, 1980; Khomeini, Imam, *Islam and Revolution,* Algar, H., (translator), Mizan Press, Berkeley, 1981; Schimmel, A., op. cit., 1981; and Shariati, A., *On the Sociology of Islam,* Algar, H., (translator), Mizan Press, Berkeley, 1979.
43. Fischer, op. cit., 1980.
44. Yusufzai, op. cit., 1983.
45. Islam, op. cit., 1976.
46. Pervez, op. cit., 1983.
47. Geertz, C., 'Religion as a Cultural System', in *Anthropological Approaches to the Study of Religion,* Banton, M., (editor), ASA Monograph 3, London, 1973, p. 19.

Part Two
Ethnicity and Leadership

5

Order and Conflict in Waziristan

The Waziristan case-study, in part, attempts to pose some answers to questions about what is stirring in the Muslim world and in part to learn the causes by examining the principles of social process in contemporary Muslim society with special reference to Pakistan.[1] The answers may help us understand the tension between tradition and modernity in Muslim society in these last decades of the twentieth century. This tension remains largely unstudied, and on the surface, inexplicable. Its complexity, and the diversity of the context within which it appears, defies easy analysis.

Social Revolution in Muslim Society

Perceptible beneath the ferment are shadowy figures: *mullah, maulvi, sheikh* or *ayatallah*. These explicitly challenge the ideological tenets of the modern age. They emphasize the central role of God and a reversion to fundamental ideology and express revulsion against materialism as the philosophy and code of life. Their target is not the king, or President, as symbol of the state, but the modern western-oriented state apparatus itself. Furthermore, contrary to accepted common thinking, the unrest — or movements — are a result of general economic betterment, not deprivation. The movements are revolutionary in form and content, death and destruction follow in their wake. Transformation of social and political structures, not merely a change of government, is desired; not only the kings of Islam are sleeping uneasily.

Traditional analysis of these movements casts them as revolt against legitimate authority — translated from notions of state and nationhood, order and rebellion, the major themes of modern political discussion. A corollary of this hypothesis is the placing of such endeavours simplistically within an anti-western framework. Muslim revolts and their leaders, from Sudan to Swat, have interested the West over the last centuries. They have provided the prototype of the 'Mad Mullah,'[2] and the implicitly hostile reaction of the West to contemporary movements and their anti-establishment religious leaders in Islamic society may be partly explained as a historically conditioned response to this prototype.[3] During the colonial phase of modern Islamic history the movements were explicitly anti-western and anti-colonial. This is not the case today. In fact, the phenomenon is much more complex than it appears. The movement is aimed primarily *within* society and is worked through recognizable local, social, and ethnic patterns. The opposition to established authority, whether Islamic or extra-religious, is a secondary, but, interconnected consequence of the movement.

In the last few years, the movements have taken place in widely different regions: Kano, Nigeria at one end of the Muslim world, and Wana, Pakistan at the other. In the centre, in Saudi Arabia, a similar upheaval was reported: the attack on the mosque at Mecca, the very core of the Islamic world, illustrates the seriousness and significance of the contemporary Muslim mood. Recent events in Iran provide dramatic evidence of the revolutionary aspects of Islamic movements. It is not difficult to postulate that other similar upheavals may have taken place, perhaps unreported because of lesser scale or drama, and more will take place.

The attempt to understand these movements and their long-term impact on social structure and organization is fundamental to Muslims and those dealing with Muslim societies. The present study is one such attempt; the anthropological method may provide useful tools for the analysis of traditional and small Muslim groups in situations of change and conflict. However, certain specific methodological adjustments for such analysis are suggested.

· The study of power, authority, and religious status, the central issues of Muslim society, by political scientists, sociologists, and historians has rested largely on traditional method and analysis. Their studies have tended to concern themselves with problems of rulers, dynasties, legitimacy, succession, control of armies and finances, on the one hand, and literature relating to issues of orthodoxy and legality on the other. Conceptually, the canvas and the configurations are large; the span in area and the time-periods covered are also large. I suggest it may also be useful to look *under* the surface of the large configurations of Muslim society and *away* from their main centres of power when examining social structure and process, especially with reference to Pakistan—from where our data are derived. However, we should look not too far beneath the surface—not at the typical anthropological village—but at the critical intermediary level, the district[4] or Agency, the study of which remains relatively neglected.[5]

Three broad but distinct spheres of leadership, interacting at various levels, are identified and demarcated in the paradigm at the district or Agency level of society: traditional leaders, usually elders, official representatives of the established state authority and religious functionaries. The last group is the least defined, and hence ambiguity in its locus and elasticity in its role are apparent. The groups are symbolically defined in society by their bases, situated in uneasy juxtaposition to the others at the district headquarters and which, respectively, are: the house/houses of the chief or elders, district headquarters (flying the government flag) and a, or the, central mosque.

Personnel from the three spheres of leadership vie for power, status, and legitimacy in society. The competition is further exacerbated by the fact the major participants are

Muslims; there are no simple Muslim *versus* non-Muslim
categories to fall back to as in the recent colonial past. Some
form of alliance and collaboration between traditional leaders
and district officials is characteristic of district history. It is
the religious leader who must clash with the other two if he is
to expand space for himself in society. This leads to an
important question which will be reflected in this study: who
speaks for society?

Once we have identified certain core features in society at
the district level we may proceed to construct what may be
termed 'the Islamic district—or Agency[6]—paradigm' of
socio-cultural process; one that is conceptually precise and
empirically based and placed within the regional political
framework. The Islamic district paradigm may assist us in
discovering meaning and structure beneath the wide range of
diversity found in contemporary Muslim society. The paradigm, it is suggested, is a predictive model. It will assist us
therefore, both, in examining Muslim society and predicting
developments in it.

At the core of the Islamic district paradigm I shall place
ethnographic analysis which, in our case, works around an
extended case-study based on traditional agnatic rivalry[7] in a
tribal Agency in Pakistan, the central actor of which is the
Mullah[8] of Waziristan.[9]

The district paradigm, by definition, suggests the perpetuation of one aspect of the colonial encounter. The district
structure and personnel, with its official head, the District
Commissioner—or the Political Agent in the Agency—were
imposed on society by the British. Since colonial times,
status and authority in the district have rested largely with
district officials as representatives of an omnipotent central
government. District officers were the *mai-baap* (mother-
father) of South Asian rural peasantry.

The continuing importance of the district and its personnel
after Independence, in spite of its clear association with the
colonial past, heightens tension in local society. Although
'native' the administrative personnel reflect ambivalence in

their dealing with the other groups in society, and may be viewed as distant and insympathetic by society. The contemporary power and importance of district officials is further exaggerated by the suspension of normal political activities (a common phenomenon during periods of martial law).

The district paradigm so constructed may be of direct utility for a study of the other tribal Agencies of Pakistan, perhaps also for the other districts of Pakistan. It is suggested, although with reservations regarding the contextual framework, that it may also be usefully applied in other South Asian countries with large Muslim populations where British colonial administrative structure survives, such as Bangladesh, and even outside the region, as in Nigeria. Let us acquaint ourselves with the extended case-study regarding the *Mullah*.

The Waziristan Case-Study

The case in hand is based in South Waziristan Agency, Pakistan. The Agency population, according to the last official census in 1972, was about 300,000, divided into two major tribes, the Mahsud, and the Wazir. The tribes, segmentary, egalitarian, acephalous, and living in low production zones are somewhat similar to other Muslim tribes in North Africa and the Middle East.[10] The Mahsuds number about 250,000 and the Wazirs 50,000. Smaller nomadic groups also live in the Agency.[11] The Agency is about 3,936 square miles in area and the largest and southern-most Agency of the North-West Frontier Province's seven Federally Administered Tribal Agencies (see map on page 76). The Political Agent heads the administration and represents government. The Political Agent's powers are vast and the tribes call him 'King of Waziristan' (*de Waziristan badshah*). South Waziristan shares borders with Afghanistan in the west and Baluchistan, eparated by the Gomal river, in the south. Desolate valleys and barren mountains, for the most part, distinguish the Agency.

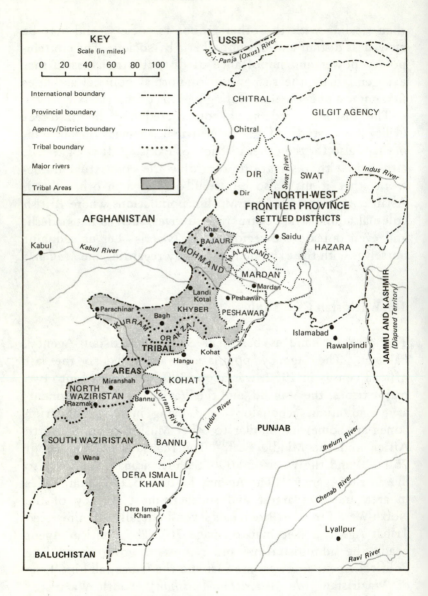

NORTH-WEST FRONTIER PROVINCE OF PAKISTAN

Recent colonial history is important to Waziristan. Count-less British troops have died here in savage encounters. In the thirties, there were more troops in Waziristan than on the rest of the Indian subcontinent. In 1937, an entire British brigade was wiped out in the Shahur Tangi. The ability of the tribes as fighters is well-recognized: 'the Wazirs and Mahsuds operating in their own country, can be classed among the finest fighters in the world'.[12] To those, like John Masters, who fought in Waziristan, the tribes were 'physically the hardest people on earth'.[13]

Some famous British Imperial names are associated with Waziristan, for example, Curzon, Durand, Kitchener, and T.E. Lawrence, whose note to the South Waziristan Scouts is on exhibition in the Scouts Mess, at Wana, the summer head-quarters of the Agency. Tradition, in name and custom, is preserved. The main western gate in the Wana camp is still called the Durand gate and the main picket guarding Wana camp is Gibraltar. Bugles still announce the passage of the day and play at sunset as the Pakistan flag is lowered and the entire camp comes to a halt for those few minutes. Farewells to officers are conducted in traditional and ritualistic manner in the Scouts Mess with the band—kilts and bagpipes—provi-ding music. The romantic aspect of the colonial encounter which created a 'mystification' in British eyes is perhaps most evocative in Waziristan.[14] The participation in the Great Game between Imperial Russia and Imperial Britain further added to the importance of the Waziristan tribes.[15]

The case-study may be examined in a diachronic perspec-tive, beginning in the late sixties, when a *mullah* among the Wazirs of South Waziristan Agency mobilized Islam to activate specific tribal ideology into a political movement against the cousin tribe, the Mahsuds, accusing the administra-tion of supporting them. The *Mullah* first appears, after migrating from the neighbouring Bannu District, as the builder of a beautiful mosque at Wana, unique in the Tribal Areas, and a complex of schools and dormitories around it.

With his emergence in the politics of the Agency, the mosque came to symbolize the *Mullah* and his policies.

The late years of the sixties and early years of the seventies were characterized by new sources of wealth – internal[16] and external, such as remittances from employment in the Arab States and the Persian Gulf.[17] For the first time, the tribesman with initiative could make considerable money. Some of the Wazir money was diverted to the *Mullah*. He appeared as their champion and he needed funds for his organization. The *Mullah's* religious organization supported complex economic networks. He invested some of the money in items that confer social prestige among Pukhtuns: Japanese cars, buses, guns, and lavish feasts to visiting politicians. Recent Waziristan history may be viewed as a function of the *Mullah's* emergence and politics.

Two important economic developments in the Agency coincided with the construction of the new mosque at Wana. First, a market (*adda*) sprang up between the mosque and the main road. In the late fifties and early sixties encroachments had resulted in a cluster of small, mud shops. The Scouts protested, as this violated rules which prohibit civil construction near their posts and camps. Numerous letters passed, and meetings were held between the Commandant of the Scouts, the Political Agent, and his senior, the Commissioner. The market, in spite of several setbacks, continued to grow. Because it was on the property of the Mughal Khel Wazirs, it came to be known as *Adda* Mughal Khel. Eventually some 400 shops, not more than a small room or two each, were constructed. The market became a thriving centre for commerce and trade for the Agency. The organization of the mosque and the market were interlinked by their guiding genius, the *Mullah*. The mosque was popularly called *Adda* Mughal Khel Mosque, that is, the mosque of the Mughal Khel market.

Second, a major dam, the Gomal Zam Project, was started by the Government of Pakistan in Wazir territory. Wazirs provided labour and were given building contracts. Both developments generated local money.

A magnificent mosque costing between 700 to 800,000 rupees,[18] was soon completed. The minarets and dome were resplendent with tiles and glass of many hues. The interior reflected depth and space. A stream passed through the mosque and contained a variety of coloured fish which fascinated visitors. Indeed no monument as splendid had been seen in that—or any other—tribal Agency until then. Elders from other Agencies came to marvel at the mosque and compliment its builder. The *Mullah* basked in his accomplishment and concentrated his energy in further expanding an organization around the mosque. He built a *madrasah* (religious school) adjacent to the mosque and dormitories for visiting *tulaba* (scholars). Most of the *tulaba* were sons of Wazir elders. A set of rooms was built for the *Mullah* on the second floor of the mosque overlooking its courtyard. As a mark of deference, people now referred to him as *Maulvi Sahib* and not by his name.

Here, I wish to look briefly outside Waziristan. In 1971, after Pakistan's war with India which resulted in the breakaway of East Pakistan, Zulfikar Ali Bhutto emerged as the political leader of Pakistan, rallying a dispirited nation. In his political style Bhutto appeared to offer a viable model of politics. The *Mullah* watched and learned. Both were relatively young leaders with considerable political skill and organizational ability who relied on their charisma and oratory to secure and stir their followers. Both spoke in the language of hyperbole and poetic populism. Personally, their demeanour bordered on arrogance and they brooked no opposition. Their critics accused them of opportunism. The politics of the seventies in Pakistan were to be cast in the mould of Mr. Bhutto. My concern is not with Pakistan politics during the Bhutto era (1971-7) but their indirect impact on Waziristan.

The Mullah after assessing the time as ripe in the early seventies made a bid for the control of the minds of the

Wazir. He was moving from a religious to a political role. For instance, he forbade the use of radios in the *adda*. It was un-Islamic, he announced. Having banned the radio, the *Mullah* listened to the programmes avidly. Selecting information from the radio commentary or news, he would 'predict' national events at the Friday congregation in the mosque. His announcement of the National Pay Commission is one such example. The *Mullah* informed his followers that he was praying for increase in pay of the poorly paid Wazir *khassadars* (tribal levies) and Scouts' soldiers (who received about 200 to 250 rupees a month). Increase in official salaries was being debated nationally during 1972-3 and an announcement on the matter was imminent. When the government announced an increase in salaries, people took it as an example of the *Mullah's* powers to predict and influence events. The *khassadars* were particularly impressed and committed a monthly contribution of four rupees each for the mosque fund.

At the same time, the *Mullah* imitated and developed some of the formalistic aspects of bureaucracy associated with the Political Agent, the official head of the Agency. Armed guards escorted him wherever he went, *mulaqats* (meetings) with him were arranged after formal, often written, requests through his supporters. He issued chits to his followers ordering admission to official schools or medical dispensaries, and on notes, he asked officials to give interviews 'to the bearer of the note'. His requests were honoured and his whims humoured: these were visible symbols of his growing importance in and to society. By appropriating some of the form and content of the Political Agent's function, he was setting himself on a collision course with that office.

A sense of destiny now marked his self-assessment. Addressing himself in his diary he noted: 'God Almighty has given you status and influence matched by few men in history'. In his diary, he referred to himself in the third person, traditionally used by royalty. Indeed, the theme of royalty was not far from his mind: 'when they insisted you address the gathering they introduced you *as the uncrowned king of Wana*', he observed in another place in his diary. The title of king was underlined by the *Mullah*. But, as we know, there was another claimant to the title in the Agency, the Political Agent. It is a notorious principle of history that no realm can long support two kings.

Three economic issues formed the main platform of the *Mullah*: first, he emphasized the Wazir nature of the market at Wana, the summer headquarters and main settlement of the Agency; second, he challenged Mahsud rights to the timber funds from Wazir forests in the politically inaccessible Birmal area that were distributed among the Agency tribes; and third, he demanded an alternative route for the Wazirs to the Settled Districts along the Gomal river that bypassed the Mahsud area. Each demand had clear social and political implications.

The *Mullah*, after a steady campaign and increasing tension in the Agency, which resulted in several incidents, damned the Mahsud as *kafirs* (non-believers). Employing religious idiom for tribal rivalry, he declared *jihad* against the Mahsud.

Sure of his power, the *Mullah* set the Wazirs on a collision course with the political administration, which he saw as a tool of the Mahsuds. Issuing *fatwas* (religious instructions) from the mosque, the *Mullah* declared that the Wazir struggle was an Islamic one. The primary objective, he declared, was to secure the Gomal road. To die in this cause, the cause of Islam, was to gain paradise. If, he declared in his fiery sermons, a Wazir killed a Mahsud it would be the equivalent of killing a *kafir*. If, on the other hand, a Wazir was killed by a Mahsud, he would become *shaheed* and win paradise, as he had been killed by a *kafir*. Wazirs were inflamed by his rhetoric.

The Mahsuds, not being able to dismiss the *Mullah* as an 'unbeliever,' stepped up their attack on his character, claiming he was a debauch, a practitioner of black magic, etc., which indirectly reflected on Wazir morality. The Mahsuds impugned the *Mullah's* 'Pukhtunness' and accused the Wazir of being without shame. Mystification of Pukhtunness was a strategy employed by the Mahsud to balance the accusation of being *kafir* by the *Mullah*. An ethnic counter-attack was made to a religious attack. Feelings on both sides ran high.

The *Mullah* opened a new front which would divert attention and keep the Wazir war spirit from flagging. He ordered the main Agency road to be blocked. In late December 1975, a Wazir war-party (*lashkar*) gathered at Dargai in the Maddi Jan area for this purpose. Traffic was entirely suspended and the Agency was cut off from the outside world. The Prime Minister of Pakistan ordered the opening of the road. The Political Agent, accompanied by a strong Scouts force, moved from Jandola towards Wana to enforce the order. Army tanks were moved into the Agency from the Settled Districts. Simultaneously, a strong Scouts column moved from Wana towards Jandola. Movement on foot or in vehicles for Wazirs was banned by the administration. A fierce and bloody encounter took place at Maddi Jan on that day in which five soldiers were killed and more wounded. It was estimated that 30 Wazirs were killed or wounded. Other clashes also took place on the same day, causing loss of life.

The Wazirs remained defiant and a few days later, once again, blocked the Agency road. The sequence of events would be repeated, it appeared. Orders from Islamabad were issued to ensure opening of the road 'at all costs'. The Scouts moved in considerable strength from Jandola, but they met no opposition. The Wazirs had melted into the night and the road was deserted.

The *Mullah* then made an abortive attempt to involve Wazirs from outside the Agency. Involvement of Wazirs from the North Waziristan Agency or Afghanistan would extend the theatre of conflict beyond the Agency borders and create serious complications for government. Already Kabul was watching developments in Waziristan with interest. Ideal material was at hand for their Pukhtunistan propaganda, which claimed Pukhtuns in the North-West Frontier Province wished to secede.

The *Mullah* now ordered a general civil disobedience movement. Wazirs blocked the main roads, shot at the Scouts, and at the climax of the movement imposed a physical boycott of the Wana camp. Major clashes between Wazirs, Mahsuds, and the administration took place, involving the deaths of tribesmen and Scouts' soldiers. The Agency was in flames, and on the Durand Line such a situation has international ramifications. After obtaining clearance from the Prime Minister, the administration acted in May 1976. Army tanks were moved into the Agency and the air force was alerted. The Scouts took action and the Wana markets of the Wazir were destroyed, the *Mullah's* 'cabinet' arrested and after a while the *Mullah* himself. The *Mullah* and his key men were tried, found guilty, and sent to jail in Hazara, across the river Indus, where they languish. The action, possibly the most severe of its kind in the history of the Tribal Areas, became the centre of controversy.

After the action, the Wazirs were in disarray, the Mahsuds jubilant, and the administration self-righteous.

The action in Wana, and events leading up to it, had been followed with interest in Kabul, as mentioned earlier. Propaganda had shaped the conflict as a simple Pukhtun struggle for autonomy against a Punjabi-dominated central government. Indeed, not since the merger of the Frontier States, Swat, Chitral, Dir, and Amb, in 1969, had such a live issue presented itself to Kabul. The situation was tense with potential and possibilities. Kabul underlined the ethnic nature of the *Mullah's* struggle and pointed out that some of the key men in the drama—the Central Interior Minister, the Chief Secretary of the Province, and the Political Agent of the Agency—were non-Pukhtun and hence, they argued, unsympathetic to Pukhtuns.

Religious Leadership in Society

Let us try to pose some questions which are relevant to the study. Why did the Wazir tribe respond to the *Mullah*? Was it clan or lineage pride, based on memory of agnatic humiliation at the hands of the Mahsuds? Or was it promises of economic betterment? Certainly some of the central issues were economic in nature. Was it the hope of a separate Agency with its political, and social implications? Or was it the *Mullah's* wealth, with which he could patronize elders and the poor in society? Or the Papa Doc Duvalier syndrome: irrational fear of the evil eye and the immediate fear of *thugs* who could rough up doubters or harm their economic interests as by closure of shops in the market?

The Wazirs thought they were using the *Mullah* to say and do things that they could not themselves. In the end, did the Wazirs use the *Mullah* or did he use them? The answer is that perhaps both are partly true.

Here it is only relevant to point out the intensely democratic, and egalitarian nature of ideal Pukhtun society. Is the *Mullah's* emergence and success in peace time an aberration from the Pukhtun model? What are the social factors that caused it? Such questions are important for the study of leadership, social structure, and organization among Pukhtun tribesmen.

To the Wazir, the *Mullah* appeared as a rational, and sympathetic religious leader determined to establish their honour and rights. To his followers, the gross and blatant tilting of administration to the Mahsuds, the arrest of the *Mullah* and the 'capture' of the mosque are tantamount to heresy. They argue that the house of God was desecrated and his faithful servant, the *Mullah,* arrested. Their continuing boycott of the mosque is explained as an Islamic response to a captured house of worship. Religion is not merely metaphysics. For all people, the forms, vehicles, and objects of worship are suffused with an aura of deep moral seriousness. It bears within it a sense of intrinsic social obligation; it not only induces intellectual conformity, it enforces emotional commitment. The *Mullah's jihad* not only induced intellectual conformity, it enforced emotional commitment. The commitment is still explicitly expressed in society.

The *Mullah* relied largely on his charisma, composed of his powerful rhetoric, personality, and organizational skills to win the hearts of his followers. Above all, he gave them group pride and identity. He was palpably neither a *qazi* (*qadi*) learned in the *Sharia* nor a saint, nor Sufi, with a reputation derived from lifelong abstinence, meditation or scholarship such as the traditional Muslim 'scholars, saints, and sufis'.[19] None of this mattered to the Wazir. There are well-known *Pukhto* proverbs which sum up the relationship of the believing followers to their *pir* such as 'though the *pir* (saint) himself does not fly his disciples would have him fly'.[20] The Wazirs saw their *pir* in miraculous flight. They entertained high hopes, partly due to their needs for a saviour figure who could deliver them from their enemies. The ground was thus ripe for the emergence of a leader who, at one and the same time, could organize cultural and religious forces on behalf of his followers. 'Now, it is at such times—when a genuine sense of injustice, or danger etc., reaches a certain point—that a closed cultural complex opens up to the transcendent religious', notes Professor F. Rahman in a personal communication.

Islamic religious groups providing leadership in society may be broadly divided into three overlapping categories. The first two are defined by their function in society and the third, by genealogical links with holy ancestors. The first, the *ulema,* defined by religious and legal learning, include *mufti, qazi, maulana,* and *maulvi*; the second category, defined by esoteric, sometimes unorthodox practice, include groups such as the Sufis; and the third, defined by religious genealogy and descent and thus claiming superior social status, includes the Sharif or Sayyed (descended from the Prophet), and the *mian* (descended from holy men).

What is of interest to our argument is the difficulty in placing the *mullah* easily in any one category. The difficulty is not simply taxonomic but related to the ambiguity and elasticity surrounding his social role. Not quite the learned *mufti,* sure of his orthodox Islamic knowledge, nor the Sufi, sure of his inner Islamic faith, the *mullah* is forced to define and create his own role. He may, indeed, borrow from all three categories elevating himself to *maulvi* in one place (as in this study) and *mian* in another.[21] In general the *mullah* occupies a junior position in the religious hierarchy and is defined as 'a lesser member of the religious classes'.[22] The *mullah* restricts himself largely to the village level of social and political life except in extraordinary circumstances. He appears to thrive in crises. Although the *mullah's* role is one of the most interesting, and important, in village and rural society it is also one of the least studied. The serious writing of the *ulema* or the Sufis, with their imaginative external practices appear to attract most scholarship.

Among Pukhtuns the *mullah* remains subordinate to the lineage elders and usually does not feature on the genealogical chart.[23] The observation is confirmed by archival material based on contemporary records for Waziristan.[24] Mahsud scholars confirm this.[25] As illustrated in another work[26] Pukhtun elders saw political activity as their preserve and restricted the role of the *mian* or *mullah*: 'mian-mullah saray —a *mian* or *mullah* man'[27] to specified pacific religious functions. The important function of the *mullah* is to organize and supervise rites of passage based on Islamic tradition.

In any case, the *mullah* in a Muslim society has no proselytizing function. He must, perforce, explore other areas if he is to enhance his role and authority in society.

The *mullah* may rise to power in extraordinary times, rallying Muslims against invading non-Muslims.[28] In the Tribal Areas and *nang* (honour) society, *mullahs* have led widespread revolts with singular courage and conviction against the British, as in 1897.[29] Their bold stand provides a contrast to those quiescent elements in society, who preferred to sit on the fence in the struggle against the British (traditional leaders and bureaucrats, in terms of the district paradigm). Men such as Adda Mullah, Manki Mullah, Palam Mullah, and Mastan Mullah, and in Waziristan, Mullah Powindah, and the Fakir of Ipi, seemed to appear from nowhere to mobilize society and lead the struggle. Some like Mastan Mullah of Buner in Swat, known as *sartor baba*,[30] claimed, or were believed to possess, magical powers in their fight for Islam. The struggle, to the *mullahs*, was interpreted as *jihad*, a holy war for Islam to be conducted irrespective of success. Their extreme devotion to the Islamic cause, as they interpreted it, and consequently its militant expression provided the British with a prototype of what became popular as the 'Mad Mullah' or the 'Mad Fakir'[31] as noted earlier.

The *Mullah* of Waziristan provides an interesting example of a *mullah* who mobilized an entire tribe by creating a religious battle hysteria against kin groups belonging to the same sect and local administration in peace time. The Waziristan study may be interpreted as the rejection of his traditional role by the *Mullah*. The rejection creates problems in society, as it affords possibilities for the *Mullah*.

Based on subjective criteria we may understand what made Wazirs respond to the call for *jihad*. This raises questions regarding the orthodox mould from which we have employed the derivative. As *jihad* is an important concept in our study I would like to discuss it in some detail.

For the orthodox Muslim, the crime of Akbar the Mughal, the most famous case of Imperial heresy in South Asian Islam, lay in his attempt at redefining Islam; for the majority Muslims of the Agency, the crime of the *Mullah* lay in his redefinition of *jihad*. What is *jihad*?[32] Scholars of Islam have held different opinions on the exact nature of *jihad*, a discussion that began from the time of the Prophet. However, its importance for the believer is not in doubt.

For our general purposes, *jihad* may be defined as 'a holy struggle in the way of Allah'. There are thus no theological sources to support *jihad* against fellow Muslims. However, *jihad* becomes operative when *takfir,* declaring someone an unbeliever or non-Muslim, is involved. The point leads to a more complex argument as to who is a Muslim. The Holy Quran and Prophet define him simply as a person declaring his belief in Islam through the *kalima.* The Mahsuds neither fitted the non-believer nor heretic categories. To condemn them as *kafir* was in itself an act of considerable audacity. The *Mullah's jihad* clearly rested on a weak theological, but strong sociological base. It tells us more about the Muslim society within which *jihad* is articulated than Islamic theology or law. The idiom of *jihad* in Waziristan was not entirely successful. Aware of the ambiguity in his usage of the term, the *Mullah* turned to a particularistic interpretation of it by defining it in cultural terms. His political acumen lay in recognizing the shadow areas in between; his success lay in manipulating from those areas. But there are also at hand examples of more universalistic interpretations of *jihad* which the orthodox would approve, indeed, applaud: the Mahsud fighting the *kafir* in Kashmir in 1947-8, or the Wazirs fighting them in Afghanistan today. The difficulty lies, for us as well as for the actors, in attempting to reconcile the two disparate interpretations. What, for instance, was the Mahsud response to the *Mullah's jihad?*

Undaunted by the *Mullah* branding them as *kafir,* the Mahsud responded with consummate skill. Their response to the campaign of the *Mullah* was the mystification of Pukhtun-ness. The Wazirs were condemned as deviating from the Pukhtun ideal; by following the *Mullah* they had become 'without honour' and 'without shame.' In mystifying Pukhtunness, the Mahsud underscored the essentially sub-ordinate role of *mullahs* in the Pukhtun universe; the Wazir '*Maulvi Sahib*' was reduced to a plain 'Mullah.' The mystifi-cation also allowed the Mahsud to make another point which neatly cancelled the Mullah's condemnation of them as *kafir.* Rejecting his status as a religious leader, the Mahsud saw the

Mullah as a diabolical figure, the devil himself (*shaitaan*). The counter-attack was as neat as it was effective. There is hope for the *kafir* (he can convert to Islam), none for the *shaitaan* (his defiance of God is unpardonable) in Muslim mythology. Point and counter-point, thrust and counter-thrust in society between protagonists are articulated through an Islamic idiom. The use of the idiom is as generalized as it is imperfectly understood.

The opposed categories in society — *Mullah versus shaitaan, kafir versus* Islam — and the passion they arouse would indicate the importance of religion in Waziristan. The question arises how Islamic are these tribes? In a sociological and cultural sense they may be defined as Islamic; they do so themselves. The self-perception explains the high incidence of Islamic symbolism in Muslim society. What is significant is not that the symbols seem to appear everywhere but that they do so in the least expected situations. The strength and ubiquity of Islamic symbols in Muslim society cannot be challenged. What can be challenged is their use in society and the assumption of theological support it implies. We know the Wazir *jihad* against the Mahsud was not justified by Islam, nor was it in the Islamic cause, but the understanding of religion is not the issue; the affective and conative power of its symbols in society is. Correcting the misuse or misunderstanding of Islam by Muslim tribesmen is a task for the orthodox *ulema*. We are, as anthropologists, concerned with how society perceives religion, not how religion sees itself.

In spite of the strength of Islamic symbols in society, anthropologists have studied Muslim groups without reference to the Islamic framework.[33] The tradition in anthropology of studying tribal society in isolation without reference to a larger framework perhaps derives from the study of non-Islamic African tribes.[34]

The question of relating the tribal identity to a larger religious identity has engaged anthropologists studying both Pukhtun tribes[35] and tribes elsewhere.[36] The exercise in itself serves little purpose and the debate generated could be sterile. We may more usefully pose the problem, as the tribesman himself views it, by examining the relationship in terms of Islam *and* Pukhtunness, and not Islam *versus* Pukhtunness. To the tribesman, Islam provides specified political and socio-religious formations within which his Pukhtunness operates. The two are in harmony and *he* sees them as a logical construct. The two are deeply interrelated, and Islam so internalized into Pukhtun structure as to suggest the dichotomy is false.

The case-study in this paper illustrates that Islam and Pukhtunness coalesce and overlap. The interiority of the latter in the former is seen as axiomatic in society. Indeed, the success of the *Mullah* is partly explained by his recognition of this equation. The mosque, as we know, remained the base of the *Mullah's* operations, and remains a key symbol of Wazir identity. Once Islam was equated to kinship his success in leading and consolidating the Wazirs was ensured. Yes, the dichotomy separating Islam and Pukhtun is false.

Perhaps a rephrasing from Islam *versus* Pukhtunness to bringing Pukhtun custom and tradition into accordance with Islamic tradition, that is, Islam and Pukhtunness, may be a more useful method for studying the problem. The discussion could be more fruitful if it analysed the role of religious leadership, such as that of the *Mullah,* and their usage of Islam to consolidate their position especially in changing times. The discussion then shifts from the ideological base of the tribesman to questions of strategy and choices open to him.

Conclusion: The Problem of the Islamic District Paradigm

Early in the study I had incautiously promised to consider the question of who speaks for Muslim society. At the end of the study I appear to have no definite answer. It is the same question, perhaps differently worded, which teases the minds of men and causes problems in the resolution of social and political issues in Waziristan. The definition and location of spokesmen and chiefs reflects a crisis within society. The very title *badshah*, king, has been applied to each major actor, the tribal Malik (the word itself means king), the Political Agent, and the *Mullah*. Does the Malik speak for society? Although he is from within society, unlike the other two, the *teeman*, tribe-at-large, do not reflect much confidence in him. The Political Agent speaks more *to* society than *for* society. It is the *Mullah* alone who appears at one stage of his career to have won a following which cut across boundaries of lineage, hierarchy, and age. For a while he spoke for society. But in his heart he, too, wished to speak to them, not for them. And it was not long before the Political Agent wrested the title of spokesman—*badshah*, if we will—back from the *Mullah*. It is precisely the method by which the Political Agent won back his title which underlines the structural weakness of his position in society.

The internal tension between the main groups these men represent is not resolved. The disparate nature of the three groups—the first characterized by tribal code, lineage identity, cousin rivalry; the second, Indo-British, secular, liberal, service traditions; the third, Islamic lore as locally understood—suggests the problem may be irresolvable. It may be irresolvable because the major actors are all Muslim; each one claims to know and speak for society. The strength of this conviction, rooted in the characteristic traditions of their group, ensures that each leader perceives society and its fundamental issues in a different perspective to the other. We are confronted by the problem of defining the key terms of society.

When explaining the use of the word Islamic in the paradigm I had pointed out its sociological rather than theological content. Nonetheless, the paradigm suggests a certain exclusivity to Muslim society. Its applicability to other societies appears to be limited. The reason may lie in two characteristic features of Islam which other societies, monotheistic (Christian) or polytheistic (Hindu), may or may not share. Let me simplify for purposes of the argument. The Prophet's well-known saying 'there is no monkery in Islam' testifies to this. First, Islam does not sanction an official priesthood. Yet we have seen the *Mullah* appropriate for himself the role of high priest; and the Wazirs acknowledge that role. It is this ambiguity which proves difficult to resolve in, and provides the dynamics of, an Islamic district paradigm. By comparison, the priesthood in Christianity or Hinduism is defined by sets of rules based on theological literature and custom; it is clearly separate from the domain of Caesar. Whatever conflict exists between Church and State — and for Christianity it forms one of the main themes of medieval European history — their respective roles remain defined in orthodox religion. Today, the *padre* and priest remain largely confined to a religious role.

Second, Islam possesses a highly developed sense of community, *ummah,* which transcends national and tribal boundaries. The concept of *ummah* dominates Muslim political thinking in cycles every few generations, as in the Pan-Islamic movements. The Hindu community, in contrast, is defined within the geographical entity called *Bharat Mata,* Mother India; those leaving its shores risk losing caste. Contemporary administrative boundaries confining Muslim groups within them negate the principle of *ummah.* These boundaries also create rival loyalties based on the district, province, or state. In the Islamic district paradigm the administrator wishes to maintain boundaries while the religious groups wish to expand them (in a different context, reflecting the same principle, we saw the *Mullah's* attempts to involve tribes outside the Agency and the resistance of the administration). The problems of the paradigm are related in a direct manner to the original template of Muslim society.

To understand our contemporary paradigm better we must, therefore, refer to the earliest — and for Muslims the authentic —model of society. The paradigm provided by early Islam is fundamentally different in structure and organization from our contemporary model. In the early model, the caliph combined in one role the functions of tribal elder, government spokesman, and religious leader. The caliph spoke for temporal as well as religious issues in society. The functions of the Malik, the Political Agent, and the *Mullah* were fused into one at the appropriate level of society. It is the division of functions and the creation of separate roles which create problems in our contemporary paradigm of society. The division, as we know, is one legacy of the European colonial period: the Malik in part and the Political Agent in whole are a product of that period.[37]

Muslims are the same everywhere in certain ways and their societies are yet different everywhere. The range of Muslim society is wide and their historical experience varied. The general application of the Islamic district paradigm to Muslim society, therefore, presents us with problems. With this in mind let me continue to simplify and suggest areas where the paradigm may be most usefully applied. First: in those Muslim majority countries with a colonial background similar to Pakistan's (and here a parochial clause is added: the British colonial experience is of primary importance to our paradigm) concrete structures and values which derive from British educational and administrative systems are associated with our paradigm. Bangladesh, Malaysia, and Nigeria are countries which fall in this category. The total population of the countries in this category may account for about half the entire Muslim population of the world.

Second, it may partly be applied to those Muslim nations ruled by other colonial powers, the French in Morocco, or Dutch in Indonesia. This may be a useful exercise if only to reject the paradigm. The rejection may illuminate interesting discrepancies in religious roles within the Muslim world. Does the *mullah* exist in, for instance, Morocco? If not, who performs his functions in rural society? The agurram of the holy lineage? And what socio-historical factors account for the *mullah's* absence in Morocco? The answers will help us understand why he emerged in Iran and South Asia. Conversely, this will help explain the relative unimportance of institutionalized, Moroccan-type, holy lineages in Pakistan. Other related questions would also be clarified: does the role of the Malik provide comparisons with that of the tribal chiefs—the *caids*? How does the role of the contemporary official *caids* compare with that of the Political Agent? How much of their colonial origins is reflected in the present administrative structures?

India provides a third category: large Muslim groups living as a minority in a nation which has constitutionally declared itself secular. Although the Indian Muslims live within the administrative structure devised by the British, the major clause of the paradigm is missing: neither the contending groups nor their main leaders are Muslim.

In concluding, let me throw caution to the wind and cross into Africa from Asia to apply the paradigm. My example is based on the case of the *Mullah* of Kano in Nigeria.[38] Briefly, Haji Muhammad Marwa, arrived from the Cameroon at Kano, and in the sixties and seventies organized a fundamentalist movement, a *jihad,* demanding change in society. Several warnings were delivered to Marwa from the Governor ordering him to cease his activities or face expulsion from Kano. With his expulsion matters would revert to normal.

In late 1980, Marwa led his followers in a series of revolts against the administration, culminating in the attack on the Governor of Kano. The main mosque at Kano was almost captured. The Nigerian Army and Air Force were eventually called in to quell the revolt. Reports in early 1981 suggest over 1,000 people were killed in the carnage, including the *Mullah,* who died after a gun-shot wound. The administration accused Marwa of employing *juju* or black magic to influence his followers. His followers believed in his magical powers and with bows and arrows were prepared to face the army, which was using bazookas and bullets. Reports of missing girls and boys also pointed to the *Mullah* and suggested nefarious deeds. A high-powered tribunal was appointed by the Nigerian Government to report on what became known as the Kano disturbances.[39]

Certain similarities with the Waziristan case are notable: the emergence of an *outside* charismatic *mullah* with powers of oratory and organizational skills who understands both social structure, and psychology, accusations of employing black magic to influence followers by detractors, the real and symbolic importance of the mosque to the *Mullahs* who ultimately derive their authority from religion and the revolt against established *native,* not colonial or Imperial, authority (for Governor of Kano equate the Political Agent of South Waziristan Agency). The ambiguity of declaring *jihad* against Muslim rulers of the land is apparent in both cases. The social structure and organization of the tribes among whom they lived provide further similarities; in both areas patrilineal, segmentary tribal groups live in low production zones. International interest and outside money, mainly from the Arab world (directly, it was believed, in Nigeria, and indirectly, through labour remittances, in Pakistan) also add to the complexity of the cases. Tension and conflict are created in society which appear to be resolvable only after a bloody climax. But tanks and bazookas do not necessarily win in any permanent manner arguments based on deep ethnic or religious divisions (yes, it would seem in the earlier Nigerian example of Biafra and no, in the Pakistan-Bangladesh one).

Do the events that took place in remote parts of Nigeria and Pakistan predict future political patterns in Muslim society? Are the Kano and Wana *Mullahs* to be seen as modern revolutionary leaders or traditional products of traditional Muslim structure and organization? Are we witnessing a shift in style and loci of leadership away from urban, westernized, bureaucratic elites? Conceptually, may we relate these movements to the current waves of fundamental revivalism surging in many Muslim countries? And finally, can universal principles of behaviour, suggesting models which predict and forecast, be adduced from these case-studies? Although tentative answers may be suggested in the affirmative, it is too early to provide long-term and clear answers. To make matters worse, there is almost no literature or information on such leaders and movements in the contemporary Muslim world. The Kano and Wana examples foretell what may be in store for Islamic governments and societies in the coming decades. Their examples suggest the strength and universality of what I refer to as the Islamic district paradigm in this study and the need for a fuller investigation.

I have attempted here to raise several methodological and theoretical questions, some of which invite, in my view, hypotheses of underlying cultural-demographic and possibly psychological mechanisms. Although it is speculative and exploratory in nature, I hope that areas for future research have been indicated. The formulation of questions as well as the provision of answers must surely remain one of the major heuristic functions of social studies.

NOTES

1. Themes in this study are explored at greater length in Ahmed, A.S., *Religion and Politics in Muslim Society: Order and Conflict in Pakistan,* Cambridge University Press, 1983.

2. Talhami, G., 'The Muslim-African Experience'; and Voll, J., 'Wahhabism and Mahdism', papers presented to the Islamic Alternative Conference, The Arab Institute, 5-6 June, 1981.

3. The apprehensions which have revived as a result of recent developments are expressed by one of the leading western authorities on Islam: 'The Iranian Revolution and the (already disquieting) Muslim fundamentalist movements whose hopes it nurtured, changed all that, helped by the rising price of that petroleum with which Allah endowed his followers in such ample quantities. Once again the Muslim world became an entity jealously guarding its uniqueness, its own culture, comprising much more than just spirituality. And might not this entity again become a threat, as it had only three centuries ago when the Ottoman armies laid siege to Vienna? Might the way of life so valued by the West be in serious danger?' Rodinson, M., *Muhammad,* Carter, A., (translator), Pantheon Books, New York, 1980.

4. The district was the basic and key unit of administration in British India, (Woodruff, P., *The Men Who Ruled India,* Vol. 1, *The Founders,* Vol. 2, *The Guardians,* Jonathan Cape, London, 1965). The district was further subdivided into sub-division and *thana.* In turn, the district formed part of a division, which was part of a province. The Agency in the Tribal Areas corresponded to the district in the administrative universe. Although I call this intermediary level *district* to help conceptualize the unit of analysis, district (or Agency) boundaries do not

always correspond with ethnic ones, a fact which continues to create political problems. In some cases, new ethnicity was formed as a result of new districts, such as Hazarawal in Hazara District. An understanding of the district structure and its personnel is therefore necessary in order to understand what I call in this study, the Islamic district paradigm. Pakistan, like India, retains the administrative structure it inherited after Independence in 1947. Most districts and Agencies remain profoundly rural in character and somewhat isolated from national developments. There is a vast literature on the subject, much of it written by British district officers themselves. For a fresh contribution see Hunt, R., and Harrison, J., *The District Officer in India 1930-47,* Scolar Press, London, 1980; the latter was once a member of the elite Indian Civil Service. The fact that I have been a district officer perhaps assists me in viewing the problem from inside the structure and thereby making some contribution.

5. The academic neglect may be partly due to methodological considerations, for the district does not correspond either to the larger subject matter—state, nation or region—traditionally studied by political scientists, sociologists, and historians, or to the smaller micro-village society studied by anthropologists. However, as mentioned in the previous note, there is no dearth of general memoir-type writing on district life.

6. I shall refer to the paradigm as district rather than Agency because the former is older in history, indeed it is the forerunner of the Agency, and more widely known.

7. In place of the technical anthropological term Father's Brother's Son's I shall employ the lesser jargon, agnatic rivalry, which I define as rivalry between males descended in the patrilineage from a common ancestor.

8. *Mullah* is a generic name for a religious functionary—a 'Mohammedan learned in theology and sacred law', (Oxford Dictionary, 1975, p. 792). I refer to the Waziristan *Mullah,* the principal actor of our study, with a capital 'M' to distinguish him in the text.

9. Waziristan, when used generally, refers to the area of North and South Waziristan Agencies. The name derives from the Wazir tribe. Wazir in Arabic and Urdu means 'minister'.

10. Ahmed, A.S., and, Hart, D.M., (editors), *Islam in Tribal Societies: From the Atlas to the Indus,* Routledge and Kegan Paul, London, 1984.

11. Ahmed, A.S., 'Nomadism as Ideological Expression: The Case of the Gomal Nomads', in *Nomadic Peoples,* IUAES, Summer 1981. See also Part Three, chapter 14.

12. General Staff, *Operations in Waziristan 1919-20,* compiled by the General Staff, Army Headquarters, India, Superintendent Government Printing, Calcutta, India, 1921, p. 5.

13. Masters, J., *Bugles and a Tiger,* Four Square, London, 1965, p. 161.

14. Ahmed, A.S., 'The Colonial Encounter on the NWFP: Myth and Mystification', in *Journal of the Anthropological Society,* Vol. IX, No. 3, Oxford, 1978. See chapter 7.

15. Ahmed, A.S., 'Tribe and State in Asia: The Great Game Revisited', paper for SOAS-SSRC Seminar, London. Revised version 'Tribes and States in Central and South Asia', in *Asian Affairs,* Vol. XI, (O.S. Vol. 67) Part II, 1979 and 1980 respectively. See chapter 8.

16. Ahmed, A.S., *Social and Economic Change in the Tribal Areas,* Oxford University Press, Karachi, 1977.

17. Ahmed, A.S., 'The Arab Connection: Emergent Models of Social Structure and Organization among Pakistani Tribesmen', in *Asian Affairs,* June 1981 and op. cit., 1980.

18. About ten rupees equalled one US dollar at that time.

19. Keddie, N.R., (editor), *Scholars, Saints and Sufis: Muslim Religious Institutions since 1500,* Near Eastern Centre, University of California, Los Angeles, 1972.

20. Ahmed, op. cit., 1973.

21. Ahmed, op. cit., 1980, p. 167.

22. Algar, H., *Religion and State in Iran 1785-1906,* University of California Press, Berkeley, 1969, p. 264.

23. Ahmed, op. cit., 1980.
24. Bruce, C.E., Lieut.-Col., *The Tribes of Waziristan: Notes on Mahsuds, Wazirs, Daurs, etc.,* His Majesty's Stationery Office for the India Office, 1929; Curtis, G.S.C., *Monograph on Mahsud Tribes,* Government of NWFP, 1946; General Staff, op. cit., 1921, p. 4; *Summary of Events in North-West Frontier Tribal Territory, 1st January 1931 to 31st December 1931,* Government of India Press, Simla, India, 1932; and *Military Report on Waziristan 1935,* fifth edition, Government of India Press, Calcutta, India, 1936; Howell, E.B., *Waziristan Border Administration Report for 1924-5,* Government of India, 1925; Johnson, H.H., Maj., *Notes on Wana,* Government of India, 1934 (a) and *Mahsud Notes,* Government of India, 1934 (b); and Johnston, F.W., *Notes on Wana,* Government of India, 1903.
25. Mahsud, Minhaj ud Din, *Impact of Education on Social Change in South Waziristan Agency,* M.A. thesis, Punjab University, 1970.
26. Ahmed, op. cit., 1980.
27. Ibid., p. 162.
28. Ahmed, op. cit., 1976.
29. Ibid.
30. *Sartor* is literally 'black head', the name implies one whose head is un-covered as a result of poverty, grief, or some personal obsession; here it would signify an obsession for the cause of Islam; *baba* is a term of respect for an elder.
31. Churchill, W.S., *Frontiers and Wars,* Penguin Books, Harmondsworth, 1972, p. 29.
32. *Jihad* has been translated in the contemporary world in dramatically non-traditional ways. For instance in April 1981 an Indonesian Muslim group calling itself Komando Jihad or Holy War Commando hijacked a DC-9 passenger aeroplane belonging to the Garuda Indonesian Airways. Indonesian commandos successfully foiled the attempt at Bangkok airport killing all five hijackers. Although the idiom of *jihad* was employed during the hijacking the case remains clouded in obscurity. *Jihad* is also used for other daily, even secular activity. There is at least one daily newspaper called *Jihad* in Pakistan.
33. Professor Barth, perhaps acknowledging the criticism, has recently re-examined his earlier work *Political Leadership among Swat Pathans,* Athlone Press, London, 1972 in 'Swat Pathans Reconsidered', in *Selected Essays of Fredrik Barth: Features of Person and Society in Swat; Collected Essays on Pathans,* Vol. II, Routledge and Kegan Paul, London, 1981. See also Ahmed, op. cit., 1976.
34. Fortes, M., and Evans-Pritchard, E.E., (editors), *African Political Systems,* Oxford University Press, 1970; Gluckman, M., *Politics, Law and Ritual in Tribal Society,* Basil Blackwell, Oxford, 1971; and Middleton, J., and Tait, D., (editors), *Tribes Without Rulers,* Routledge and Kegan Paul, London, 1970.
35. Anderson, J.W., 'How Afghans Define Themselves in Relation to Islam', paper presented to A.A.A., Washington, D.C., December 1980; Beattie, H., 'Effects of the Saor Revolution in the Nahrin Area of Northern Afghanistan', paper presented to the A.A.A., Washington, D.C., December 1980; Canfield, R.L., 'Religious Networks and Traditional Culture in Afghanistan', paper presented to the A.A.A., Washington, D.C., December 1980; Ghani, A., 'Islam and State-Building in a Tribal Society: Afghanistan 1880-1901', in *Modern Asian Studies,* Cambridge University Press, XII, 2, 1978, pp. 269-84; '*Sharia* in the Process of State-Building: Afghanistan 1880-1901', and 'Disputes in a Court of *Sharia*', (forthcoming papers); and Tavakolian, B., 'Sheikhanzai Nomads and the Afghan State', paper presented to A.A.A., Washington, D.C., December 1980.
36. Geertz, op. cit., 1968 and *The Interpretation of Cultures,* Basic Books Inc., New York, 1973; and Geertz, C., and Geertz, H., and Rosen, L., *Meaning and Order in Moroccan Society: Three Essays in Cultural Analysis,* Cambridge University Press, 1979; Gellner, E., *Saints of the Atlas,* Weidenfeld and Nicolson, London, 1969(a); op. cit., 1969(b); and *Muslim Society,* Cambridge University Press, 1981; and Vatin, J. C., Introduction, *Islam, Religion et Politique,* Revue de l' occident Musulman et la Mediterranee, 1-1980, 1980.
37. Although the division was originally a feature of Mughal Imperialism all the British did was improve it.

38. For one of the few sociological comments on Marwa's movement, see Lubeck, P., 'Islamic Political Movements in Northern Nigeria; The Problem of Class Analysis', paper, 9-11 May, Islamic Conference, University of California, Berkeley, 1981; for a factual account see Okoli, E.J., 'After the Kano Rioting', *West Africa*, 3311, 12 January 1981.

39. A four-man judicial tribunal was appointed by the President of Nigeria to prepare a detailed report. It was headed by a Justice and called the Kano Disturbances Tribunal of Inquiry. An understanding of the events in Kano within the context of the Islamic district paradigm, in which tribal administration and religious organization interact, will remain incomplete unless those who could comment professionally on such interaction are consulted. Anthropologists, in particular, may have a useful contribution to make in analysing the Kano disturbances.

6

Hazarawal: Formation and Structure of District Ethnicity

The creation of Pakistan in 1947 was a consequence of its leaders correctly assessing the political compulsions of Indian Muslims. Pakistan's chronic problems—including the breakaway of Bangladesh in 1971—are a result of its leaders failing to appreciate its ethnic compulsions. The problem has assumed the form of a paradox for the central government: the greater the need to come to terms with the problems of ethnicity in Pakistan, the greater the tendency to dismiss them with ideological abstractions.[1] This is often done by claiming that the ideology of Pakistan is in danger. Neither the ideology nor the nature of the danger have been successfully defined since 1947. Clearly, ethnic tensions exist in spite of the fact that the majority of the nation belongs to one religion.[2]

The two major approaches to the question of ethnicity may be crudely categorized as 'circumstantialist' and 'primordialist'.[3] The first regards ethnicity as a dependent variable, created in the main by a combination of external interests and strategies, both ecological and political.[4] 'Ethnicity,' to social scientists who approach it this way, 'is shown to be essentially a political phenomenon'.[5] To those who adopt the 'primordialist' approach, ethnicity derives from and reflects elemental 'atavistic' loyalties and 'primordial attachments'.[6] Such writers stress that members of ethnic groups give equal attention to past memory and to future strategy. They are concerned with what has been called 'the dynamics of cultural autonomy'.[7] In this chapter, I explore another expression of ethnicity which may be called 'district ethnicity.'

Hazara District Ethnicity

The formation of district ethnicity is neither a result of political alliances pursuing defined interests (circumstantialist) nor an expression of traditional loyalties (primordialist). District ethnicity is artificially created and fostered as a consequence of externally imposed administrative arrangements by a powerful central government. When the central authority is colonial, as in this case, its decisions become difficult for the concerned native parties to challenge.

The British acquired the areas constituting Hazara from the Sikhs in the mid-nineteenth century. Under the Sikhs, these areas were associated with and part of their Punjab Empire. The British created a separate district to define the areas and called it Hazara.[8] The district was about 8,300 square km and its population in the first census (taken in 1869) was 343,929 (2,007,575 in the 1972 census). When the North-West Frontier Province was formed from the Punjab province in 1901, Hazara was attached to it. There was an ethnic logic to the attachment, as the majority of the people of Hazara claimed Pukhtun origin. However, they were in the process of forgetting their language, Pukhto.[9]

The defining of administrative boundaries laid the foundation for the transformation of local ethnicity. The district was the key administrative unit in British India.[10] When Hazara became a district, records of ownership, rights, births, deaths, and so on, specifically associated individuals in the area with Hazara District. Four to five generations have come of age in the area the British named Hazara, and the people of Hazara, caught as they are between two large and aggressive cultures, have developed a new identity which they identify as 'Hazarawal,' or 'person from Hazara.' This Hazara ethnicity assumes an exaggerated identity because it is caught between the two major ethnic groups in the northern half of Pakistan: the Pathans and the Punjabis.

Pathan society is in general a segmentary system based on genealogical charters and possessing a developed tribal code, the *Pukhtunwali*.[11] The tribe reflects egalitarianism in its political behaviour and economic arrangements. The boundaries of its universe are defined in terms of the lineage and the tribe itself. In contrast, Punjabi social structure reflects a more settled and agricultural society.[12] Village boundaries define its universe, which is largely self-sufficient.

Although I refer to two major ethnic zones for the sake of simplicity, there are more extraethnic zones beyond and around Hazara. To the north, in the Gilgit Agency, are people who are neither Pathan nor Punjabi. To the east, there are Kashmiris. Central and South Asia meet in Hazara. Gilgit, which marks the boundary between them, also borders on Hazara at the Babusar Pass, north of the Kaghan valley. Hazara is thus a cultural and geographical 'transition zone' or 'shatter zone'.[13]

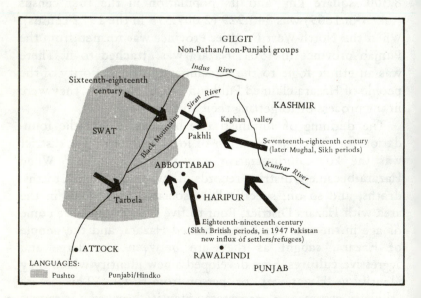

Figure 6.1: Ethnic Thrusts into Hazara: Sixteenth to Twentieth Centuries

The Hazara model is one of ethnicity artificially created
by colonial administrative arrangements which incorporate
socially and economically distinct groups living in border
zones between major cultural systems. It is therefore a
system that incorporates the variety to be found in a transi-
tional zone. The system sometimes achieves a successful
cultural synthesis, sometimes not; it is in part tribal and in
part peasant, remaining in the two worlds but not belonging
to either of them. The Hazara model might appear to be
unique but in fact it is not. The structural and organizational
features of the Hazara model may be recognized in other
areas of Pakistan, for example, in the district of Dera Ismail
Khan. Conversely, the Derawal ethnicity (between the North-
West Frontier Province and the Punjab) may be better understood with reference to the Hazara model.

History is embedded in the genealogical charter of the
tribes in the Tribal Areas.[14] In Hazara, ethnicity is embedded
in the history of the district (Figures 6.1 and 6.2). The
history of the areas now constituting Hazara reflects changing

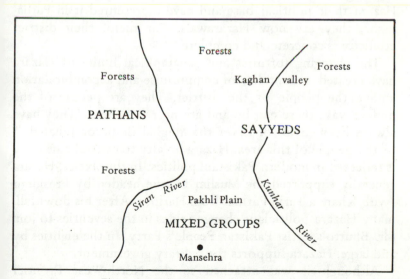

Figure 6.2: Ethnic Groups in Mansehra: 1980

ethnic domination based on different religious affiliation. In the Middle Ages, the Turks and, following them, the Mongols, invaded Hazara; then the Mughals ruled Hazara and called it Pakhli Sarkar—a name that survived until the nineteenth century.[15] Swat Pathan tribes, themselves ousted by the Yusufzai Pathans, then invaded north Hazara and laid claim to its forests and valleys. Under Sikh rule, place names such as Haripur, derived from *Hari*, appeared in Hazara. Next the British ruled in Hazara, which explains names like Abbottabad (from Abbott, the first Deputy Commissioner of Hazara District in 1849). In 1947, Hazara became part of Pakistan.

Abbottabad, the headquarters and centre of Hazara, symbolizes ethnic diversity and, to some extent, ethnic accommodation. In terms of my argument, this implies the blurring of primordial ethnic boundaries and the creation of new ones. Numerous non-local settlers, including retired government officials, have bought land and built houses in the valley and live there as Hazarawal. National leaders, too, like Asghar Khan and Qaiyum Khan (both from Kashmir), and Begum Mahmooda Saleem (from the Punjab), have made Hazara their political base and have represented it in Parliament; they are now Hazarawals. For them, their district ethnicity is concrete and complete.

The changing fortunes and geographical limits of Hazara have created a mentality of compromise and accommodation among the people of the district. They are people of the middle way; there can be and are no rebels here. 'They have always been loyal' observes the Mughal Emperor Jahangir[16] of the people of this area. Hazara loyalty to central authority is reflected in modern Pakistani politics. In the sixties, Hazara generally supported the Muslim League headed by President Ayub Khan, a Tarin Pathan from Haripur. After his downfall, many Hazara politicians changed sides in the seventies to join Mr. Bhutto's leftist Pakistan People's Party. In the eighties by and large, Hazara supports the military government.

Although it was attached to the North-West Frontier Province, Hazara is mentioned only in passing by the standard books on the Pathans and the Frontier.[17] What appears to interest analysts of the Frontier are the famous tribes in the Tribal Areas, such as the Mohmands, Afridis, Wazirs, and Mahsuds, or the Yusufzai of the Peshawar valley. Anthropologists, too, appear to have overlooked Hazara. When he raised the important question of Pathan ethnic boundaries and boundary maintenance in Afghanistan and Pakistan, Barth[18] omitted mention of the Pathan groups of Hazara. He did discuss the Hazara tribe—not related to Hazarawals—in Afghanistan[19] but did not mention the Hazara District or its Pathans. Indeed, other scholars further minimize the association of Hazara with Pathan culture.[20] This blind spot is explained by the Hazara model, which deals with the grey areas *between* the Pathan and Punjabi zones that are seldom seen as critical.

The failure to recognize Hazara as a distinct ethnic group is due to the tendency of theorists and ethnographers to view it as an extension of one of the major ethnic zones bordering it. In contrast, this chapter argues that Hazara is not a *stage* or part of a process of assimilation to one or the other zone but a discrete form in itself. It is precisely the greyness of the area which accounts for the success of district ethnicity. The critical focus of this investigation thus becomes the grey areas in between the major zones. This greyness raises certain seemingly irresolvable problems of cultural identification for the Hazarawal.

To the Pathan across the Indus, Hazarawal indicates non-Pathan identity and association with the Punjab. Paradoxically, to the Punjabi, Hazarawal means a Pathan identity and association with the Frontier. Hazarawals, whether Pathan or not, confront this dilemma when they leave the Hazara Division. 'When we are in the Punjab they call us *"Khan Sahib"* [a Pathan] and when we are in Peshawar they call us "Punjabis". We don't know where we really stand but both groups disown us. Hazarawal is neither Pathan nor Punjabi'. This sentiment was quoted to me by many Hazarawals, including young Awan students as well as powerful Swati

Khans.[21] Hazara ethnicity may be frustrating and create ambiguity, but it has its advantages.

The benefits that accrue from the Hazarawal identity are many and varied. Although the foundations for district ethnicity were laid in the middle of the nineteenth century, the concept found its fullest expression after Independence in 1947. The people of Hazara—neither quite Pathan nor quite Punjabi—discovered they could use their situation to advantage. For instance, the Hazarawals in Frontier politics form a natural and distinct group, balancing the extreme Pukhtun nationalists of the National Awami Party (Peshawar and Mardan Districts), on the one hand, and the religious party of the southern districts (Bannu and Dera Ismail Khan), on the other. As a result, the Hazarawal lobby has skillfully obtained key positions for members it puts up as compromise candidates, including the chief ministership of the province. The lobby also successfully upgraded Hazara District to division status in 1973. The upgrading meant a corresponding increase in government employment, educational institutions and projects, and so on. Hazara emerged as the fourth division of the Frontier province, along with Peshawar, Dera Ismail Khan, and Malakand. The upgrading was seen as a triumph for the Hazara lobby. Recently, a medical college was acquired for Abbottabad as a result of Hazarawal lobbying. The Hazara lobby also keeps a jealous eye on and firm control of its forests. For instance, the Hazarawal lobby pressed for the forest minister's post in government. Hazarawals also apply pressure through political and official networks on those officials disinclined to go along with their demands for illegal cutting of their own timber. Uncooperative forestry officials thus find themselves facing premature transfer, or even retirement.

Hazarawal ethnicity has provided a base for returning individuals, too. Gohar Ayub Khan, the son of President Ayub Khan, returned to Hazara to contest the 1977 elections after a long absence spent making his fortune in Karachi. Rejecting association with any one Hazara group, he appealed to broadbased Hazara ethnicity, both Punjabi and Pathan. In turn, he was seen as being in a position to benefit Hazara Division through his economic and political connections throughout Pakistan. By winning a seat in the National Assembly against a candidate of Mr. Bhutto's party, he emerged as a serious candidate for high office in Pakistan.

Although the expression of Hazara district ethnicity serves to suppress primordial attachments, they may re-emerge in the context of political conflict internal to Hazara, as will be seen later. In Hazara, primordial attachments that are presumed to have faded are activated as a result of circumstantialist factors. The Hazara case thus illustrates an important structural component in the dynamics of ethnicity. As Fortes[22] argues,

> ethnicity is now widely recognized as a 'diacritical' element in inter-group and (at some levels) inter-individual relations in all politically or economically stratified or segmented societies, whether or not they conform to the Furnivallian model of the plural society. Ethnicity or quasi-ethnicity can appear as a 'diacritical marker' of structural divisions even in traditional tribal societies. . . . [The diacritical markers are connected] with differential rights of access to scarce resources, be they merely means of subsistence or the goods and services, the legal statuses or mobility opportunities, and so forth, of modern industrial societies.

In the Hazara case, as in modern industrial societies, the right of access to scarce resources lies at the root of the ethnic problem, both in relations of conflict between Hazara and other major ethnic groups as well as in conflict among the groups constituting Hazara.

Diacritical Features in Hazara Society

Beneath its district ethnicity, Hazara society remains polyethnic, reflecting what has been termed 'structural pluralism'.[23] For purposes of analysis let me divide the people of Hazara into two broad categories, the 'dominant' and 'dominated' groups. The dominant group includes the traditional leaders of society, the Pathans (from Swat, hence

Swatis) and Sayyeds. The dominated group includes the
other groups in Hazara, such as Awans, Gujars, Tanaulis,
Mughals, and refugees (from India). The dominated group is
exclusively non-Pathan, and of these the Awan and Gujar are
the most populous and important. They have a famous
saying: 'Hazara district is difficult to live in' (*zilla Hazara
mushkil guzara*). Thus, there is a clear ethnic basis for social
and economic divisions within Hazara society.

Hazara society has created stereotypes for each group, and
the individual is expected to behave accordingly. The stereotypes are sometimes reduced to social caricature: for
example, a Swati Pathan must be aggressive, a Sayyed must
be gentle, and an Awan or Gujar must 'know his place' (i.e.,
be humble). Pathans are expected to be headstrong or obsti-
nate in conformity with their belligerent reputation. Gujars
are considered the most lowly and have been hitherto
'invisible'.[24]

Although other cultural models offset it, the dominant
ideology in Hazara remains that of the Pathans, with its
characteristic martial values of bravery and honour, in spite
of the recent emergence of primordial ethnicity among the
dominated group. Other Hazara groups have until recently
accepted the status of the Pathans, in an implicit admission
of Pathan hegemony. Recent awareness of separate ethnic
identities has not yet created a separate ideological framework for the Awan or Gujars. Both are aware of their own
identities as distinct from the Pathan but still tend to identify
with Pathan values and ideas. Ethnic consciousness has not
yet created ideological distinctiveness. Although Pathans may
no longer explicitly dominate Hazara, their ideology remains
the pre-eminent cultural framework for the Hazara groups.

As a result of this dominant Pathan ideology, there has
been a clear 'Pathanization' or 'Swatiization' process of social
mobility at work in Hazara, similar to Sanskritization in
India.[25] The Awans, in general conversation, identify themselves as Pathans, freely using Khan to signify Pathan origin
after their names, while the richer Gujars often refer to

themselves as Awans. Both groups have undeniable origins in the Punjab.

Historically, the Pathans have monopolized the forests and the fertile valleys to build a sophisticated system of irrigation for their fields. They pushed the Gujars to the poorer lands on the hilltops where there was no irrigation and where their single crop depended entirely on rainfall. The Gujars perforce remained poor herdsmen.

The spokesmen of Pathan society are the Swati Khans, who often own hundreds of acres of forest lands and used to own thousands. These Khans were often known by the forests they owned, as were the Khans of Tanglai, Giddarpur, and Agror. Poorer Swatis are critical of the bigger local Khans for destroying the forests for their own purposes when in political power. The Khans are seen as selfish and power-hungry.

There appear to be numerous mechanisms in Hazara society for the dominant groups to perpetuate cultural boundaries and maintain exclusivity. Between different groups there are differences in life-style, demographic patterns, household arrangements, cultural values, and even clothes. There is strict endogamy in Hazara. Marriages are ideally contracted within the ethnic group and rarely outside it. The ideal is only now breaking down in individual cases, due to the general economic affluence of the dominated group and the decline of the dominant group.

Language is jealously preserved by Pathan groups as *their* language. Pushto is a key criterion defining Pukhtun ethnicity[26] and therefore is necessary for Pathans to maintain in the face of strong extraethnic influences. But it is significant to note that the younger Swati generations are forgetting Pushto, which creates certain dilemmas and tensions in their society. Although less than 50 per cent of Swatis speak Pushto, there remains a high awareness of the language as a diacritical feature. Only 7 per cent of Sayyeds, who rely on more universalistic features, speak Pushto, and the dominated groups do not speak Pushto at all. Hindko—akin to Punjabi—

is spoken by the dominated group. Urdu is commonly understood and spoken throughout Hazara.

There is a clear correlation between genealogical memory
and high status. Although junior and less important lineages
invariably 'forget' or 'lose' ancestors, senior lineages retain
their memory, 'telescoping' unimportant ancestors in the
process. While 30 per cent of Swatis and 80 per cent of
Sayyeds remembered the names of male ascendants up to
four generations back, the figure for the Awans and the Gujars
was zero.

There are other figures which correlate status and ethnicity.
For instance, there is a correlation between high status and
education (Table 6.1). Also, the dominant groups live in
better housing than the dominated groups. Figures for the
Swatis and Gujars clearly illustrate the point: the highest
figure for houses with some cement construction is among
the former, 27 per cent, and the lowest among the latter,
7 per cent. 20 per cent of Sayyed and 12 per cent of Awan
houses are cement. The general poverty in the rural areas is
underscored by the fact that about 80 per cent of the total
population still live in mud houses (Table 6.2). There is also a

Table 6.1: **Education: Secondary School and Above**
(Percentages)

	Swatis	Sayyeds	Awans	Gujars
Yes	20	19	10	7
No	80	81	90	93

Table 6.2: **Housing Materials**
(Percentages)

	Swatis	Sayyeds	Awans	Gujars
Mud	73	80	88	93
Cement	27	20	12	7

correlation between high status and landownership. Swatis own the most land and Gujars the least (Table 6.3).

Thus, ethnicity inside Hazara has a multi-criteria base, which helps to explain the complex social situation in Hazara and the interethnic relationships that prevail. Other factors such as physical characteristics are also important in defining ethnicity underneath the surface similarities of district ethnicity.[27] But the traditional correlation of ethnicity and status in Hazara is being affected by changing national politics.

Ethnicity and the Democratic Process

With democratic politics and adult franchise, benefits such as education are no longer seen as a monopoly of the dominant group. In fact, too rigid a proclamation of ethnicity may be counter-productive for Khans seeking votes from the dominated group. We thus observe a paradoxical trend in Hazara: while certain Swati Khans still maintain language and hospitality as symbols of primordial ethnicity, other Swati Khans are busy discarding them and emphasizing unity in society based on Hazara district ethnicity. The shift in strategy is largely a response to the emergent and changing politics of Pakistan.

Change in Hazara society is a consequence of three factors: the national elections in 1970, which for the first time made the dominated group aware of its potential strength; the breakup of East Pakistan from Pakistan in 1971, which emphasized the importance of ethnicity in society; and

Table 6.3: **Landownership**
(In acres)

	Swatis	Sayyeds	Awans	Gujars
Irrigated	1.0	1.8	0.1	0.1
Unirrigated	8.2	6.4	1.4	0.7

the labour migration of many members of the dominated group to the Arab states, which opened new sources of income for them and provided them with an escape from the traditional structure. These factors caused interconnected results in Hazara. The traditional model of society, the world view of the dominant group, was no longer accepted as universally valid, and, in consequence, there was a revival and rediscovery of ethnicity in Hazara groups. Many Hazarawals who had successfully completed the Swatiization process were rediscovering their primordial origins. As a result, a 'retribalization' process is apparent.[28] A good example is Sarfaraz Khan of Mansehra, a retired civil servant. When I was posted in Mansehra (1969-70), he called himself 'Sarfaraz Khan Swati' (even on his visiting cards) and was active in the politics of the Swati Pathans. He spoke Pushto and his hospitality was well-known. In 1980, he proclaimed his Awan origin and mobilized Awan voters around himself.

The regrouping around ethnic consciousness assumed a political form and provided a natural base for certain national political parties. For instance, the Pakistan People's Party and its leftist manifesto—and often populist politics—found willing followers among the dominated group. The impact of national and local politics sharpened social cleavages and ended with confrontations at various levels. The traditional order in Hazara was changing (Figure 6.3).

The dominated group woke to their power in Hazara with the elections of 1970. Unlike the earlier periods, the Khans now went to the houses of the voters, however humble, to canvass. Well-known politicians of Pakistan, like Hanif, and his brother Badshah, lords of the Hazara forests and ministers, visited small villages and wooed the dominated group. It was the twilight period of the Swati lords of Hazara. The incidents in the seventies, in which Pathan and Sayyed landlords, in the Siran and Kaghan forests respectively, shot and killed tenants in a desperate bid to turn the clock back, were probably the last of their kind in this area. The Sacha incident in the isolated Siran forests was a straightforward massacre of the dominated group.

The incident in Kaghan in 1974 was more complex and reflects the processes of social and ethnic change in Hazara. It was a consequence of the success of the recently introduced potato crop grown by the dominated group in the Kaghan valley, especially in the Batakundi area. Earlier, the Sayyed landlords had watched with interest the potato experiment among their tenant farmers. Once it was successful, they demanded half the crop according to custom. Backed by the Pakistan People's Party, the tenants refused. The Party's

TRADITIONAL

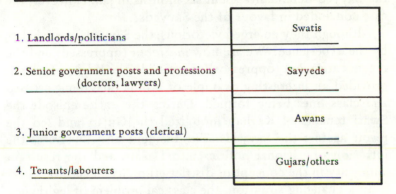

1. Landlords/politicians — Swatis

2. Senior government posts and professions (doctors, lawyers) — Sayyeds

3. Junior government posts (clerical) — Awans

4. Tenants/labourers — Gujars/others

TRANSITIONAL/CONTEMPORARY

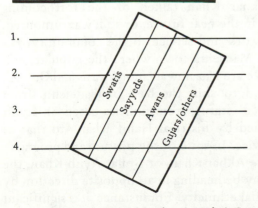

Figure 6.3: Changing Ethnic Status in Hazara

leaders came from outside Hazara and encouraged the tenants to stand firm. Encouraged by the national support and attention, the tenants took their potatoes directly to the market without paying their landlords any share. The landlords mobilized support and obstructed the tenants in the quarrels that followed. The landlords, who were well armed, gained the upper hand. In one incident 2 tenants were killed, 10 were injured, and 80 received mild injuries. The case was registered and numerous Sayyeds were arrested. Akbar Khan, a prominent Swati lawyer, represented the tenants. After a high court acquittal, an appeal was made by the tenants and the Sayyed defendants spent six months in jail. However, the case concluded in favour of the Sayyeds.

Although they emerged victorious, the Sayyeds were shaken by the experience: 'We are now *mazloom* (oppressed) and the tenants are *zalim* (oppressor)', they said. The Kaghan incident provided an interesting example of ethnic lines being crossed and class lines being formed. During the entire episode the Swati tenants of Kaghan mobilized the Gujars and led the revolt against the Sayyeds. The incident also illustrates the intrusion of national politics into Hazara and the resultant ambiguity in the concept of district ethnicity in Hazara.

In a changing situation, the classical problem of legitimacy — how men are credited with the right to rule over others — is acute. In 1980, Akbar Khan talked of the forthcoming elections, to be held in the near future, or so it was rumoured. He emphasized his work and service to the community. His political base was in Mansehra town where the population is largely non-Swati. 'We are Hazarawals, not Swatis and Gujars', he stated. He wished to shift the base of leadership from 'ascribed' to 'achieved' status; from politics based on forest wealth — as exemplified by his rival Hanif Khan — to that of talent and public service. In spite of the posture and prognosis of Hazara leaders like Akbar Khan, or Gohar Ayub Khan, the politics of Hazara may be heading in an opposite direction by emphasizing primordial ethnicity. For instance, it is significant that in the last elections the Gujars, for the first time in their history, fielded a Gujar candidate in Abbottabad. Although unsuccessful, he won the entire Gujar vote, about 10,000. Primordial loyalties in this case were triumphant.

Ethnicity, Forests and Politics in Hazara

The semantic, conceptual, and organizational linking together of ethnicity and forests is nicely expressed in the politics of Hazara.[29] The big Swati Khans own and exploit the forests for political purposes. The more wealth a man extracts from the forests, the more extensive the networks he establishes and the greater his investment (and success) in politics. Success in politics, in turn, is reinvested into acquiring more forests. It is a cycle of success and corruption. The successful ones are the lords of the forests. But to many in Hazara—like Akbar Khan or Sarfaraz Khan—they are no more than 'thieves of the jungle' (*jungle chor*).

The relationship between forests and politics is clearly explicated in society. From time to time a landlord obtains an official permit from district forest officials to cut wood from the forest. He may end up cutting ten times the amount allowed on the permit. Stories of rags to riches as a result of cutting timber illegally circulate widely in Hazara. 'In the sixties, some notable *jungle chors* drove old condemned jeeps; now they own Mercedes cars', Akbar Khan complained. There was a recent widely reported case in which a Khan fraudulently bought jungles in Kohistan worth 8,000,000 to 9,000,000 rupees and sold them to Karachi businessmen for enormous gains.

The new and expensive hotels which appeared in Hazara in the late seventies and early eighties are the visible signs of financial success. The Sarband Hotel is said to have cost 7,000,000 to 8,000,000 rupees and is owned by a forest contractor of the Frontier province. The Zarbat, Gomal, Springfield, and Purush are also owned by forest contractors, one of them a Chief Minister .

The relationship between forests and politicians has made Hazarawals bitter about their politicians. Akbar Khan and Sarfaraz Khan complain: 'There were six ministers and one President (Ayub Khan) from Hazara, yet they did nothing for Hazara'. The bigger the *chor,* the bigger the politician, and vice versa, they say.

Those who stand to gain most from the wealth of the forests are the loudest in proclaiming Ḥazara district ethnicity. The Swati Khans traditionally own and claim access to the forests. They argue that the forests belong to Hazara and should be utilized by and for its people only. The owners have invested heavily in larger politics to ensure that their views prevail. On various occasions attempts to nationalize the forests or rationalize cutting have been sabotaged by the bigger Khans. By ensuring minimum administrative inter- ference from outside Hazara Division, the Khans maintain their monopoly over the forests and their political dominance in Hazara. For them, district ethnicity—especially proclaimed outside Hazara—reinforces superior social and economic status inside Hazara. Conversely, for the dominated group, rediscovery of primordial ethnicity involves a reassessment of district ethnicity. They view the Pathans as manipulating district ethnicity to maintain their hold over the forests. The politics of ethnicity in Hazara are thus related to its forest wealth.

The flow between forests, ethnicity, and politics should now be apparent. People of all ethnic groups and economic classes are acutely aware of this flow and connection, and the

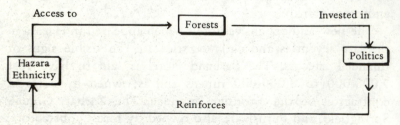

Figure 6.4: Flow between Ethnicity, Forests and Politics

crucial factor of ethnicity is never far from social or political activity (Figure 6.4).

Conclusion

The chapter points out that in Hazara society two opposed trends with regard to ethnicity are articulated simultaneously: the formation of Hazara district ethnicity – the Hazarawal – and, underneath it the survival of deeper primordial ethnicity. For general purposes, interaction *outside* Hazara by Hazarawals is marked by overt signalling of Hazara district ethnicity. However strong the primordial loyalties may be inside Hazara, the notion of Hazara district ethnicity has a momentum of its own. In part artificial, in part real, Hazarawal ethnicity defines the people of Hazara both to themselves and to outsiders.

It is too early to make a final comment on Hazara ethnicity. It is a complex and changing situation allowing large areas of anomaly and ambiguity. Emergence (as among the Awans and Gujar) and submergence (as among the Swatis) of ethnicity may derive from similar reasons – changing political or economic factors. The durability of Hazara ethnicity depends to some degree on the political trends of the country. There are three possible ways in which the situation might be transformed: by general elections where the question of supporting an ethnic candidate or the most suitable Hazarawal candidate is relevant; by a political revolution – an unlikely possibility in the near future – in which the dominated group, along with poorer members of the dominant group, challenge the established order through armed confrontation and attempt to overthrow it (ethnic cleavages will generally reinforce economic ones in this case); and finally, a continuation of the present system, martial law, where existing structures remain frozen. In the last event, Hazara district ethnicity will continue to be the dominant mode of articulation of regional politics. District ethnicity, I argue, is related to larger political developments in the nation.

NOTES

1. Because ethnicity is such a sensitive topic, traditional 'socio-economic' surveys have collected useful economic data but have ignored the ethnic factors in Hazara. See Hussain, M., *A Socio-Economic Survey of Village Baffa in the Hazara District,* Peshawar Board of Economic Inquiry, NWFP, Pakistan, 1958.

2. This is true of Muslims elsewhere, as in Malaysia. Different religions within national borders may further complicate ethnic problems. Muslims in south Thailand and the southern Phillipines—or non-Muslims in the southern Sudan—are examples of this. See Barth, F., 'Pathan Identity and its Maintenance', in *Ethnic Groups and Boundaries: The Social Organization of Cultural Difference,* Barth, F., (editor), Allen and Unwin, 1970; Cohen, A., *Two-Dimensional Man: An Essay on the Anthropology of Power and Symbolism in Complex Societies,* Routledge and Kegan Paul, London, 1974 (a) and *Urban Ethnicity,* (editor), ASA Monograph No. 12, Tavistock, London, 1974(b); De Vos, B., 'Ethnic Pluralism: Conflict and Accommodation', in *Ethnic Identity: Cultural Continuities and Change,* De Vos, G., and Romanucci-Ross, L., (editors), Mayfield Publishing, Palo Alto, CA, 1975; Geertz, C., *The Interpretation of Cultures,* Basic Books Inc., New York, 1973; Glazer, N., and Moynihan, D.P., (editors), *Beyond the Melting Pot,* MIT Press, Cambridge, 1965 and *Ethnicity: Theory and Experience,* Harvard University Press, Cambridge, 1975; Hsu, F.L.K., (editor), *Kinship and Culture,* Aldine, Chicago, 1971; Keyes, C.F., Introduction in *Ethnic Adaptation and Identity: The Karen on the Thai Frontier with Burma,* Keyes, C.F., (editor), Institute for the Study of Human Issues, Philadelphia, 1979 and *Ethnic Change* (editor), University of Washington Press, Seattle, 1981; Kuper, L., and Smith, M.G., (editors), *Pluralism in Africa,* University of California Press, Berkeley, 1969; Lambert, R.D., Ethnic/Racial Relations in the United States in Comparative Perspective, AAPSS Annals 454, 1981, pp. 189-205; Maybury-Lewis, D.H.P., (editor), *Dialectical Societies,* Harvard University Press, Cambridge, 1979; Nagata, J., (editor), *Pluralism in Malaysia: Myth and Reality,* E.J. Brill, Leiden, 1975; Schermerhorn, R.A., *Comparative Ethnic Relations: A Framework for Theory and Research,* University of Chicago Press, Chicago, 1978; Weiner, M., *Sons of the Soil: Migration and Ethnic Conflict in India,* Princeton University Press, Princeton, 1978; and Young, C., *The Politics of Cultural Pluralism,* University of Wisconsin Press, Madison, 1979 and *Patterns of Social Conflict, State Class and Ethnicity,* Daedalus 3 (2), 1982, pp. 71-98.

3. Glazer, N., and Moynihan, D.P., (editors), *Ethnicity: Theory and Experience,* Harvard University Press, Cambridge, 1975.

4. Barth, F., 'Pathan Identity and its Maintenance', in *Ethnic Groups and Boundaries: The Social Organization of Cultural Difference,* Barth, F., (editor), Allen and Unwin, London, 1970; Caplan, L., *Land and Social Change in East Nepal,* University of California Press, Berkeley, 1970; Cohen, A., *Custom and Politics in Urban Africa,* Routledge and Kegan Paul, 1969 and *Urban Ethnicity,* ASA Monograph No. 12, Tavistock, London, 1974(b); Dahya, *et al.,* in Cohen, A., *Two-Dimensional Man: An Essay on the Anthropology of Power and Symbolism in Complex Societies,* Routledge and Kegan Paul, London, 1974(a); Foster, B., Ethnicity and Commerce, *American Ethnologist* 1, 1974, pp. 437-48; Haaland G., 'Economic Determinants in Ethnic Processes', in *Ethnic Groups and Boundaries: The Social Organization of Cultural Difference,* Barth, F., (editor), Allen and Unwin, London, 1970, pp. 58-73; and Leach, E.R., *Political Systems of Highland Burma,* London School of Economics, London, 1954.

5. Cohen, op. cit., 1974(a), p. 15.

6. Geertz, C., (editor), *Old Societies and New States,* Free Press, New York, 1963; and Parkin, D., *The Cultural Definition of Political Response: Lineal Destiny among the Luo,* Academic Press, London, 1978.

7. Parkin, op. cit., 1978.

8. The area was known by the Mughals as Pakhli. Hazara is said to derive from *ming* (a thousand) or *hazar* (the unit of the Mongol Army), used by Taimur's invading forces. But there are other theories: that the name derives from Abisara, a mountain chief who was a contemporary of Alexander, or even from Urag, a district mentioned in the *Mahabharata.*

9. Pukhtuns are called Pathan, and Pukhto is Pushto in Hazara. Both are Anglo-Indian corruptions and neither are used by Pukhtuns themselves.

10. *Gazetteer,* Hazara District (Settlement Census), and Hazara District, Peshawar, Government of Punjab, Lahore, 1883-4 and 1907; Woodruff, P., op. cit., 1965. For extended contemporary case-studies involving district principals in the Tribal Areas, see Ahmed, op. cit., 1983.

11. Ahmed, op. cit., 1976 and 1980; Barth, op. cit., 1970 and 1972; Caroe, O., *The Pathans, 550BC-AD1957,* Macmillan, London, 1958; Raverty, H.G., *Notes on Afghanistan and Part of Baluchistan: Geographical and Historical,* Eyre and Spottiswoode, London, 1888; Spain, J.W., *The Pathan Borderland,* Mouton, The Hague, 1963.

12. Ahmed, A.S., *Mansehra: A Journey,* Ferozsons, Pakistan, 1974 and 'Hazara District: Land and Legend', in *Pieces of Green, the Sociology of Change in Pakistan,* Royal Book Co., Karachi, 1977; Ahmad, op. cit., 1973 and 1977; Alavi, H., 'Kinship in West Punjab Villages', *Contributions to Indian Sociology,* (NS) 6, 1972, pp. 1-27 and 'Peasant Classes and Primordial Loyalties', in *Journal of Peasant Studies,* 1, 1973, pp. 23-62; Balneaves, op. cit., 1955; Darling, op. cit., 1925, 1930, and 1934; Eglar, Z., op. cit., 1960; Ibbetson, op. cit., 1883; and Pettigrew, op. cit., 1975.

13. Barth, op. cit., 1953.

14. Ahmed, op. cit., 1980.

15. Hugel, C., *Travels in Kashmir and Punjab,* with notes by Major T.B. Jervis, John Petheram, London, 1845.

16. Jahangir, *The Tuzuk-i-Jahangiri,* Beveridge Rogers, (editor), Alexander, R., (translator), Vols. 1-2, Sang-e-Meel Publications, Lahore, 1974, p. 126.

17. Caroe, op. cit., 1958; Elliot, J.G., *The Frontier 1939-1947: The Story of the North-West Frontier of India,* Cassell, London, 1968; and Spain, op. cit., 1963.

18. Barth, op. cit., 1970, p. 119, map.

19. Ibid, pp. 125-6.

20. Rittenburg, S., 'Continuities in Borderland Politics', in *Pakistan's Western Borderlands,* Royal Book Company, Karachi, 1979.

21. The matter of Hazara ethnicity is vigorously discussed both in and outside Hazara. At various levels of national politics it is debated whether, for instance, President Ayub Khan, from Hazara, was a Pathan or a Punjabi. The answer becomes relevant when claiming dispensation or apportioning real or imagined grievances by political parties. Ethnically, he was the former, but as he neither spoke Pushto nor lived across the Indus, many Pushto-speaking Pathans consider him the latter.

22. Fortes, M., 'Anthropology in South Africa', *Royal Anthropological Institute Newsletter,* 37, London, 1980.

23. Smith, M.G., 'Some Developments in the Analytic Framework of Pluralism', in *Pluralism in Africa,* Kuper, L., and Smith, M.G., (editors), University of California Press, Berkeley, 1969, pp. 415-58.

24. Cohen, op. cit., 1974(a).

25. Srinivas, M.N., *Social Change in Modern India,* University of California Press, Berkeley, 1966.

26. Ahmed, op. cit., 1980; and Barth, op. cit., 1970.

27. Isaacs, H.R., 'Basic Group Identity: The Idols of the Tribe', in *Ethnicity: Theory and Experience,* Glazer, N., and Moynihan, D.P., (editors), Harvard University Press, Cambridge, 1975; Horowitz, D.L., 'Ethnic Identity', in *Ethnicity: Theory and Experience,* Glazer, N., and Moynihan, D.P., (editors), Harvard University Press, Cambridge, 1975; and Parsons, T., 'Some Theoretical Considerations on the Nature and Trends of Change of Ethnicity', in *Ethnicity: Theory and Experience,* Glazer, N., and Moynihan, D.P., (editors), Harvard University Press, Cambridge, 1975.

28. Cohen, A., *Custom and Politics in Urban Africa,* Routledge and Kegan Paul, London, 1969. Another result is that numerous works which I would describe as narcissistic ethnic studies (see my Foreword in Afridi, O.K., *Mahsud Monograph,* Tribal Affairs Research Cell, Peshawar, Pakistan, 1980) have been written by Hazarawals. In such studies, the author writes uncritically and with

unrestrained admiration of his own group. For example, Ayub Khan (1967) enlarges on the role of his tribe, the Tarin, in the Hazara struggle against the Sikhs. Hazara histories written in Urdu are plainly narcissistic. Swati history is glorified by the Swati author Samiullah Dhudial in *Swati History, Tarikh-i-Swati*. The author's ascendants die fighting the Sikhs. Sher Bahadur's *Hazara History, Tarikh-i-Hazara* exaggerates his (Pathan) virtues to the detriment of other groups. Turk glory is recounted by the Turk author Irshad Khan in *Hazara History, Tarikh-i-Hazara;* he traces Turk rule to Sultan Mahmud of Pakhli. The Awans are glorified by Hawari in *Awan History, Tarikh-i-Awan*.

29. It is noteworthy that parliamentary constituencies are divided along the major forest zones providing the base for political and economic strength. For instance, the 5 parliamentary seats for Mansehra are Kaghan, Mansehra, Pakhli, Upper Pakhli, and Tanaul.

7

An Aspect of the Colonial Encounter in the North-West Frontier Province

The story of colonization is not a pretty one. To the Pathans living in the North-West Frontier Province of what is now Pakistan, and particularly in its Tribal Areas, it has meant destroyed villages, water-tanks and grainstores and a non-ending series of 'butcher and bolt' raids: an almost total failure in communication between two systems. Colonization scars the colonized as it dehumanizes the colonizer.[1] To the Pathan in the Tribal Areas it meant a complete rejection of the twentieth century which in his eyes the British represented: for instance in 1947, when the British left there was not a single school, dispensary, electric bulb, or government post in, for example (what is now) the Mohmand Agency area. Here was one of the most barren meetings of cultures possible. The lack of synthesis does not indicate an inherent structural flaw or weakness in either culture, it merely reflects on the form of the encounter. Nevertheless, a miasma of romance and mystification enveloped the encounter on the Frontier. I shall examine here the causal factors that created this mystification and the social needs they satisfied.

Let me hasten to add that I speak of larger cultural encounters and Imperial systems that leave little room for the role and character of individuals. On the latter level, the Frontier has produced some of the most celebrated figures of Empire. The legendary heroes of Victorian India grew to stature here: Edwardes of Bannu, Abbott of Hazara, and Nicholson, one of the heroes of Delhi. These officers provided the Victorian era with a prototype: dashing, bold, and often killed on duty in the prime of their lives like Burnes, Nicholson, Mackeson, and Cavagnari. Later years produced Frontier officers like Howell, Cunningham, and Caroe—often more Pathan than the Pathans themselves. Their tribute to the Pathans living in the Tribal Areas is summed up in the following statement. It speaks with the voice of sincerity as it is an excerpt from an official report not written for publication and marked 'confidential': 'I spoke above of political officers as the custodians of civilization dealing with barbarians. Against this definition, if he were to hear it, I am sure that Mehr Dar, or any other intelligent Mahsud Malik, would emphatically protest. Their argument, which is not altogether in a subconscious plane, may be stated thus—"A civilization has no other end than to produce a fine type of man. Judged by this standard the social system in which the Mahsud has been evolved must be allowed immeasurably to surpass all others. Therefore let us keep our independence and have none of your *qanun* [law] and your other institutions which have wrought such havoc in British India, but stick to our own *riwaj* [custom] and be men like our fathers before us". After prolonged and intimate dealings with the Mahsuds I am not at all sure that, with reservations, I do not subscribe to their plea'.[2]

Their affection for 'their tribes' or 'people' ('my people. . . my people; the phrase rings like a bell through all that he [Abbott] wrote'[3]) contrasts strangely with the attitude of local administrators after Independence: 'Men I can lead. Animals like those villagers I must drive'.[4]

The North-West Frontier Province remains one of the most fascinating areas and memories of the British Empire. Myth, legend, and reality overlap here and one is not sure where one stops and the other begins. The Frontier was where careers, including those of Indian Viceroys and British Prime Ministers, could be made and unmade; where a simple incident could escalate rapidly into an international crisis and where in 1897 in the general uprisings in the Tribal Areas[5] the British faced their greatest crisis in India after 1857. I shall quote a passage to portray the sense of drama and history that permeates the Frontier stage: 'Both Alexander the Great and Field Marshal Alexander of Tunis served here; and between them a great scroll of names – Tamerlane, Babar, Akbar, and with the coming of the British, Pollock, Napier, Lumsden, Nicholson, Roberts, Robertson, Blood, Churchill, Wavell, Slim, Auchinleck, and even Lawrence of Arabia. Apart from soldiers, the Frontier has involved generations of administrators, politicians, and statesmen; Palmerston, Disraeli, Gladstone, Dalhousie, Lawrence, Lytton, Curzon, Gandhi, Nehru, Attlee, Jinnah, and Mountbatten have come to power or fallen, through their Frontier policies. The Frontier has not only been the concern of Britain, India, and Afghanistan (and recent years Pakistan); the mysterious pressure it generates have involved Russia, China, Persia, Turkey, and even France; on two occasions these pressures have brought the world to the brink of war'.[6]

The world's greatest conquerors, Alexander, Taimur, and Babar have not succeeded in subjugating the Pathan and have had to come to terms with him to use his passes to the subcontinent. With small populations and severely limited resources he has shattered the armies of the world's mightiest empires at their zenith: Aurangzeb the last great Mughal Emperor's army was shattered in the Khyber Pass in 1672 (10,000 killed, 20,000 captured). In 1920, an entire British brigade was decimated at Ahnai Tangi in Waziristan: killed 366 (including 43 officers) and wounded 1,683. Pathan tribes in Afghanistan, and before their 'assimilation' by Amir Abdur Rahman later in the century, provided British military history with one of its most dramatic and chilling moments with the appearance of the half-dead and half-crazed Dr. Brydon on the cold January morning in 1842 at the Jalalabad garrison; a moment visually immortalized by Lady Butler's famous painting in the Tate Gallery, London. The Doctor was the sole survivor of the grand Army of the Indus. The impossible had happened in the Victorian era and at high noon of British military might: an entire British Army had been wiped out.

Two types of writers created the myth of the Frontier: people who had lived and served in the area and those who bowdlerized the subject for popular appeal. Of the former, let us look at the most celebrated. The romance of the Frontier was to reach its literary apogee with Kipling, troubadour of Empire. His most popular stories feature Pathan characters like Mahboob Ali in *Kim*[7] and even enter children's stories like *The Jungle Book*[8] in Shere Khan. Kipling reflects sympathy for the under-dog and his ethnic references are not wilfully malicious, but the African native is still 'Fuzzy-Wuzzy', and a 'big black boundin' beggar',[9] and the Indian prototype, the low-caste 'Gunga Din', 'of all them blackfaced crew the finest man I knew'.[10] The African and the Asian are 'the White Man's burden':

> Your new-caught, sullen peoples,
> half devil and half child.[11]

Contrasting strongly in theme and tone of address is the encounter between the Pathan, in this case an Afridi outlaw, and the Britisher in perhaps the best known of his Imperial poems, 'The ballad of East and West'. The theme and literary tone are grand and Imperial, they manifestly transcend colour and race. Here is a meeting of two races on equal footing reflecting a mutual admiration and acceptance of each other's ways:

> But there is neither East nor West, Border, nor Breed, nor Birth,
> When two strong men stand face to face, though they come from the ends of the earth.

At the end of the poem the 'two strong men' have come to terms:

> They have taken the Oath of the Brother-in-Blood on fire and fresh cut sod,
> On the hilt and the haft of the Khyber knife, and the Wondrous names of God.[12]

A certain respect for the rough and wild tribesmen emerges that contrasts with the open and general contempt for natives in the Empire.[13] It is the Pathan in the Pass that forces questions and doubts about the 'Arithmetic on the Frontier' where:

> Two thousand pounds of education
> drops to a ten rupee jezail.[14]

Missionaries,[15] doctors,[16] soldiers,[17] administrators,[18] and women[19] have contributed over a century to multi-dimensional and intimate accounts of Pathan social and political life wherein he emerges as an Indian version of the 'noble savage'. There is a peculiar love-hate relationship inherent in the concept. The two main points that emerge from the sources cited above are divided between the 'noble' half of the concept, a 'different' type of native, his 'likeability', democracy', 'frankness', 'sense of humour', and the other half of the concept, his 'savageness', 'treachery', and the dangers of duty on the Frontier. Every Frontier hand had tales of sudden and violent death to tell. Nonetheless and on balance, 'everyone liked the Pathan, his courage, and his sense of humour. . . although there was always the chance of a bullet and often a great deal of discomfort'.[20]

The second category of writing is highly romanticized novels with titles like *Lean Brown Men, King of the Khyber Rifles,* and *Khyber Calling*.[21] It is not surprising that Flashman begins his adventures in the First Afghan War.[22] These novels were complemented by popular 'B' films like the *'Brigand of Kandahar'* or *'North-West Frontier'*. The worst novels of the genre create names for people, places, and situations not even remotely accurate. In such novels the economic, sociological, and historical attempts at approximating to reality are thrown to the wind. A good example is the series written by Duncan Macneil and currently popular with titles like *Drums Along the Khyber* and *Sadhu on the Mountain Peak*. Their inaccuracies may gratify and conform to images of rebellious tribesmen east of Suez living a life of luxury and sin but little else.

On the Frontier today, the romance engendered by the colonial encounter is still preserved. It began from the

moment of the Independence of Pakistan in 1947 when Sir
George Cunningham, an ex-Governor of the North-West
Frontier Province, was recalled from Glasgow by Mr. Jinnah,
the Governor-General of Pakistan, to become the first
Governor of the Province. Memories of the colonial encounter
remain untouched. The billiard's room in the Miran Shah
North Waziristan Scouts Mess is still dominated by the
portrait of Captain G. Meynell V.C., Guides Frontier Force,
and 'killed in action Mohmand operations – 29 September
1935'. Lt.-Colonel Harman (immortalized by Howell's account
of him)[23] stares from a painting in the dining room of the
Wana Mess in South Waziristan. A note in T. E. Lawrence's
hand thanking the South Waziristan Scouts for their hospitality is enshrined in a glass box in the Wana Mess Library. On
the Shabkadar tower that dominates the entire area the
plaques commemorating fallen soldiers are still clear. The
graveyard, too, is undisturbed, and the headstones tell their
tale clearly. Both a testimony to the Mohmand encounters
between 1897 and 1915. The new 'Gate of Khyber' at
Jamrud, the mouth of the Pass, quotes Kipling's lines from
'Arithmetic on the Frontier' on a marble slab.

The continuing romance of the Frontier is best captured
for me by a story Askar Ali Shah, the editor of *The Khyber
Mail* (Peshawar), recounted of an old retired British officer
who had served in the Frontier Scouts and who was recently
given permission, obtained with difficulty, to visit Razmak,
North Waziristan, with his wife. He requested the commanding
officer to be allowed to accompany the local Scouts on a
'recce' trip (*gasht*) and wore his uniform still splendid after
all the years. He observed that evening that he would go
home and was now ready to die. Perhaps with the death of
his generation the romance will also fade and die.

It is important to distinguish that the symbols of the
romance of the Frontier are maintained by political and
military administration. Perpetuation of tradition is itself
part of the romance. No such symbols of Frontier romance
or nostalgia are visible among the tribes themselves. It is

essential to underline that this is a one-way nostalgia. Pathan tribes saw the encounter as extraethnic, extrareligious and, in many cases, extrasavage. Because tribesmen were left to themselves in the Tribal Areas by and large, and social contact and administrative control were at a minimum, they remained tribal in the most profound sense and in the same sense, unencapsulated by larger state systems and civilizations. At the same time, colonization on the Frontier was not the total uprooting and destruction of a civilization as in other parts of the world by other European powers.[24]

What caused this halo of romance to float over British endeavour on the Frontier and continue to grow after it was all over? The answers are many and I shall consider them briefly on various levels. Racially, the British found that across the Indus there was a different world, the people were fairer and taller and some, like Afridis, had blue eyes and blonde hair which helped create, and perpetuate, romantic theories of Greek origin.[25] Geographically, the climate, and the physical environment reminded the British of home.[26] Psychologically, the British by the turn of the century found themselves with no new worlds to conquer on the subcontinent: India lay passive and quiet. The major military preoccupation was with the unruly North-West Frontier tribes; peripheral crises on the periphery of Empire. Imperial security bred a confidence in one's values and as a consequence of this confidence understanding of those of a remote and tribal people. Socially, the type of civil and military officer after India became a colony of the Crown in 1858 and no longer the business of a commercial company, represented the middle and upper classes of the most powerful nation on earth who were often driven with a zeal to serve, civilize, or convert, and thereby make a name for themselves. It is this answer to the question that I shall consider now.

The cream of the Indian Civil Service and the military formed the new Indian Political Service Cadre serving mainly on the Frontier.[27] The mystification of the Frontier encounter was bred by changed Imperial circumstances and the type of

its personnel. It was not always so. Early contacts with
Pathans in the middle of the nineteenth century after the
subjugation of more complex, sophisticated, and affluent
Indian States, and people spoke of them as 'absolute barbarians
. . . avaricious, thievish, and predatory to the last degree'
(Temple, Secretary to the Chief Commissioner of the Punjab
in 1855).[28] Ibbetson thought Pathans 'bloodthirsty, cruel,
and vindictive in the highest degree; he does not know what
truth or faith is, in so much that the saying *Afghan be iman*
(i.e., an Afghan is without conscience) has passed into a
proverb among his neighbours'.[29] These attitudes were to be
converted to those bordering affection, respect, and even
admiration two generations later.

Like schoolboys in a state of boredom and security the
new breed of officers at the turn of the Frontier century
craved some excitement: the Frontier was the French leave,
the excitement involving an out-of-bounds adventure, the
forbidden drink; the innocently exciting infringement of
school laws and social taboos, that the 'likeable rogue' at
school attempted without being caught.

Social reality drew its symbols from public-school life of
which it appeared an extension, a confirmation, and a parody.
The concepts of 'sportsmanship', 'games', 'honour', 'word',
'playing the referee', 'gentlemanly', and 'winning fairly or
losing honourably', the key symbols of idealized British social
behaviour found almost exact contrapuntal equivalents in
Pathan society: 'word' (*jaba*), 'honour' (*nang*), 'gentlemanly'
(*Pukhtun*), and 'courage' (*tora*). Certain things were either
'done' or 'not done'. Life was seen and understood through
these mutually recognized symbols. There was a particular
Frontier Code of its own that evolved as a consequence of
the encounter: 'It became, therefore, a point of honour with
us never to leave a wounded man behind. So if one of our
men was wounded we counterattacked in order to get that
wounded man back'.[30] But above all the Frontier tested the
man: 'To run away or to show cowardice on a Frontier
campaign and come and wine or dine with your brother

officers in the evening was a far worse punishment than risking death'.[31]

The Pathan was just the sort of person to fit in with concepts of 'honour' and the 'code' with his own equivalent concepts: 'Frontier officers were a rather special breed of the British and they were sometimes almost converted to the Pathan's sense of honour and usually to his sense of humour; it did not often happen the other way round. The same kind of stories recur whenever people talk about the Frontier; they remember, for instance, the Zakka Khel men in 1908 crowding round Roos-Keppel, once their Political Agent, when the expedition against them was successful and the fighting over. 'Did we fight well?' they asked and he replied: 'I wouldn't have shaken hands with you if you hadn't'.[32]

The Pathan was placed in a different social category to the other natives on the subcontinent: 'There was among the Pathans something that called to the Englishman or the Scotsman — partly that the people looked you straight in the eye, that there was no equivocation and that you couldn't browbeat them even if you wished to. When we crossed the bridge at Attock we felt we'd come home'.[33]

The colonial encounter was reduced to the nature of a cricket match, it was 'our chaps' *versus* 'your chaps'. The Pathan-British encounter is seen in straight 'game' analogy: 'It is a game — a contest with rules in which men kill without compunction and will die in order to win, in which kinship and friendship count less than winning — but in which there is no malice when the whistle blows and the game is over. And the transfer of an important player may be arranged at half-time while the lemons are being sucked'.[34]

Life on the Frontier was itself part of the Great Game played two continents by international players. Even the sordid business of bombing tribesmen was cast in a 'sportsman-like' mould and a proper 'warning notice' issued before air-raids. Otherwise it simply would not be cricket:

Whereas *lashkars* [war-parties] have collected to attack Gandab [Mohmand] and are to this end concentrated in your villages and lands, you are hereby warned that the area lying between Khapak-Nahakki line and the line Mullah Killi-Sam Chakai will be bombed on the morning of [date] beginning at 7 a.m. and daily till further notice.

You are hereby warned to remove all persons from all the villages named and from the area lying between them and the Khapak and Nahakki Passes and not to return till further written notice is sent to you. Any person who returns before receiving such further written notice will do so at his own risk.

Signed Griffith-Governor, dated 4th September 1933.

Little wonder that a leader in the *Statesman* disapproved of this stance on the Frontier and warned that 'war is not a sentimental business and there will be no end to it so long as there is the least tendency to romanticize it as a gentlemanly and heroic and admirable pastime'.[35]

Above all, the Frontier represented a male world and its masculine symbols a system that translated easily into classic British public school life. Women, on both sides, were generally invisible — and when encountered honoured. No stories of rapes, abductions, and mistresses are told on either side. In any case almost the entire Tribal Areas was strictly a 'no families' area for officials. It was this absence of the *'Mem-Sahib'* that gave life on the Frontier its special public-schoolboy flavour, and their presence in large numbers after the opening of the Suez Canal late last century has been considered as the final ethnic and social barrier between Indians and the British.[36]

The mystification of the Frontier encounter created a mythical tribesman worthy of the honour to play opposite the British in the Frontier Game. It popularized a universal image of the Pathan embodying the finest qualities of loyalty, courage, and honour that transcend race, colour, and creed[37] and one that approximated to the Pathan's own notions of ideal Pathan behaviour as understood in terms of his code. Contemporary British accounts end on a romantic and emotional note of contact with a people 'who looked him in the face'[38] and speak of 'an affinity born of a hundred years of conflict, a mutual sense of honour, affection, and esteem'.[39] This romantic nostalgia is not restricted to British

writers alone for most writing on the Frontier in Pakistan is
in a similar vein; for instance, articles on the Frontier in
magazines and newspapers have titles such as 'The Romance
of Tribal Customs, Traditions' etc.[40]

This romantic gloss does not change the savagery or determination of the encounter: barbed wires and bombing do not
win friends, but for the British it helped create a special
ethnic category of people who they could elevate to 'noble
savages' above the general run of 'savages'. It was an elevation
not based on sophisticated intellectual or cultural criteria but
an extension of the public-school analogy: someone not at
your school but who could take a beating in the boxing ring
or rugger without complaining and give as good as he got.
The map of British India was dyed with various colours: red
for British India, yellow for the 'protected areas' of the
Indian States and so on. To these categories was added a
special one, an acknowledged 'no-man's-land', of the Tribal
Areas. A land beyond the pale.

For purposes of my argument here the British left the tribal
structure largely untouched. Whether they could or could not
occupy and hold the Tribal Areas is not the point. As a logical
result of the traditional romantic attitude to the Frontier in
colonial eyes, tribal structures were allowed to function
uninterrupted and untouched; their tribal 'purity' was thus
ensured. External imperial expansionism worked in two
opposing directions within Pukhtun society. External pressure
created homogeneity within the tribe which ensured safeguarding and preservation of tribal cultural values. An aspect
of this pressure applied as 'big-power' strategy had another
opposite effect: allowances, estates, and titles exacerbated
and deepened internal conflict based on agnatic rivalry.
External history is seen locally as unending sequences to
aggrandize, interfere, or encapsulate and mainly explains
suspicion regarding official schemes sponsored by larger state
systems.[41]

NOTES

1. Fanon, F., *The Wretched of the Earth,* London, 1967.
2. Howell, E., Mizh: *A Monograph on Government's Relations with the Mahsud Tribe,* Preface, Simla, 1931.
3. Caroe, op. cit., 1958, p. 341.
4. Bailey, F.G., *Stratagems and Spoils,* Oxford, 1970, p. 172.
5. Ahmed, op. cit., 1976.
6. Swinson, A., *North-West Frontier,* London, 1967, p. 11.
7. Kipling, R., *Kim,* London, 1960.
8. Kipling, R., *The Jungle Book,* London, 1964.
9. Kipling, R., *Selected Verses,* London, 1977, p. 163.
10. Ibid., p. 166.
11. Ibid., p. 128.
12. Ibid., pp. 99-103.
13. Kiernan, V.G., *The Lords of Human Kind,* London, 1972.
14. Kipling, op. cit., 1977, p. 13.
15. T.L. Pennel.
16. H.W. Bellew, H. Holland.
17. W.S. Churchill; J.G. Elliott; J. Masters; R.E. North; H.G. Raverty; R.T.I. Ridgeway; F.M. Roberts; G.S. Robertson; and H.C. Wylly.
18. A. Burnes; O. Caroe; H.B. Edwardes; M. Elphinstone; W.K. Fraser-Tytler; B. Goodwin; E. Howell; D.C.J. Ibbetson; L.W. King; P. Mason; W.R.H. Merk; A. Stein; and R. Warburton.
19. L.A. Starr.
20. Woodruff, op. cit., 1965, Vol. 2, p. 292.
21. North, R.E., *The Literature of the North-West Frontier of India: A Select Bibliography,* Peshawar, 1945.
22. Fraser, G.M., *Flashman,* New York, 1969.
23. Caroe, op. cit., 1958, Appendix D.
24. Wolf, E., 'The Spanish in Mexico and Central America', in *Economic Development and Social Change,* Dalton, G., (editor), New York, 1971, p. 231.
25. Bellew, H.W., *A General Report on the Yusufzai,* Lahore, 1864; *A Grammar of the Pukhto or Pushto Language,* London, 1867; and *The Races of Afghanistan,* London, 1880.
26. Ahmed, op. cit., 1974 and 1977, pp. 123-48.
27. Coen, T.C., *The Indian Political Service,* London, 1971.
28. Wylly, H.C., *From the Black Mountain to Waziristan,* London, 1912, p. 5.
29. Ibbetson, op. cit., 1883, p. 219.
30. Allen, C., (editor), *Plain Tales from the Raj,* London, 1977, p. 207.
31. Ibid.
32. Mason, P., *A Matter of Honour,* London, 1976, pp. 337-8.
33. Allen, op. cit., pp. 197-8.
34. Ibid.
35. *Statesman,* Delhi, 13 September 1935.
36. Spear, P., *The Nabobs: A Study of the Social Life of the English in Eighteenth Century India,* Oxford University Press, 1963. See also Allen, op. cit., 1977.
37. Caroe, op. cit., 1958, p. 344; and Mason, op. cit., 1976, pp. 338-9.
38. Ibid., 1958, xiii; and Elliott, J.G., op. cit., 1968, p. 293.
39. Caroe, O., in Preface to Elliott. op. cit., 1968.
40. *Dawn,* Karachi, 10 June 1977.
41. Ahmed, op. cit., 1980.

8

Pukhtun Tribes in the Great Game

This chapter seeks to adduce certain principles pertaining to the complex relationship between tribes,[1] whose role has been highlighted by recent events, and states[2] in Central and South Asia, particularly, Afghanistan and Pakistan (or, before 1947, British India). The relationship is not of war or peace, black or white, but shades of grey; one that reflects the continuing socio-political dynamics of a special, indeed unique, situation that has prevailed in the region. I will attempt to explain the causal factors responsible for the special relationship between the tribes and states and their continued relevance in the area. I will consider the effect of the state and its policies on tribal economies, culture, and political organization, and the relevance of concepts such as 'encapsulation'.[3] I shall attempt to identify what elements of tribal culture (in the broadest sense) can be interpreted as reflecting attitudes to or interaction with the state as a source of political, cultural, or religious authority and orthodoxy.

The shortage of written material regarding my subject, its inaccessibility, and the sensitive political nature of the region, may perhaps result in raising more questions than answers. I shall be exploring various ideas and raising numerous questions which will not necessarily be entirely or satisfactorily dealt with but may suggest future areas of research and interest.[4]

I will be examining the problem as a political anthropologist working in the Tribal Areas of the North-West Frontier

of Pakistan. I shall be viewing political and historical developments in terms of tribal structure and organization; the structure, organization, and customs of the tribes will be examined
and in relation to these some of the major historical sequences
that have taken place over the last century involving tribe and
state will be explained. I shall do this by briefly discussing
four episodes in this century when tribe and state were
involved and the interaction led to various administrative,
ethnic, and religious boundaries being crossed as a result of
which great danger and confusion were created in the area.
My main aim will be to attempt to explain why it was necessary for the British at the turn of the century to allow, indeed
create formally, a buffer zone, to be called the Tribal Areas,
between their Empire and Afghanistan (and by an extension
of political strategy, Imperial Russia); and why it was imperative to, and an integral part of, what then was the most
important objective that the former had in mind, the playing
and winning of the Great Game, the term employed for the
encounter between Imperial Russia and Great Britain expanding into Central Asia in the last century. Simultaneously, and
pari passu, the Great Game allowed the tribes to play their
own little games to maintain a large degree of cultural and
political freedom and escape encapsulation into the larger
framework of Empire.

This statement in itself raises important political and
historical questions related to tribes and states in Central and
South Asia which will have to be dealt with at length, and as
such, are outside the terms of reference of this chapter.

A brief paragraph differentiating between the Tribal Areas
and the Settled Areas of the North-West Frontier Province
will help clarify the argument which will be developed. From
the time that the British incorporated the tribes that lived
along the Durand Line in the late nineteenth century into
what they called the Tribal Agencies or Tribal Areas no civil,
criminal, or judicial procedure codes were applied to them.
This was agreed to in written treaties signed by *jirgas* (councils
of elders), representing the tribes, and the state. For instance,

a man who committed murder in broad daylight and in front of witnesses in the Tribal Areas would not be tried according to the laws of the land prevalent in the rest of the British Indian Empire. He would be tried according to the laws of *Pukhtunwali*[5] (see also Part One, chapter 3) the customary and traditional Code of the Pukhtuns, as interpreted by the *jirga*. This is the fundamental difference with its wide social and political ramifications which must be underlined in terms of the administrative framework between tribal and settled social organization.

The situation in the Tribal Areas presents an exceptional, indeed unique, situation where a no-man's-land has existed almost until today; where a man can shoot his wife or cousin with impunity according to *Pukhtunwali* and still remain outside the laws that prevail in the rest of the nation. Perhaps without exaggeration, the Tribal Areas have rightly been called 'the last free place on earth'.[6]

I shall be discussing the problem of tribes and states with special reference to Waziristan, the area I have held under my charge. However, as stated earlier, I shall be discussing the problem more as a political anthropologist than a political officer.

I will attempt to show why tribal society was loosely incorporated but not quite absorbed into the Imperial state framework and left structurally undisturbed in contrast to the creation of feudal estates and even small quasi-autonomous dependent states such as Swat elsewhere. I will also show how varying social systems that are juxtaposed or connected manage to coexist and maintain their separate identity within or along larger administrative frameworks.

A conceptual framework thus exists where borders between tribes and states are deliberately left blurred by the latter and buffer zones, Frontier Regions, created alongside larger buffer zones, Tribal Areas. In any case, as I shall show, a certain ambivalence marks the relationship of the tribes along the Durand Line and on either side of it to the adjacent states. This situation poses intriguing problems for academic investigation in political sociology and especially in the Tribal Areas where no such work has been attempted to date. As stated, I will not be interested in historical sequences and dynastic periods, but in attempting to adduce the principles that underline such tribe-state encounters and which bring into relief tribal structure and organization, their characteristic weakness and their strength.

The Wazir Tribes

The Wazirs and the Mahsuds, the two major tribes of Wazir-istan, are cousin tribes, descended from Karlanri, a son of the apical ancestor of the Pukhtuns, Qais bin Rashid. Both Wazir and Mahsud trace their descent to an eponymous ancestor, Wazir, who is said to have lived some 13 to 14 generations ago (late sixteenth century). It is only recently that Mahsuds have adopted an independent identity and dropped the appellation Wazir from their names; until a few decades ago they were commonly known as 'Mahsud Wazirs'. Both tribes are acephalous, egalitarian, and segmentary in their structure and organization. They live in a highly inhospitable mountainous area broken by ravines and valleys and almost inaccessible due to the lack of roads, an area rarely ever penetrated in history by an army. According to the Government of Pakistan, 1972 Census Report based on rough 'estimates' they number about 550,000 of which 250,000 are Mahsuds (entirely in South Waziristan), about 200,000 Wazirs, 100,000 Daurs and the rest smaller tribes such as the Suleman Khel and Dottanies. The total area of the North and South Waziristan Agencies is about 5,000 square miles.

Wazir and Mahsud society is democratic and all major decisions are made through the *jirga* where each household head, *mashar* (elder) or Malik (petty chief) speaks his mind openly and may, if he wishes to disagree with the final verdict, even refuse to go along with the communal decision. The Malik is the head of the household and his status and strength in society depend on two factors: his individual reputation of leadership qualities especially wisdom, courage, etc., and the number of guns he can muster in his support, usually those of male offspring. Rarely do Maliks tower above the tribal section or subsection in leadership. The restricted economic base discourages the possibility of recruiting mercenaries.

Landholdings are small and population scattered. In any case, the *barani* (rainfed) land does not permit large accumulation of holdings and therefore does not provide leverage for any one man to emerge with economic or political superiority over his fellow men.

In earlier works[7] I had suggested that for heuristic purposes Pukhtun society in the North-West Frontier Province may be generally divided into two categories that provide two distinct models: acephalous, segmentary, egalitarian groups living in low-production zones and, on the other hand, ranked groups with super-and subordinate social positions inhabiting irrigated lands. The foremost symbol in society of the former category is that of *nang,* honour as is *qalang,* taxes, rents of the latter. Wazir and Mahsud tribes (see also Part Two, chapter 5) ideally suit the *nang* category of Pukhtun groups and I shall refer to the tribesman or group in this category as *nang* for convenience.

It is important to underline that these tribesmen, unlike those elsewhere on the subcontinent who have been subjugated and incorporated into the larger state do not suffer a sense of cultural humiliation and economic suppression.[8] In the Tribal Areas, for historical and geographical reasons, the tribesman has always emerged as one who has held his own against any larger state system whether it was Mughal, Sikh, or British. What is more important in sociological terms, he is acutely aware of his independence and the factors responsible for it. The tribesman is thus aware of his own reputation for courage, honour, etc., and inclined to exaggerate such virtues to emphasize his ethnic uniqueness on the subcontinent. This 'man to man' attitude of the Pukhtun tribesman has led to a certain romanticization of his character and his history and a mystification of the colonial encounter.[9]

Two interrelated questions arise: why have we not generally heard of Waziri martial prowess on the larger stage of India around Delhi or Bengal over the last thousand years? And why, if they are such a formidable force, have they not formed dynasties outside their area? The answers are, in part, characteristically related to the structure and organization of the tribes. Firstly, the economic and ecological limitations on such adventures. Secondly, Waziristan tribal military movements are not, for instance, patterned on Ibn-i-Khaldun's theory of the cyclical emergence of tribes, like the Berbers, who come down from the hills fresh with *asabayah* (social cohesion) to settle and start new dynasties and over three generations degenerate and are ready to be conquered by fresher tribal stock.

During military encounters in Waziristan the aim is neither to occupy or settle remote lands, for the primary principle of agnatic rivalry with Father's Brother's Son (*tarboorwali*) creates such intense jealousy that it in itself would make difficult the sustaining of a dynasty. The typical clash, invariably as a climax to *tarboorwali,* is the short raid, usually at sunrise or sunset, culminating in the capture of the village or booty, like cattle. The glory of participation in an encounter and not the setting up of a dynasty or the lengthy involvement with administration that it implies is a motivating factor. For example, all the major raids in the last hundred years from Waziristan, whether to Kabul or Kashmir, have been characterized by their *blitzkrieg* nature, by their swift irresistible penetration and by the rapid inevitable disintegration of the *lashkar* (war-party). Often the Pukhtun warrior will simply pack up and leave after a hard day's fighting without coordination with, or command from, the *lashkar.*[10]

The history of the tribes, that fall in the *nang* category as we know them in the Tribal Areas, tells of accompanying successful armies to India but not being able to consolidate empires. On their own ground they have resisted the Mughals, Sikhs, and the British, three of the most powerful Empires on the subcontinent but they have not been able to organize dynasties of their own. The contrast to the Pukhtuns who belong to the *qalang* category who have invaded India and provided Delhi with at least six Pukhtun dynasties reflects the general discipline, organization, and pyramidal authority structure of their society.[11]

The following points are of significance when examining the aspects of battle as a relationship between tribe and state in this region. Firstly, the 'seasonal' aspect of war. Tribal war is invariably linked with the pattern of crops and cultivations. Encounters tend to be fought before or after the harvest and many a leader has discovered to his dismay that his followers have tended to disperse at the climax of a battle if the current crop has to be harvested.

This leads to the important point relating to the nature and duration of tribal warfare. Because of the mountainous terrain and by its organization the tribe can ideally harass, trouble, or create problems for an invading state army in guerilla actions but because of the logistical problems cannot sustain a movement especially outside its areas for any length of time. The short-term aspect of tribal war is also related to the in-built structural democracy of tribal organization. The segmentary societies that inhabit the areas on both sides of the Durand Line are acephalous and egalitarian in the extreme, and by definition, it is difficult for them to accept the leadership of one man over a period of time. I have argued earlier that in extraordinary times of crisis, particularly involving concepts of religious war (*jihad*) religious leaders have united tribes successfully against the British. This has always proved to be a short-term social and military phenomenon and once the fighting is over the tribal groups tend to disperse and leadership again reverts to Maliks and society to what has been anthropologically termed as 'ordered anarchy'.[12]

The two fundamental features of Pukhtun tribal structure and organization in understanding this aspect of tribal warfare from an anthropological point of view are *tarboorwali* or agnatic rivalry, and an intense egalitarian sense in society. Both are interconnected and together make it difficult to sustain any tribal movements for long and under the leadership of one man. Hence it is seen that although there have been successful forays and even swift victories over neighbouring states and established armies, as I shall show later, there have been no attempts at setting up empire. Thus those tribes which I have described as *nang* as distinct from those categorized as *qalang* can and have held their ground against invading forces of superior logistical power and economic force and have incessantly hit back in the form of guerilla raids but by the very nature of their structure and organization could not sustain or consummate victory by setting up an independent administration of their own. Too often like the old Mahsud who talked to Pettigrew, the tribesman will fight a good day's fight and leave for home without orders or co-ordination within the larger context of the battle. These two key factors, *tarboorwali,* and tribal democracy, are the variables affecting both the success and failure in relationships between the tribe and the state within this region.

Waziristan

Waziristan, is divided into two Agencies, North and South Waziristan, and probably falls in a special category as the most turbulent area on the subcontinent, even in the special category of the Tribal Areas, as the literature on it offering solutions testifies. About half the Wazir tribes are placed in Afghanistan (Birmal and Matun) and half of them in Pakistan (North and South Waziristan Agencies). These tribes seldom recognize or accept the existence of the international border as a legal reality and movement between the two countries between kin clans is free and unrestricted. Added to this is the fact that no boundary commission, including the original 1894 Durand Boundary Commission, has ever visited the international border to set up posts or pillars.[13] A check or surveillance is therefore practically impossible, a factor which facilitates movement for trade or raids from either side.

It was the only area on the entire subcontinent which was at one stage directly administered by the Central High Command of the Indian Army. Up to 31 March 1924 it was considered to be an 'action service area' and political authority was vested in the force commander advised, of course, by political officers. By 1923, about 17 crack British battalions were posted in Waziristan in addition to the paramilitary forces, the South Waziristan Scouts (for South Waziristan) and the Tochi Scouts (for North Waziristan)—about 2,000 men in each Corps. During the thirties, there were almost 28 battalions in Waziristan—more troops than on the rest of the subcontinent. Such unusually large numbers were necessary to 'hold' Waziristan and its tribes who were in constant rebellion and a formidable force on their own ground. For instance, in the twenties, the Mahsuds annihilated an entire British brigade in the Ahnai Tangi.

Why was Waziristan different? And why were the tribes living here more difficult to administer than the others, themselves famous for their martial qualities, such as the Afridis and Mohmands, in the Tribal Areas? Various answers suggest themselves. Firstly, the fact that Waziristan is the only area which borders not only with Afghanistan but also with the Province of Baluchistan both providing ideal escape routes after raids. Secondly, the tribes are well armed. In 1924 'according to the latest return the armament of tribes of Waziristan, apart from other weapons, comprises 10,880 bolt action weapons of ·303 bore, of which 6,850 are said to be in Mahsud hands'.[14] And they know how to use their weapons. Generals who have commanded troops against him 'place the Mahsud highest as a fighter' in the Tribal Areas.[15] Thirdly, this is physically the largest area and the South Waziristan Agency the largest Agency in the Tribal Areas, and contains possibly the most difficult terrain in the entire area. Fourthly, Waziristan contains no fertile valleys or zones worth shedding blood for or exploitation. Finally, it is remote in terms of distance, roads, and railways, from what were the centres of British military concentration such as the cantonments at

Peshawar, Kohat, Mardan, or Nowshera. Waziristan is not on the main routes into India such as the Khyber, and hence no Alexander, Taimur, or Babar have had to cross or attempt to settle it.

In terms of the relationship between tribes and states in a historical continuum the former has been the constant factor while the latter, the unstable factor: empires have risen and fallen over the centuries while tribal society has largely maintained its political boundaries and safeguarded to a large degree its cultural and social traditions.

In 1849, the British conquered the trans-Indus Districts from the Sikhs and occupied Peshawar. But it was only after the famous attack on Tank by the Mahsuds in 1860 that Neville Chamberlain was ordered to command a field force, composed entirely of British Indian troops, into Waziristan. This was the first time in history that an army marched into Waziristan. Chamberlain advanced to Jandola and the Takkizam and returned down the Khaisaro to Bannu. He marched for 16 days through a country no foreigner had ever dared to enter. His force consisted of 3 squadrons of cavalry, 13 mountain guns, and 9 infantry battalions. In addition, there were also some 1,600 tribal levies under their own Khans and Maliks: the most formidable fighting machine ever assembled in the area.

Fearing the aims of the British in their territory, the Mahsuds had sent urgent deputations to Kabul appealing for help on the grounds that the British were annexing their country. However, the memory in Afghanistan of the First Afghan War had still not faded and the country was in no immediate mood for military adventures.

Afghan-British interests in Waziristan continued over the century with varying fortunes. As late as 1920, Wana (the summer headquarters of South Waziristan) had been reoccupied from the British by a small Afghan contingent. It was in that year that a British force of two infantry brigades advanced from Jandola through the Shahur Tangi and occupied Wana with little opposition. It was then decided to occupy Wana permanently. The road through the Shahur Tangi to Wana was also constructed.

The incorporation, however loose, into the British Empire made little impact on the tribes in the Tribal Areas and a glance at Table 8.1 clearly expresses their intransigence and persistent defiance of central authority.

The Wazir tribes were in the forefront for kidnapping from and raiding the Settled Districts of Dera Ismail Khan and Bannu: 'The raids took a heavy toll. For example, in Dera Ismail Khan District alone in 1919, the casualties were as follows: Muslims: 107 kidnapped, 54 killed, 51 wounded, Rs. 332,315 worth of property lost; Hindus: 18 kidnapped, 8 killed, 10 wounded, Rs. 738,426 worth of property lost'.[16] 'In addition more than thirty attacks were made on army personnel or establishments for the purpose of rifle-stealing'.[17]

The number of civil and military officers killed in Waziristan must be some sort of an Imperial record and at least five Political Agents, the head of the administration, have been killed on duty here. I mention these figures only to illustrate my point that the spirit of tribal independence was never fully checked by the British however savage the encounters or brutal the measures. So although the British were manipulating the tribes to their own purposes in embarrassing Afghanistan, the very turbulence and democracy in the nature of tribal structure ensured that for the British the entire affair remained a double-edged sword.

Table 8.1: **Raids by Trans-Frontier Elements on British India 1920-38**

Years	Raids	Years	Raids	Years	Raids
1920-21	391	1926-27	19	1932-33	17
1921-22	194	1927-28	18	1933-34	8
1922-23	131	1928-29	10	1934-35	21
1923-24	69	1929-30	4	1935-36	38
1924-25	39	1930-31	17	1936-37	37
1925-26	30	1931-32	21	1937-38	74

Source: Compiled from Border Administration Reports, 1920-38: Spain, J., The Pathan Borderland, The Hague, 1963, p. 187.

However, the creation of Pakistan in 1947 changed many things in the relationship between tribe and state. The *raison d'etre* for invasion, the rationale, the obvious rallying point, the logic, that is the religious motive, was abruptly removed. The *jihad* argument therefore ended in 1947 to the south and west of the Durand Line when it could have been argued that battles, kidnappings, raids into what was then British India were directed not against the local population, often Muslim, but against the rulers of the land, the British. The Wazirs and Mahsuds did come down in large numbers in 1947 but it was to occupy the shops and *bazaars* left behind by the Hindus. Today Tank is almost entirely owned by Mahsuds who own a thriving transport industry, they farm lands around Tank and are gradually acquiring the ways of the Settled Districts. The Wazirs have moved to the Settled District Headquarters of Bannu (from North Waziristan) and Dera Ismail Khan (from South Waziristan). Nonetheless, both tribes jealously maintain the independence of their houses and lands in the Tribal Areas and are not prepared to lift the facade and mystique that still hang over their lives in the Tribal Areas. The external ritual of tribal administration and tribal life in the Tribal Areas still largely continue as if little had changed and time had almost stood still.

The treaties signed at the earliest point of contact between the *nang* tribes, like the Wazirs, and the Imperial State were fundamentally different in nature, content, and tone than those between the latter and the *qalang* leaders representing emergent quasi-autonomous states such as Swat.[18] The former treaties do not reflect the expression of a subjugated or defeated people confronting superior powers. Indeed there are underlying and not very subtle notes which reduce the treaties to a worth less than the paper they were written on. For example, it is clearly hinted that the promises to 'behave' and 'forego raiding' would be promptly broken if 'allowances' were not regularly forthcoming. In political terms, the treaties hoped to prevent the tribes from raiding British India — a clause so often violated as to almost lose its legal stature and sanctity. On 5 April 1902, an agreement with a *jirga* representing the Mahsuds stipulates that the tribe 'will be of good conduct and commit no offences in areas occupied by government, that is to say, districts like Bannu, Dera Ismail Khan, the Sherani country, or Wana, or the Tochi, or roads like the Gomal or other trade routes'. The scope and area where offences could be committed are immense and left undefined. The British promised to pay the tribe Rs. 54,000, to be distributed according to *nikat* (hereditary distribution) one third each to the three Mahsud clans, the Alizai, the Bahlolzai, and the Shaman Khel. The promises for 'good conduct' were made 'in consideration of these allowances'[19] and how seriously observed may be seen by a glance at Table 8.1. The conduct of the Mahsuds over the century was recorded by the British as 'persistently and uniformly bad'.[20]

The treaties with the *nang* tribes quite specifically stipulate that the tribesman would be allowed to administer his area and organize his social and economic life exactly as he has in the past according to custom and tradition. He would however, in a rather ambivalent and not clearly defined manner, accept the fact that he now belonged to the larger entity called British India. However, the clause that he formed part of what was a 'special area' within that entity was clearly underlined. Pax Britannica was to extend to the main roads and a hundred yards either side of it in the Tribal Areas and no more. So we have a situation where the state, represented by the most powerful Empire at the turn of the century tolerated, for various historical and strategic reasons, the buffer zones stretching from Bajaur to South Waziristan Agency, almost entirely inhabited by what I have described as *nang* tribes. This situation in itself laid the foundation for the continuation of the Great Game and added a new dimension and complexity to it.

I shall mention briefly certain historical sequences to illustrate the principles of what I have been arguing above.

Waziri Tribes in the Great Game

The question arises which in fact poses the problem. Why were the Tribal Areas not incorporated and eventually 'encapsulated' in the sense the term is understood in anthropological literature.[21] The answer is not to be sought simplistically in the context of administrative frameworks or military manoeuvres in South Asia of Imperial powers but rather in the Imperial nature of these Empires, their expansion, tactics, policies, and ambitions which led to their confrontation and engagement in Central Asia. The Great Game favoured the creation of a buffer in Afghanistan. The British found it even more convenient to have a buffer to the buffer and so created the Tribal Areas zone. The historical sequences or play, if one is to employ the analogy of the Great Game, was really to move one's pawns on the chessboard of Asia without having to actually either escalate the Game into a full-fledged war or lose an important piece. But on the Central Asian board the pawns often moved with their own volition and sometimes it appeared to be more expedient to lose a king than a pawn as I shall illustrate later. Thus a paradox developed, unusual in Imperial expansionism: border tribes and areas were deliberately left independent following historical precedence and after deliberations at the highest levels. 'Such independence has always been essential to the security of any rule or dynasty in India'.[22] Buffer zones, shatter zones, scorched earth policies are common in the history of empires and on their borders. They are less common in the history of a vigorous, aggressive, and growing Empire at its zenith as the British in the last century. The British Indian Empire had finally settled on a solution to the problem of its border Pukhtun tribes: a defined zone, a no-man's-land, to be officially designated as the Tribal Areas.

The creation of the North-West Frontier Province in 1901 by Lord Curzon, himself the symbol of Empire, and its literary propagation by Kipling, the troubadour of Empire, added to the mystique of the people and area. The nature of the Great

Game provided some of the most evocative and popular writing of Empire, as exemplified by Kipling especially in his best known works such as *Kim*.[23] The Great Game itself was an analogy and extension of the public school philosophy of middle and upper class Victorian England. It was a 'game' between worthy players, with half-times, referees, boundaries, and even rules of sorts. The entire Game was cast in the mock-heroic mould and posture of Empire with its concomitant concepts that included 'honour', 'glory', with a dash of intrigue and danger in the service of 'Queen and country'.[24] On the other hand, a kind of mirror reflection exposes the tribal mind. I shall be exploring an aspect of the Great Game as seen through the eyes of the tribesmen and often turned to their advantage in this section.

The Game was complex and difficult and the peculiar nature of the problem understood as well in Delhi as in Kabul and Moscow. Accepting this, 'the tribes between the administrative border and the Durand Line were a buffer to a buffer, and the Line had none of the rigidity of other international frontiers. The countries on either side of it had each to realize that any attempt to enlarge their influence with the tribes must excite the suspicions of the other. It was the usual British compromise, but there was no other acceptable solution and, considering the complexity of the problem, it worked very well.'[25]

Although it is accepted that 'the border tribes have always played an important role in determining who was to hold power in Afghanistan'[26] the Tribal Areas were always a two-edged sword for the British who were always kept anxious and alert. However, and on balance, they could always use it to shake or knock Kabul across the Durand Line. The pious hope of international harmony contained in the Durand agreement[27] was rarely respected and the treaty constantly revoked on both sides of the Durand Line, the international border.

A series of policies emanating from Delhi over the last century reflecting minds and policies in conflict and changing circumstances were imposed on the trans-Indus areas (the NWFP): 'masterly inactivity' after the catastrophic 1857 Indian uprisings, followed by a greater show of interest in the 'conciliatory intervention' policy leading to the tougher 'Close Border Policy' and finally, by the turn of the century, to the aggressive 'Forward Policy'.[28] Throughout, British relationship with Kabul was a function of their politics in the land of the Pukhtuns, the NWFP. It is seldom realized how near Kabul is to the Tribal Areas. It is some 50 miles from the border of the Kurram Agency, less than a single day's journey by trucks and buses. For this relationship, and the playing of the Great Game itself, the situation of the Tribal Areas was found fundamental. Making a virtue of necessity the Tribal Areas were recognized as special areas; if they had not existed they would have to be created.

There were not only mighty Imperial States involved in the Great Game but also small obscure tribes living in low production zones, the tribes living along the central mountain regions that divide South Asia from Central Asia, between Afghanistan and the South Asian subcontinent. Tribesmen who matched heavy artillery and air bombardment with dated but deadly ·303 rifles that stopped and decimated entire British battalions.

In terms of structure, organization, and history of the tribes they were neither allowing themselves to play the British game, the Afghan game, or the Russian game, they were simply playing their own game. It may not have been a full blown Great Game involving major campaigns, air action, large expenditure, and sophisticated logistics on their part but it was certainly played with the unmatched brilliance of a born tactician which enabled them to remain independent over the centuries in spite of being in one of the most focal and politically important regions of Asia. A Mahsud Malik summed up the essence of the Great Game to me succinctly: 'we are like men with two jealous wives — both pulling us in their directions. Sometimes we prefer one, sometimes the other'. A thought that would have indubitably raised the ire of the Colonial Secretary in Delhi who would have assumed he was calling the shots. Thus the creation of the Durand Line added a dimension to the definition of tribal boundaries and further underlined the independence of the border tribes. Involvement with the Great Game and tribal administrators created external links with tribal society but stopped short of affecting internal structure or interfering with it. The rules were explicit: *badal, tor,* etc., the core of *Pukhtunwali,* were matters clearly beyond the laws of the new administration.

I am suggesting that apart from the romanticized aspect of the colonial encounter on the NWFP and the mystification of the Pukhtuns it generated, the Tribal Areas were an important and integral part of the strategy of the Great Game as played by the British. Afghanistan was the key and buffer state between the two superpowers in Asia, the Russian and the British Empires, at the turn of the century and the early twentieth century. The British through the Tribal Areas invariably had the edge over the Russians because of the very nature of tribal organization and structure coupled with the peculiar form of administration that was imposed on the Tribal Areas. As an example, a tribal raid or foray into Afghanistan could always be officially discouraged or disowned by the British, whereas, in fact, the British Political Agent would in most probability be financing or even directing it. So on one level he would discourage any such activity across the international border and even officially denounce it but on another level be playing his part, however, indirectly, in the Great Game.[29]

After crossing the Indus from the Punjab in the last century British administrators realized the special relationship between the tribes and the Afghan Government: 'the sentiments and tendencies of such characters are naturally antagonistic to our rule, and they can only resort to Kabul for encouragement to persist in them'.[30]

The Afghan Government cultivated leaders from Waziristan assiduously and after the last British Afghan War in

1919 treated them with an extra show of respect: 'on their
arrival at the capital (Kabul) the Maliks were received by the
Amir in person with every mark of honour and conducted
to a *sarai* [guest-house] which had been reserved especially
for their use'.[31]

Special medals and marks of honour were bestowed on the
Waziristan tribes to enlist and consolidate their sympathy:
'subsequently the Amir issued rewards and presented medals
to the Maliks. The latter were similar to those issued to his
own troops for the recent operations against the British.
Of the officers who had deserted from the militias each
received a special award of Rs. 300 and the sepoys
Rs. 100'.[32] A few years later, the Afghan strategy began to
bring rewards as Wazir and Mahsud tribes were found fighting
for the Afghans in their northern provinces. Afghan influence
among the tribesmen further increased and two corps of
Wazir militia with headquarters at Matun and Urgun were
formed with a nominal strength of 1,200. Recruiting was
opened in July 1924 and by the end of August, 400 had been
enlisted. Some of these Wazirs and a larger number of the
Mahsud militia distinguished themselves in the fighting on the
Turkestan border in the northern provinces for which services
they received generous rewards.[33] But the Indian Political
Department and its officers that manned the Tribal Areas still
had a trick or two up their sleeve and their opportunity came
when King Amanullah was deposed and his throne usurped
by Bacha Saqao in 1929.

It was not difficult for an imaginative Political Agent to
suggest to the Waziristan tribes that there was booty to be
had in Kabul, and honour and glory awaited them, if they
were to slip across the border for a few days of adventure.
In 1929, Mahsuds and Wazirs crossed the border to Khost
and joined Nadir Khan in autumn at Matun. They were in the
forefront of the force which quickly advanced and captured
Kabul by the middle of October, toppled Bacha Saqao,
and placed Nadir Khan on the throne. In his chapter on
'Waziristan' Caroe reminds us that 'this *lashkar* formed the

spearhead of Nadir's advance; it was they who took Kabul for him and made it possible for a Durrani dynasty to be restored. They were in fact the King-makers of the day'.[34] Since then they have never ceased to remind the rulers of Kabul of their chief share in that conquest.

As payment to Wazir and Mahsud tribesmen, Nadir Khan, faced with an empty treasury, was forced to allow them to loot his own capital. These tribesmen returned home by the end of the year with a great amount of loot, rifles, and ammunition. In the earlier part of the next year, a large number of rifles had been sold or exchanged for ammunition by tribesmen in Waziristan to Afghan subjects in Khost in a typical example of tribal legerdemain.

Shortly after, an insurrection almost in the suburbs of Kabul among the followers of the dead Bacha Saqao forced Nadir Khan once again to call the Pukhtun tribes to his support. This time he was able to get them home without having to let them loot Kabul in recompense. Within a few years the same tribesmen were denouncing Nadir Khan and arguing they had supported him only for the purpose of restoring Amanullah, the rightful King. The Waziristan tribes, aware that 'King-makers can as easily be King-breakers'[35] felt ready for yet another exercise in King-making and gathering of booty in addition. In 1933, they invested Matun in Khost and it was only with great difficulty that the entire Afghan army, led by the King's brother, Hashim Khan, repelled them otherwise they might well have repeated the story of 1929.

However, the game was and could be played by both parties, for the tribesman as I am arguing has always been like a double-edged sword, and it was not long before other powers attempting to fish in the troubled waters of the Tribal Areas took advantage of the situation. In the late thirties, a young Syrian from the revered Jilani family, popularly called the Shami Pir, was installed at Kaniguram, in the heart of Waziristan, from where it was rumoured he would lead an opposition army. It was not precisely clear whether against the British or Kabul. With the war-clouds gathering in Europe the British could ill afford another Waziristan adventure. Wazir and Mahsud tribal *lashkars* began to gather and the situation could have rapidly escalated for the British in their own backyard had not once again some quick-witted Political Agent acted swiftly. The Shami Pir was persuaded to fly out of Waziristan apparently, it is estimated, the richer by £20,000 in gold sovereigns. These lessons were not lost on Kabul. What £20,000 could stop a similar or smaller sum could start. Afghan subsidies to the Pukhtun tribes, especially on the British side of the Durand Line were stepped up and *Khilats* (robes of honour) were liberally distributed to visiting Maliks in royal audiences in Kabul.

The final example of interaction between tribes and states is provided with the 1947 Partition of India as a backdrop. Once again in 1947, the Waziristan tribes illustrated that they had not lost their capacity for swift and brilliant strategic military movement against larger state systems and superior and established armies. Spontaneously and voluntarily they moved in large numbers to the Muslim state Kashmir, and disputed between India and Pakistan, which was in a state of turmoil. Almost single-handedly they swept aside the regular troops and came within an ace of conquering Kashmir. They scattered battalions of Dogras, the crack Kashmir regulars and by 30 October the Pukhtun *lashkar* was at Pattan, 18 miles from Srinagar. Sikh battalions of the regular Indian Army were flown in and reached the Srinagar airstrip barely in time to deny it to the tribesmen and soon troops began to pour in from India. It was only with the massive intervention of the regular troops, with heavy armaments and superior logistics moved in by an all out airlift from Delhi, that the situation was saved for the Indians. Otherwise, the tribesmen with their dated ·303s would have captured one of the most important areas of the subcontinent and subsequently altered the destiny and history of the subcontinent. In the next 3 decades India and Pakistan were to engage in three wars over Kashmir.

Although the main battle for Kashmir was fought in the Vale, the raiders erupted into all parts of the State. The distance from home, always an important aspect in determining the length of their involvement, must be kept in mind. Srinagar is 290 miles from Fort Jamrud at the entrance to the Khyber; it is almost twice that distance from Razmak, in the heart of Waziristan. It is interesting to conjecture how the classic syndrome of Waziri war tactics would have affected their performance if the engagement has been protracted.

It is important to point out Pukhtun tribes on both sides of the Durand Line saw the Kashmir fight as *jihad* and many Wazir tribesmen in the remote Birmal areas joined the *lashkars* to Kashmir. In this situation ethnic solidarity, cutting across the Durand Line, formed the spearhead in what was seen as a straight religious war.[36] There is nostalgia even today regarding the Kashmir episode in the Tribal Areas and Maliks describe it thus: 'it was the best time of my life. We went along singing and holding our rifles. Nothing was able to stand before us'.[37] Sectional elders speaking on behalf of *jirgas* meeting political officers in the Tribal Areas even today invariably begin with '*Sahib*, we have sacrificed everything for Pakistan. We fought in Kashmir and lost kin and property. We have shed blood for Islam and Pakistan. We have a right to make demands'.

Spain's comment on the Kashmir *jihad* is particularly relevant in the context of my arguments in this chapter: 'Little attention has been paid to this, and in it lies a key to the character of the tribes and a demonstration of the limitations and potentialities of their power'.[38] I agree with the analysis in that such large-scale actions expose both the 'limitations' (jealousies inspired by agnatic rivalry in tribal structure and organization) and 'potentialities' (the formidable fighting prowess fired by a fierce sense of independence) of the tribesman.

Conclusion

The Mahsud Maliks had confronted, assessed, and rejected western civilization as represented by the British Empire and requested their Resident, Sir Evelyn Howell, to 'let us be men like our fathers before us'.[39] In the end, perhaps, one may well agree with the comment on the political administration of Waziristan made by a senior British official after he read Howell's little classic, *Mizh* that 'what a record of futility it all is'.[40] For the problem of the tribes, the definition of their boundaries in an ethnic, political, and administrative sense remained as problematic as it had been for the last century up until 1947.

Presently rapid changes are afoot with far-reaching social and economic ramifications.[41] Today there is a Mahsud Political Agent in the Tribal Areas, a Mahsud General in the Pakistan Army, and a Mahsud Development Commissioner in charge of a province. Apart from these senior officials, thousands of other Wazirs and Mahsuds serve in various departments of the State of Pakistan. Service itself implies change in life-style, change in attitudes, and eventually, changes in culture and tradition. Perhaps the distinction between tribe and state will in the future no longer be as valid as it was in the past and therefore less strongly upheld and the next generation may even see the final absorption of the tribe, its customs, and traditions into the larger state on both sides of the border.

When I ask Wazirs and Mahsuds whether they are 'men like their fathers before them' in the most profound sense of the concept, they invariably reply in the negative. 'No. We are now soft. We have become businessmen. We own shops in Tank and Dera Ismail Khan. We run transport buses. We cultivate lands in Districts (Bannu and Dera Ismail Khan) and we have given up the ways of our fathers'. Change is in the air. Schools, roads, and service are bringing fundamental changes in cultural, and social attitudes.[42]

The importance of tribes generally and the tribesmen in Waziristan in their relation to their adjacent nation states lost a dimension with the rather abrupt end of a chapter of the Great Game in 1947 when the British left the subcontinent. The tribes were 'played' by but they had also 'played off' the states, they had managed to remain politically unadministered to an extent and to retain anthropological 'purity' to a large degree. With the departure of one of the two major players in 1947 from the field a vacuum was created and there appears to be only the other major player left. The politics of the region emerging in the late seventies and early eighties are a direct consequence of the new realities and one could even suggest a prognosis and the conclusion of the Great Game begun centuries ago.

The two immediate results are that the tribesman: (i) in Pakistan sets the pace for encapsulation in his relationship to the larger state whether for economic development or political absorption as in the seventies but in an increasingly cordial relationship;[43] (ii) finds his role in the old Great Game is now severely limited with the departure of one player. The balance appears palpably uneven. In addition, even his structure and organization are in danger of being affected by the migration in thousands to the Gulf States, the acquirement of land in the Settled Areas, and involvement in administration and business in the rest of the country.

Although their structure and organization are still largely intact in the Tribal Areas economic developments, migrations, and education will most certainly have affected the martial spirit and attitudes of the tribesmen. The last military excursion and adventure on any scale involving the Waziristan tribes was in 1947-8, over 30 years, that is, a full generation ago. Whether the new generation is capable of emulating the independent spirit and martial qualities of their forefathers, or consider that model worth shedding blood for, is a question that only time and history can answer.

NOTES

1. The definition of 'tribe' is still problematic in anthropology as the title of a chapter by an eminent anthropologist studying the subject illustrates: 'The concept of the "Tribe": a crisis involving merely a concept or the empirical foundations of anthropology itself?' Godelier, M., *Perspectives in Marxist Anthropology,* Cambridge, 1977.

2. The question of the consolidation of modern nation states and their relationships with local tribes is now engaging anthropologists and is an important subject in the light of current political developments in Africa and Asia. See Colson, E., 'Contemporary Tribes and the Development of Nationalism'; and Skinner, E., 'Group Dynamics in the Politics of Changing Societies: The Problem of Tribal Politics in Africa in *Essays on the Problem of Tribe,* Seattle and London, 1971; and Dupree, L., and Albert, L., *Afghanistan in the 1970's,* New York, 1974.

3. For a comment on encapsulation I will borrow from Professor Bailey: 'Research has uncovered and made sense of societies which have no authorities and are not states and yet enable their people to live orderly lives. Furthermore, given the anthropologist's strong interest in small communities encapsulated within larger societies—in villages, tribes within nations, or colonial dependencies, sections of urban populations, and so forth—who seem to operate political structures in spite of the fact that the State authorities are only occasionally involved, he has no choice but to consider those as political structures, which are partly independent of, and partly regulated by, larger encapsulating political structures'. Bailey further underlines the relationship between encapsulator and encapsulated: 'Dependency, as the word does not imply, is always in fact a two-way interaction. Exactly the same kinds of questions about adjustment or failure to make adjustment between the encapsulated structure and its environment can be asked, even when some parts of the environment are themselves political structures'. Bailey, F.G., *Stratagems and Spoils,* Oxford University Press, 1970, p. 12.

4. I have attempted to follow at least one strand of this argument in chapter 3.

5. Generally defined as *melmastia* (hospitality), *badal* (revenge), *nang* (honour), and *tor* (bravery). See Ahmed, op. cit., 1976, 1977, and 1980; Barth, op. cit., 1969; Spain, op. cit., 1963; and Caroe, op. cit., 1958.

6. Moynahan, B., 'The Free Frontier: Warriors of the Khyber Pass', in *The Sunday Times Magazine,* London, 21 March 1976.

7. Ahmed, op. cit., 1976, 1977, and 1980.

8. Bailey, F.G., *Tribe, Caste ünd Nation,* Manchester, 1960; and op. cit., 1970: C. von Furer-Haimendorf, 'The changing positions of tribal populations in India', in *Royal Anthropological Institute Newsletter,* No. 22, October 1977.

9. Ahmed, A.S., 'An Aspect of the Colonial Encounter in the North-West Frontier Province', in *Asian Affairs,* Vol. IX, Part III, October 1978; and 'The Colonial Encounter on the NWFP: myth and mystification', in *Journal of the Anthropological Society,* Vol. IX, No. 3, 1978. See also chapter 7.

10. To illustrate the typical individualistic approach to battle, indeed life, of the Mahsud I quote a British officer who served on the Frontier: 'Nearly twenty years later Pettigrew, the author of *Frontier Scouts* (Selsey, Sussex, 1965) found himself on the Barrier (north of Sorarogha) in the course of a patrol to cover an engineer road reconnaissance. He records that he had always been puzzled by the verdict in the official history that success had been due to surprise and, meeting an ancient Mahsud on the top of the hill, he asked him if he had been in the fighting. "Of course, that is my house over there." "Then tell me, why didn't you fight hard to hold the ridge?" He shrugged his shoulders, hands palm upwards, a smile showing through his thick, untidy beard. "It was freezing. There had been snow, and we were hungry and cold, so we went away".' See Elliott, op. cit., 1968, p. 258. This independent and highly democratic attitude to tribal war is a typical characteristic of tribesmen in the *nang* category and a direct reflection of his own tribal structure and organization in terms of what I am arguing.

11. The Yusufzais of Rampur, who ruled Rampur State, trace their ancestry to Yusuf the eponymous ancestor of the *qalang* Yusufzai and have a highly developed ethnic sensibility. Elphinstone, M., *An Account of the Kingdom of Caubul,* Vols. I and II, Karachi, 1972 — reprint.

12. Middleton, J., and Tait, D., (editors), *Tribes Without Rulers,* London, 1970.

13. In the summer of 1979, with a large company of Wazir Maliks, I became the first Political Agent, indeed the first official or outsider, to visit Birmal right up to the Durand Line. The impact of this visit was tremendous. Wazirs fighting near Kabul with the *Mujahideen* or religious fighters against the Russian backed regime took time off to write to 'congratulate' me. They were highly aware that their last sanctuary had finally been 'opened'.

14. *Waziristan Border Administration Report for 1924-5: 16.* Keppel, A., *Gun-running on the Indian North-West Frontier,* London, 1911.

15. Skeen, Sir A., *Passing it on: short talks on tribal fighting on the North-Western Frontier of India,* Quetta, 1978 — reprint.

16. *N-WF Enquiry Report,* p. 15.

17. Spain, op. cit., 1963, p. 187.

18. The British signed treaties, subsequently ratified by the Government of Pakistan (Instruments of Accession), clearly specifying terms and conditions, rights and duties of the Rulers, etc., with the Wali of Swat, the Mehtar of Chitral, the Nawabs of Amb and Dir. All important matters such as defence, external affairs, ecclesiastical affairs, etc., would be directly the concern of the central government.

19. Howell, op. cit., 1931.

20. Ibid.

21. Alavi, op.cit., 1973; and Bailey, op.cit., 1960 and 1970/1977. See also note 8.

22. Elliott, op. cit., 1968, p. 53.

23. Kipling, op. cit., 1960.

24. Ahmed, see note 9.

25. Elliott, op. cit., 1968, p. 53.

26. Spain, op. cit., 1963, p. 233.

27. 'The Government of India will at no time exercise interference in the territories lying beyond this Line on the side of Afghanistan, and His Highness the Amir will at no time exercise interference in the territories lying beyond this Line on the side of India'. (Point 2 of the Durand agreement, signed in Kabul by Amir Abdul Rahman on 12 November 1893.)

28. Bruce, R.I., *The Forward Policy and its Results,* London, 1900.

29. For an apt topical comment on political administration and the Great Game, see Caroe, O., Review of *Mizh* by Howell, E., in *Asian Affairs,* February 1980, pp. 88-90.

30. Letter No. 120-P, dated 8 October 1881, written by Major Macaulay, Deputy Commissioner, Dera Ismail Khan, Proceedings 21 July 1882, Nos. 8-20, quoted on page 2 of *Waziristan Border Administration Report for 1924-5.*

31. General Staff, *Operations in Waziristan,* Army Headquarters, Calcutta, India, 1921, p. 84.

32. Ibid.

33. General Staff, *Military Report on Waziristan,* Army Headquarters, Calcutta, India, 1935.

34. Caroe, op. cit., 1958, p. 407.

35. Ibid.

36. Stephens, I., *Pakistan,* London, 1963; Caroe, op. cit., 1958; and Spain, op. cit., 1963.

37. Spain, op. cit., 1963, p. 210.

38. Ibid., p. 206.

39. Howell, op. cit., 1931 (Preface).

40. Ibid., p. 48.

41. Ahmed, op. cit., 1977.

42. Ahmed, A.S., Foreword to *Mizh* by Howell, E., Karachi, 1980 — reprint.

43. Ahmed, op. cit., 1977.

9

The Arain Ethic and the Spirit
of Capitalism in Pakistan

General Zia-ul-Haq came to power in Pakistan exactly nine years ago amidst predictions, including his own, that he would not last more than a few months. It is a good time for stock-taking.

The period has had bad moments and publicity: the hanging of Mr. Zulfikar Ali Bhutto, stories of lashings, amputations, deprivation of women's rights etc. It has also been fraught with international crises in neighbouring lands. Afghanistan—which sent 3 million refugees into Pakistan—Iran, and now, on the southern border, the Sikhs in India are in turmoil. Internal tensions have sometimes been severe as in Sind.

How has Pakistan survived, indeed in economic terms, even thrived? Perhaps the most significant factor has been the nine years of relative internal stability. Indeed, this is the longest period of stability Pakistan has enjoyed in its history after Ayub Khan's rule which ended in 1969. We may look for answers in the rural areas.

About 75 per cent of Pakistan's 90 million people are in the rural areas; rural society is the silent majority of Pakistan politics. The Province of Punjab is important because it contains about 57 per cent of Pakistan's population and its richest agricultural lands. It also dominates in the army and the civil services, the two key organizations in the country.

There are two major sources providing stability to rural society and strength to the economy. First, remittances worth about 3 billion dollars, sent annually by some 3 million Pakistanis working abroad, although there are signs that this source may be drying up. Second, the remarkable agricultural success story of the small farmers of Pakistan, a good example of which are the Arains. Their numbers are not known.

Max Weber's thesis applies to these farmers. It is an Asian version of the Protestant Ethic and the Spirit of Capitalism. Arain frugality, thrift, and hardwork fuse into an understanding of Islamic practice as puritanical and earnest. The combination makes for a successful farmer. Arains are mainstream Sunni Muslims and have not joined controversial groups like Ahmedis. In spirit and ritual, they align with fundamentalist preachings of Islam. Like the Arain head of the party, Mian Tufail, they tend to support the Jamaat-i-Islami, Pakistan's major religious party.

When Pakistan was created in 1947, the Arains migrated *en bloc* from the districts of East Punjab. They sold vegetables, fruits, and flowers and were once considered at the bottom of the Punjabi social order dominated by Rajputs, Jats, and Gujars. Arains point out some key figures in the regime such as General Zia and Dr. Afzal, until recently, the Education Minister, as Arains with a new sense of pride.

Farmers like the Arains, in an important sense, have provided the main anchor to Zia's stability (the weather has helped agriculture too). Escaping their low social position thousands are abroad, especially in the Arab States, sending home money regularly. In the UK, too, especially in cities like Glasgow and London, Arains maintain the work ethic having moved out of factories and now own thriving groceries and cloth stores. Money sent home is invested in tractors and tube-wells.

Pakistan in 1947 became a symbol for these refugee farmers, a sacred trust. ('I will tell you what Islam and Pakistan mean', said Zia in an emotional voice, tears welling in his eyes, leaving the official text at an International Conference on Islam in Islamabad in 1983, 'It is a vision of my

mother struggling on tired feet, with her worldly possessions
in her hands, when she crossed the border into Pakistan').
They crossed Sikhs leaving behind their lands and heading in
the opposite direction for East Punjab where they would
create India's most prosperous agricultural community. From
Lahore, south to Multan, and crossing into Sind — and thereby
creating friction with Sindhi farmers — the Arains worked
the land. Most of the farms are small, 2 to 10 acre, family
concerns.

The spirit of capitalism is embodied in the Arains. The
green farms of the Arains are an enchanting feature of the
otherwise generally arid landscape. They monopolize the
mandis, the agricultural market, and trade centres, in much
of the Punjab.

When the British conquered the Punjab from the Sikhs in
their drive towards the north-west regions of India they
inherited a potentially rich agricultural zone. The famous
canal colonies, built around an elaborate network of canals,
were created. New districts, named after Victorian heroes,
appeared on the Punjab map: Lyallpur, after Lyall, and
Montgomery after Montgomery (renamed recently, Lyallpur,
as Faisalabad after the Saudi King; and Montgomery, as
Sahiwal after the group which lives there). Among the small
farmers settled here were the Arains. The British called them
'peasant proprietors' (they were the 'middle peasants' of
Mao). Punjab was destined to become the 'bread basket' of
British India.

The push towards the Indus created in the farmers a
frontier spirit, not unlike that of the mid-west farmer in the
USA now in the heart of the Bible Belt. The head of the farm
relied on his own ingenuity to tame the land. Unlike the
farmers along the barren Rawalpindi-Jhelum road, descendants of warrior groups like the Rajputs, who supplemented
their incomes by joining the British Army, the Arain worked
his farm. He learned to depend on his sinews; it gave him
pride in the land. It also made him of the earth, earthy. He
was seen by the bigger landlords as socially crude.

Even today the Arain world is agricultural prices, varieties of seeds and fertilizers, and timings of the canals which bring water to his fields. He has little of the elegance and polish of the traditional feudal landlords of the Punjab, Noons and Tiwanas, of Rajput origin. Afternoon tea parties, partridge shoots, or polo are not associated with Arains. Nor does he waste his energies on dancing girls, or drunken evenings listening to poetry, or numerous marriages, a pastime of the landed gentry through which they alienated their lands.

If Zia symbolizes Arain values, Mr. Bhutto symbolizes those of the other, the aristocratic landlord, class. In a sense, the confrontation between these two is an important theme of contemporary Pakistan politics. But it was not only between two kinds of politics in Pakistan. It also reflected two distinct social ideologies and classes.

Zia is, as we know, an Arain, and reflects Arain values. The son of a junior officer, Zia is self-consciously proud of his humble background and hence aware of the distance he has travelled to high office. In spite of critics' accusations – of hypocrisy, lying, etc., – and of life in the westernized elite armoured corps and at the president's palace, he is still known for his abstemious piety, and humility.

Bhutto, on the other hand, was born with a silver spoon in his mouth. The world was his oyster. Berkeley and Oxford added flair but failed to conceal the characteristics of the Sindhi landlord. His charisma and brilliance were personal but his political style reflected north-Indian feudalism. For Bhutto's class, Arain values were lowly and contemptible. Interestingly, neither Zia nor Bhutto publicly identified with, or claimed to speak for their group; one pushed outward, to Islam, the other downwards to the common people.

Recent World Bank reports suggest Pakistan, presently with a per capita income of about 350 dollars, is on the threshold of joining the middle level nations of the world leaving behind its neighbours in South Asia, notably India and Bangladesh. A sort of 'green revolution' that characterized Ayub Khan's era is afoot. One sign is that Pakistan is exporting wheat, rice, and sugar. Unsung and little known, the small farmer like the Arain may well be the hero of Pakistan's success story in agriculture.

The story provides a stable and prosperous foundation to society and gives Zia's vision of Pakistan a legitimacy and his politics a base. It also sustains the extravagant ideological ambitions of those who dream of Pakistan's special destiny.

Part Three
Contemporary Issues

10

The Afghan Refugees

'A Pathan took revenge after a hundred years and said it was too quick' is a common proverb of the Pathans, the major ethnic group of Afghanistan and the North-West Frontier Province of Pakistan. It is only 6 years since the summer when events unfolded in Afghanistan which would invite the Russians. As a result of those events, almost 3 million refugees poured into neighbouring Iran and Pakistan. Today, the refugee problem in Pakistan is assuming serious proportions both for hosts and guests. Over both, hangs the question of the future of the refugees.

The problem really stems from the type of refugees the Afghans are. They are a swaggering, armed, aggressive lot. Their bearing adds to their historical image of themselves as conquering warriors. They are quite unlike the refugees who came to Pakistan from India in 1947, and the Biharis from Bangladesh in 1971. Those refugees, their lives permanently broken, their destinations unknown, were grateful to accept whatever they could get. In any case, the Afghans do not accept their own role as guests passively.

'This land', Afghans aver, 'was conquered by our ancestor Ahmad Shah Abdali' (see also Part One, chapter 1, notes 4 and 14). Indeed, Ahmad Shah the extraordinary first king, indeed creator of modern Afghanistan, ruled most of what is now Pakistan in the eighteenth century. Never known for their fear of trespassing south of the Khyber Pass, India has been ruled by at least five or six Afghan dynasties—they do not feel trespassers. Pakistanis, especially those unacquainted with Pathan history as in the Punjab and Sind, find this kind of assertiveness uncomfortable. They would like to see more gratitude, perhaps even some humility, on the part of their guests.

On crossing into Pakistan, Afghans were received as fellow Muslims and, equally important, fellow tribesmen. The government set up one of the best refugee organizations of the world. They were given a tent, subsistence allowances and, most critical of all for refugees, hope. But, there was a price of a sort. They became part of an international argument in geopolitics. Their private agony was put on display. They played a part in the circus arranged for VIPs to Pakistan, mimicking anger, and swearing revenge. From Princess Anne to Kirk Douglas celebrities applauded them and had photographs taken in their camps. One of Pakistan's major foreign policy planks, and strengths, became the presence of the Afghan refugees.

Among the refugees, there is a painful survival of the fittest process at work. Afghans have muscled into various enterprises such as trucking, selling cloth, etc., from Peshawar down to Karachi. Some have reverted to more traditional employment such as hold-ups. Their tribal networks, crossing international boundaries, allow them to traffic in banned weapons and drugs.

The anarchy that is revolution, a world turned inside out, is reflected in the camps. Families are dispossessed, their unity shattered. Young men disappear in turns to fight the holy war, *jihad,* in Afghanistan. Women and children wait. Squalor and despair are evident. More important, the kaleidoscope of traditional patterns has been shaken — leadership, women, and even children are affected. New voices, are being heard, new values emerging. Afghan society will never be the same again. Perhaps also affected will be their reputation as invincible warriors, the Jacks who slay giants in the shape of super-powers.

The Afghans are reacting in a traditional manner to the crisis. There is talk of raids, revenge, and guns — the stuff of

Pukhtunwali, the Pathan Code of honour (see also Part One, chapter 3). There is a great deal of rhetoric. But it is mimicry. Their mock aggressiveness and mock fanaticism have become a substitute for substance, serious thinking, and concerted action. The clarity of their political vision remains obstructed by petty squabbles and personal jealousies. Repeatedly, the major half dozen parties have failed to unite. Recently, their mutual animosity has resulted in expulsion orders from Peshawar. Their attempts to blow up rivals with explosives were making Pakistanis in the Frontier Province nervous. These Afghans do not quite fit the romantic mould of the dashing tribesman in *Kim* or *The Far Pavilions*, created by the novelists of the British *Raj*.

The romantic image of the Pathan was that of a fearless, blue-eyed, hawk-nosed warrior silhouetted, with his *jezail*, on a mountain ridge. Heroic deeds from the past littered the barren land. Sir Olaf Caroe, a British Governor of the Frontier Province, was one of the main authors of the image through his classic work *The Pathans*. Some years before his death, he expressed the opinion that writers who lived and worked in the Frontier Province, were partly responsible for this image. Indeed, he could only think of one or two examples, Wali Khan, for instance, of those who approximated to the ideal. The actuality did not match the ideal. It needed a test, a jolt, to be exposed. One victim of the Afghan crisis may well be the romantic image of the Pathan warrior (see also Part Two, chapter 7).

In contrast to the Pathans who were expected to perform well, the performance of non-Pathans has been notable. The best known resistance fighter, Ahmad Shah Massoud, of Panjsher valley fame, is not a Pathan.

Whatever Afghan Government reports of consolidation in Afghanistan, the price has been a high one—3 heads of government assassinated, 3 million refugees living just outside national borders, and a state of civil war in the country.

The world whose capacity for concentration is infantile has grown indifferent to the sufferings of the Afghan refugees.

It seeks its news of tragedy with morbid fickleness elsewhere — a famine in Somalia last year, a communal riot in India early this year, a tribal massacre in Uganda this summer. Had it not been for the efforts of the State Department in Washington, in keeping the Afghan issue alive, for their own Great Game with the Soviets, perhaps this interest would have been further weakened.

Revenge and honour — the core themes of Pathan folklore — still sound in the village *hujras* where men sit in discussion. But the Pathan code has become a burden. The world has moved swiftly for the Afghans and the tribal code appears bankrupt in dealing with its new problems. Behind the vitality which shines in the eyes of young Afghan children in the camps, there are flashes of despair. There is a growing neurotic uncertainty about the future for the elders. An uncertainty which is contagious for Pakistanis.

In the trans-Indus Provinces, Baluchistan and the Frontier, people wait. They wait for dramatic solutions to seemingly irresolvable problems. And in their despair they have nothing but traditions, including proverbs, to cling to. The Afghans still have time, 94 years, to take revenge. This raises a host of questions for apprehensive Pakistanis. Will this period be spent in Pakistan, if so, will the refugees become permanent residents? How will the presence of thousands of battle-trained armed Afghans affect life in Pakistan? And will the enemies of Pakistan use the refugees as part of a Trojan horse strategy? The answers have wide ranging social and political implications for South Asia.

An Afghan Refugee Grows Up

Returning to the scene of a great tragedy is not easy; it is more difficult when the tragedy is not over. On a visit to Peshawar, northern Pakistan, I talked with Afghans involved in various degrees with the problems of their country.

Javed, whom I last met a couple of years back as a boy of fourteen, appeared older, more in command of himself.

There was a hint of new strength in him. Javed talked of his father who had disappeared since his last incursion into Afghanistan as a guerilla fighter. Deep inside Javed was a conviction that perhaps something had gone wrong. His new maturity attempted to hide his unease. He had a mother and three sisters to worry about now. The honour of his women —a cardinal feature of the Afghan moral and social code— was his new anxiety. He was still too young to cope with this responsibility. It was a chilling awareness of a new pain. His pain touched me. But I had nothing to offer. For me he symbolized the Afghan resistance —and the Afghan tragedy.

Exile diminishes anyone. Yet to many Afghan refugees Pakistan is historically a second home. Culturally and ecologically they are in familiar surroundings. Peshawar and Quetta are known cities to many Afghans. Their exile is therefore partial and complex.

The refugees feel they may be in Pakistan for an indefinite period. Mud and brick rooms are replacing tents in the refugee camps. Aza Khel, a few miles from Peshawar, is perhaps the most famous camp because it is on the itinerary for foreign dignitaries. Today, Aza Khel has the appearance of a permanent, well-organized bustling little town. Pakistan, too, appears to have resigned itself to this idea. Opposite Aza Khel, on the other side of the Grand Trunk Road, the government has recently built gigantic godowns to hold wheat and other commodities.

It is a paradox of the Afghan situation that the 'Pukhtunistan' problem has been abruptly killed. Killed not by political machinations but as a result of the refugee situation. 'Pukhtunistan', Afghan propaganda once claimed, would be a homeland for the Pukhtun tribes of Pakistan and eastern Afghanistan. The idea was rooted in the memory of Afghan conquerors who once ruled the Peshawar valley up to the river Indus before the British came. Today, the Afghans are in Peshawar but not as conquerors. And those Pakistanis who toyed with the 'Pukhtunistan' idea in the Peshawar valley are showing signs of impatience with their guests. As a result of the 300,000 refugees in Peshawar (of an estimated 3 million in Pakistan) prices have risen sharply. Accommodation is difficult to find and competition for cultivated land heightens local tension. But this does not detract from the struggle in Afghanistan.

'How is the fighting in Afghanistan?' I asked Javed and his friends. The answer was not simple. Both adversaries are learning from and adapting to each other. The classic Afghan strategy of capturing the heights to stop an enemy (so effective against the British) is proving ineffective. The Russian gunships simply fly in from behind to attack and dislodge the snipers. The Afghans have learned not to destroy captured Russian equipment as they did in the early days of the conflict. Now they cannibalize tanks, for instance, and use the parts with an ingenuity born of adversity.

The fight in Afghanistan is also linked with a larger global pattern, Javed explained. 'If', he said, 'we are getting weapons we need from Egypt the death of one man there – Sadaat – could affect our supplies'. Not for the first time in their history an Afghan war was becoming part of a Greater Game in world politics.

Two interlinked themes appeared strongly in Javed's talk: the determination to return home, and the realization that the path home will not be easy. The realization of his refugee status, the greater convulsions in his life, the struggle for the future had pushed a bewildered young boy prematurely into adulthood. He was consumed by the desire to return – and the need for restoring honour. 'We have a saying', he told me, 'an Afghan took revenge after a hundred years and said "I took it too quickly" '. Javed was already filling his father's shoes.

How to Aid Afghan Refugees

In the North-West Frontier Province of Pakistan, about 2 million refugees have crossed the border from Afghanistan and are temporarily living there; another 700,000 are in

Baluchistan. I shall not touch on the political genesis of the problem or on its continuing political ramifications, except to forecast that the refugees will be living on this side of the Durand Line longer than most people expect. Hence the urgency for planning, especially long-term planning.

Awareness of social factors is almost absent from the entire refugee scene. For instance, in a discussion with some United Nations officials, I discovered that some of them were in Pakistan for the first time in their lives, and knew nothing or little about the area or its history. As they were West European, they could not appreciate the administrative situation in the Tribal Areas or the historical nuances of the Great Game. Some of them manifested little of the missionary spirit which one imagines is necessary for such a task. They appeared more concerned about hotel rates, and taking precautions against local diseases such as malaria. After staying in air-conditioned, four-star hotels, removed from the filth and chaos of the refugee camps, for two or three weeks, they would rush to Geneva to write a report with suggestions on the camps. The depth, perception, and even validity of the conclusions were to my mind open to doubt.

While relief agency staff are often short-term visiting specialists, the Pakistani administrators are invariably from the Civil Service (now the Tribal Area Group and the District Management Group). District administration in the subcontinent is based on the philosophy of maintaining law and order, not inducing change. Yet a refugee crisis demands staff prepared and trained for dealing with rapid change. Anthropologists too must adapt their methods to take account of change and upheaval.

Both relief agencies and host country administrations tend to be exclusive and over-concerned with questions of procedure. The staff is largely conservative.

The role of the host country administration is as interesting as it is difficult. It is that of a broker between relief agencies and refugees, often attempting to interpret one to the other. The role requires imagination and understanding, for whereas

relief agencies reflect some of the more advanced achievements of the twentieth century (computers, international
organizations, etc.), refugee problems are familiar since the
Middle Ages. A need for understanding of local culture and
structure is all the more apparent.

It is not uncommon for refugees to complain and often
play off the relief agencies against the administration (in any
case most of the elders in one form or another have played
their parts—indeed are still playing—to some degree in the
Great Game over the decades). It goes to the general credit of
Pakistan that so far no major complaints have been lodged by
refugees. Most of the complaints by these refugees are against
their own leaders, who have formed political parties and tend
to attract publicity to and assistance for their own groups,
based largely in Peshawar.

The problem is compounded for the administration. How
does an official explain to a relief agency that the Tribal
Areas are a part of Pakistan and yet a 'special' part, and that
for various historical and political reasons it is not advisable
for foreigners to roam around in them? Without knowledge
of the history of the region, the proposition that there is a
large area within a country not fully administered by it does
not make sense. The point is fundamental and anyone dealing
with the problem must be aware of it. There are no criminal,
civil, or revenue laws applicable to the Tribal Areas. What
crimes are committed are dealt with by tribal elders according
to custom and tradition. A man may commit murder, killing
his wife or his cousin, and yet will not be condemned to
death if the tribal group agree it was done according to tradition. There are no courts or judges in the Tribal Areas (see
also Part One, chapter 3, Part Two, chapter 8, and Part Three,
chapter 13 for a discussion on the subject).

Over the last thousand years, Afghans have repeatedly
crossed the mountains of the North-West Frontier Province
on their way to India. But they have done so as conquerors.
The Khiljis, the Surs, and the Lodhis, tribal groups from
Afghanistan, were rulers of Delhi. One of the last invaders

was Babar, from Farghana, who established the Mughal Empire. These memories lend a fierce pride to the Afghan tribesmen, and underline their present plight. They have not crossed the mountains as conquerors but have fled from homes that have been invaded. For the first time in their history they are crossing into the subcontinent as a consequence of a major invasion of their land from the north. Hence a sullen pride and determination to return and restore the old order.

Some refugees are nomads who have migrated annually from Afghanistan in winter across the international border to Pakistan, and back in summer, and were in a manner of speaking nationals of both countries (see chapter 14). They spent their winters in Pakistan and made the long trek back on camels and on foot to summer pastures in Afghanistan. The tradition was established over the centuries when modern international borders did not prevent them from moving as they willed. These nomads were and are called *powindah* 'one who travels on foot' in Pakistan or *kochi* 'one who travels' in Afghanistan, words derived from Persian. The main refugee problem arises from political changes in Kabul begun in the seventies as a result of successive and increasingly pro-Soviet *coups*. The trickle of refugees crossing over soon became a flood and by the summer of 1979 there were some 200,000 in Pakistan. In December, when Russian troops moved into Afghanistan, a further impetus was given to refugees, and in mid-1980, there were almost 700,000 of them in Pakistan. But in addition—and I suspect the figure is not fully assessed by officials—are the large nomadic groups stranded on this side of the border with their summer pastures in Afghanistan blocked to them since 1979.

The refugees have been treated generously by the Government of Pakistan. Generously in terms of the resources available to Pakistan, for Pakistan has had to pay for them from her own coffers, and from some charity donated by individuals and institutions all over the country. Refugees receive 4 rupees a day (about 20 pence) per adult and subsidized

essential rations such as wheat, sugar, and vegetable oil.
Recently the rates have come down to 2 rupees a day but a
fixed amount of rations is provided free.

In South Waziristan Agency, about 50,000 refugees are said
to be living. Of these, about 20,000 are officially registered
and therefore entitled to the standard measurements of
official aid. About half of these are *powindah* tribes, Sultan
Khel, Sulaimanzai, and Dottani, and the other half *muqami*
tribes, Kharoti and Tajak, from across the Afghan side of
Birmal. About 30,000 live in the vast and inaccessible Birmal
area of the Agency, and one of the reasons they prefer to
wait it out on the border is the hope of returning soon to
their villages, a short distance from their present location.
Birmal officially 'opened' in the summer of 1979 with the
first ever visit of a government functionary in the history of
the area; yet, the absence of a road and other facilities
prevents a full scale penetration and, therefore, the area still
remains partly inaccessible. As they are not registered, the
Birmal refugees do not receive any aid. In South Waziristan
Agency, out of a total population of 300,000 tribesmen some
50,000 are 'outsiders'. A proportion of 1:6 of such outsiders
in any total population is a high one to feed and support. The
problem is more acute in North Waziristan Agency where the
number of officially registered refugees is almost 120,000
(making the refugee-local ratio 1:2).

One of the reasons that South Waziristan Agency does not
face this problem so acutely is that in November 1978, when
I took charge, I anticipated events in the area, and was sure
that a mass exodus of refugees was in the offing. The local
administration would be in danger of being swamped by
them, and eventually their presence would create tensions
with the Agency tribesmen and result in a deterioration of
law and order. This was the period when groups were crossing
into Pakistan and requesting that they be allowed to camp or
open up centres in the Agencies. Little thought was given to
the problem in a long-range perspective, and a rather haphazard attitude prevailed depending on the policies of the local

administration. I was firm in my orders regarding refugee camps. I turned down requests to set up camps either at Wana, or beyond Wana towards the Durand Line, because I was aware that such camps might sooner or later harbour military groups or guerrillas and thereby create international complications.

We fed the first groups and recommended that they move down to the Settled District of Dera Ismail Khan where camps were organized for them. Most of the registered 20,000 refugees moved down to Dera Ismail Khan to escape the harsh winter of Wana. Apparently, such precautions were not then taken in other Agencies, and the result was vast, unorganized, often highly politicized camps, some of them sitting right on the Durand Line in, for instance, North Waziristan and Kurram Agencies.

South and South-East Asia have seen violent upheavals over the last few decades. In 1947, the subcontinent of India was partitioned, and millions of people crossed the borders from and to the new country of Pakistan. Killing, rape, and looting were common stories during the summer of 1947. In the seventies, Indo-China was a land of turbulence as a result of changing political fortunes, and millions were displaced and killed. Today, into the eighties, the world faces the problem of the Afghan refugee. The difference between the refugees who came to Pakistan in 1947, from India, and the Afghan refugees 30 years later, is that Afghans are determined to return to their lands, however long and bitter the struggle; they have not come to stay.

After the Russian invasion, heads of government, and heads of armies, and other VIPs paraded in Peshawar and the Khyber Pass. They visited the refugee camps and expressed sympathy. Suddenly the Afghan refugee was discovered and the VIPs descended on them. The camps had become like a tourist resort. World leaders were photographed nodding their heads in sympathy and pointing portentously to the Khyber Pass. But this interest is, I fear, a temporary one; for when the political dust has settled down and other areas of interest absorb the leaders of the world, the Afghan refugee will be left largely to fend for himself. His problem of food, shelter, and sanitation will remain as pressing as before.

Alas! the world and mass media respond to these great human tragedies with only momentary interest and passing enthusiasm. Sometimes the main interest is a sensation of viewing suffering on such a magnitude. The political climate also determines length of interest. It was only when the Russians moved into Afghanistan with some strength in late 1979 that the world woke to the problem of the Afghan refugees. Which suggests that there was a political motivation in the response and not primarily a humanitarian one. Even after the Russians entered the scene it was a problem of degree and not kind. No doubt some fresh major disaster will divert the attention of the world from the problem of the Afghan refugees. They have no country and an uncertain future, and are increasingly desperate: classic ingredients for another Palestine.

Today, there is considerable pressure to view all refugee activities including the most mundane in a global context. Such a demand is now a compelling element of the intellectual orientation of the relief agencies, and yet it is inevitably unacceptable to social scientists working in and representing the Third World. The agencies insist, as they are insisting in Pakistan, that aid should be 'meaningfully employed', that 'income-generating activities' should be encouraged, by which is meant more agriculture or land-use. An increase in cash crops or even planting seasonal crops rationally would generate some income, it is argued. This argument betrays a blissful ignorance of the Tribal Areas where the majority of the Afghan refugees are placed. According to tradition and custom, refugees cannot buy or own land in Tribal Areas. Therefore, they cannot embark on agricultural activities. No local tribesman is allowed to sell land to any outsider which could permanently alienate it from the subsection or clan. In any case, scarce water and barren lands do not make agriculture a feasible short-term project. Nonetheless, I have heard official insistence and considerable petulance from agency staff. In any case, the host country officials have a difficult time explaining the local administrative situation in the Tribal Areas, which is one of the most peculiar in the world to the relief agencies. Those agency staff who have little knowledge or experience of South Asia, unlike some of the older British, find it difficult to understand the Tribal Areas.

Another example of a similar misunderstanding of local needs is the standard one of giving the wrong items of aid. For instance, certain foods such as tinned sardines and cheese, have been brought in bulk for the refugees. Blankets of excellent quality have also been given to the administration for distribution. Both the food and the blankets are sold in the Peshawar markets and find their way to Islamabad and Lahore, and even as far as Karachi. The agencies are once again upset as the news trickles in, and the administration has difficulty both in controlling the position and in explaining it to the agencies. The fact is that refugees will not use either item. They will not eat foods such as sardines and cheese, for their diet is restricted under any conditions to wheat bread (*dodai* or *nan*); and they use quilts for sleeping in, and never blankets. To turn to blankets from quilts would be as repugnant as turning to trousers from the loose *pyjama*-type dress (*partog*) worn by the local population (on both sides of the border). What the refugees need in this situation, living in their canvas tents, are small, cheap, tin oil-stoves to cook food and a plentiful supply of kerosene oil. They need temporary income-generating sources at hand, such as employment in manual work, on roads, or on building sites — employment which can easily be provided through the local administration.

The point is borne out by my experience, some 16 years ago, in 1970, when I was in charge of Manikganj Subdivision in East Pakistan as a Subdivisional Officer. I had to cope with the havoc caused by the fierce and terrible cyclones that hit the land from the Bay of Bengal in autumn. The cyclones displaced millions, and an estimated half million people were killed in East Pakistan. The scale of the catastrophe, and what they saw as the indifferent and insensitive attitude of the bureaucracy, was one of the factors that convinced Bengalis to take their political destiny into their own hands. The irrelevance of certain commodities of aid that were given to East Pakistan that autumn, aroused as much indignation as bewilderment. I was in charge of relief operations in a low-lying area almost flooded by swollen rivers and incessant rain. We were provided with tinned food which village Bengalis did not eat, with fine blankets which they did not use, and western clothing. Such items invariably found their way to the town markets after distribution to the villagers. The international agencies were soon wondering whether aid items were being misused by the official machinery or even distributed at all in the first place. Had a social scientist been attached to the government teams, they would have learned that Bengalis, even when confronted with a disaster on such a scale, do not know what use to make of tinned food, blankets, and western clothes. In the villages, such items are not traditionally acceptable even to numbed victims of disaster.

A certain flexibility, which implies imagination, is important in dealing with such problems. Intentions, however noble, may be frustrated by larger regional problems. Examples are provided from the Tribal Areas where the Pakistani administration has little control beyond the main roads and government centres. Many of the camps are in areas where there is little direct government authority. Apart from this political aspect, there is a cultural aspect too. For instance, the refugees in South Waziristan, and especially the *powindah* nomadic elements migrated from Wana to Dera Ismail Khan, some 150 miles away as they would in winter, to escape the severe winter of the Wana plain (at a height of 5,000 feet) in a journey that takes 3 to 4 days. Technically, they were now moving from one refugee zone to another, and therefore creating problems for those who keep records and accounts. Nonetheless, under no circumstances would these refugees have lived in their tents facing the harsh winter of Wana. Similarly, they will once again migrate from the plains when it becomes uncomfortably hot in summer.

Compassion or feeling for people, which one imagines to be a major prerequisite for administering aid to refugees, is apparently missing or at best buried under bureaucratic procedure. Refugees are reduced to numbers and lists of names in obscure registers in minor offices. Yet the refugee is living in a state of social and psychological shock as a result of the dislocation of his life. And so the work of someone like Dr. Dahl, at the Mission Hospital in Tank, has an immediate and wide impact. He provides free medicine to refugees and sees an average of a 1,000 refugee patients a month. He is always accessible to the refugees who have come to Tank, to their women and their children. His female staff are of great help to the women in particular. A smile, some attention, and some medicine go a long way to ease problems.

Some knowledge of social structure and organization, of the history and culture of a group, and of its domestic economy, are important in helping to administer aid effectively. For instance, the Cambodian household will be different to the Afghan, and therefore they have to be handled differently. It was therefore, a pleasure to meet and discuss refugees with the Austrian aid relief team, the head planner of which is Alfred Janata, a well-known anthropologist. The team had with them Dr. Bernt Glatzer, an anthropologist who had worked in Afghanistan, and within a few minutes the difference in approach was apparent. Relevant questions regarding the nuclear family, household economy, seasonal migrations, etc., were being asked. The difference in perception and understanding between this and other teams was clear.

What can anthropologists do to help practically?

Most important, *the social organization and structure of the groups* could be identified. This identification is fundamental in trying to understand how many and what types of groups are being dealt with. For instance, very few agency or government officials recognize that inspite of surface and cultural similarities, the Afghan refugees can be demonstrably categorized into nomads and non-nomad groups with different structural characteristics.[1] This difference is recognized in the Tribal Areas, and tribesmen refer to the first as *powindahs* and contrast them with the second as *muqami*, local, land-owning groups. The official Afghan refugee register does not recognize this difference and a column entitled 'name, parent-age, and tribe' glosses over it. *Powindahs* are transhumant and migratory and their economy is based on their animals and around their tent-homes. *Muqami* refugees dress, eat, and live differently to *powindahs* and are mostly small landowners exhibiting characteristics of the peasant farmer. The needs of *powindahs* and *muqami* are different; as is their motivation for becoming refugees. Migration is escaping the situation for the *powindah*, but a strategy for the *muqami*.

Problems arise from the distribution of tents. The *powindah* has lived in a tent all his life and adjusts his household around it. In the heat of summer, he spreadeagles the tent and nails it in such a manner that it is a foot off the ground. This allows circulation of air and has a cooling effect. The *muqami* groups are stifled in the heat. They have not only placed their tents on the ground but also made mud walls around them. *Purdah* remains a key factor in their lives. The heat is oppress-ive in their tents and many of them live under adjoining bush and stick sheds. The tents are used as store-rooms.

Again, all along the Durand Line *powindahs* have moved in long-range spans (Waziristan to Dera Ismail Khan, for instance) while the *muqamis* have short-range spans, often of a few miles (as the Salarzai and Mohmands in Bajaur or the Zadran and Gurbaz in North Waziristan).

Other questions the anthropologist can answer are: What is the authority structure of the two categories? Which are their major senior lineages? What are the affiliated or occupational groups attached to the main groups?

The clear distinction between the *powindah* groups and the other *muqami* groups in their organization, structure, economy, seasonal migrations, and attitude to income-generating activity would help agency and government officials understand the refugees. *Powindah* and *muqami* are tribal, and both adhere to generally similar religious and cultural codes, yet, their society and economy are fundamentally different. Knowledge of these groups would help those setting up new camps to decide where to place, for instance, senior lineages. Nearer the main lanes or roads? Nearer the water supply? Where to place the occupational groups? Concepts of pollution and proximity are here involved.

The *powindahs* would want to move with the seasons, irrespective of any constraints, and this has to be taken into consideration. The *muqami* groups, on the other hand, would not be moving in response to the seasons and, therefore, a different type of camp, perhaps a more permanent one, would suit them better. Therefore, planning should be prepared and implemented on different levels with different objectives for both the groups. To the best of my knowledge, no such analysis of local groups has been made.

Another problem among refugees would be that of *leadership*. Who are the 'elders'? The men 'who carry the gun'? Their relevance is immediately apparent in any council, for they speak for the group. They will decide how and in what proportions to distribute aid among the group. They will decide where and when assistance is needed, for example, in the shape of veterinary assistance for their animals. They will decide whether the *mullah* (see also Part Two, chapter 5) attached to certain groups would be best employed in teaching children at newly introduced primary schools, rather than newly inducted staff. They could respond to the suggestion that in the absence of doctors their local *mullahs* or medicine men might be provided with medical kits to deal with minor cases.

Thirdly, *the role and status of women,* particularly in the household and its economy, can be identified. The household economy of the *powindahs* is to a large extent dependent on the activities of women. They look after the animals, and can, if given assistance, weave carpets and rugs to create an extra income source (see Part One, chapter 3). Similarly attention could be given to poultry-raising in the tent household by women, and selling of eggs, etc. This is a traditional income-generating activity and it could be emphasized, rather than non-traditional methods being suggested. Problems of health, child-bearing, and sanitation are tied up with the problem of women in general. Fertility is yet another problem and, for instance, would the fact that men are more or less stationary in the camps with few social diversions increase fertility over a 9 month period? I would guess so.

In a survey of 1,400 refugees conducted for himself at the Tank Mission Hospital, Dr. Dahl found significant differences in diseases that afflicted *powindah* as opposed to *muqami* refugees. These are partly explained by the household structures and modes of living. For instance, *powindah* women are changing from breast-feeding to bottle-feeding of infants. This has disastrous consequences. Filth, flies, and dirty hands ensure the nipple of the bottle is infected. The baby is, therefore, continuously ill with severe intestinal trouble, tuberculosis, and diarrhoea. Either the mother must return to breast-feeding or keep the milk bottle impeccably clean. A regular systematic effort by female medical staff has to be made to convey this point to the *powindah* women.

For such analyses, female social scientists would be essential. Given the Pathan tribal structure, male anthropologists would find it next to impossible to have access to women. So far, no such provisions have been made.

Knowledge of local norms and culture based on *Pukhtunwali*, the Code of the Pathans,[2] would be of immense assistance in understanding local culture. Anthropologists could be of help in describing what local groups wear, what they eat and how they live. These answers to some key questions will also include items that would be locally rejected. For instance, Muslims do not eat pork and Muslim tribal women do not generally wear mini-skirts, etc. The categorization of refugees will tell us that many *muqami* groups, such as Tajiks, speak Farsi. Most *powindahs* speak Pushto. Male doctors would not be allowed to attend to females. Under no condition will refugees wear trousers, which are associated specifically with colonizing western powers, and have a long history of adverse connotations. But coats, especially overcoats for winter, will always be welcome. I would recommend that certain standard books be made available for reading to relief agency staff when dealing with local groups. Some knowledge, for instance of Pathan social structure, and organization, and their history, is imperative to anyone dealing with these groups. As also for useful background information, Granada Television's two films on the history and sociology of the region, *Khyber* and *The Pathans* both by Dr. Andre Singer and his Time-Life book, *The Pathans* ('Peoples of the Wild' series). Certain writings from the colonial period is still valid and provides excellent material for tribal groups. Captain J. A. Robinson's *Notes on Nomad Tribes of Eastern Afghanistan*, written almost 50 years ago, is still important and accurate, and I may add a fair account of nomads including those that pass through South Waziristan, such as the Sulaiman Khel (see chapter 14).

Cultural codes are also tied to larger religious ones. *Religious mores and tradition* do not allow the drinking of beer or the eating of ham, and sending these commodities as aid would be not only useless but counter-productive in creating ill-will among refugees. There is the problem of the village or tent mosque. Some knowledge of religion would also reveal that there is a tendency for differentiation in structure and organization among the major sects of Islam. The Shias seem to be more hierarchical and pyramidal in their social and religious structure than are the Sunnis. This would help in knowing whom in authority to talk to among these sects. Kurram Agency has a chronic Shia-Sunni problem, compounded by the fact that while Shias occupy better lands and are more educated, Sunnis are more numerous in population. The influx of Sunni Jajis among the Shia Turi alarmed the latter and local hostility was responsible for the refugees moving towards Peshawar. The Shias feared that the balance would tilt irrevocably in favour of the Sunnis.

Another consideration for relief agencies is the possibility of associating or employing Muslim personnel to work among Muslim tribal groups. Although these may belong to different nationalities, the common bond of Islam is of assistance in establishing an immediate rapport which goes a long way to open local doors and create the right atmosphere for effective communication. One of the most successful relief agency staff that I have met was an official from a Muslim country. He could travel around not only among the camps but also in the Tribal Areas without any fear or cultural hang-up as a result of historical tensions between certain colonial powers in the region.

For some of the reasons enumerated above, the association of social anthropologists with the efforts of relief agency and government officials must be recommended. In turn, anthropologists must be prepared to abandon their classroom 'pure anthropology' attitude and to roll up their sleeves. They must leave their notes and papers aside and be prepared to utilize their knowledge for less privileged groups.

Resistance may be as fierce from within anthropology as from the agencies and government administrations. British academic anthropology is in the main oriented towards teaching, and continues to show a reluctance to apply knowledge. The reluctance is rooted in the last two hundred years of British academic traditions and ideology. Knowledge must be practical if it is to be applied and utilized in Third World situations. It is of little relevance to know that a paper has been read in a small department in the West, to a group of two dozen specialists, and accepted as successful. What we are concerned with is, how this knowledge can benefit large groups of people in predicaments where they need help. If local sociologists and anthropologists are available, that would be of maximum benefit to all parties. But an area specialist who has worked in a Middle Eastern tribal society with generally similar religious, geographical, and economic frameworks as the Pathans, will have little difficulty in rapidly knowing and understanding Pathan structure.

An anthropologist must be attached to every major administrative unit of the relief agencies, particularly in the field. We cannot expect government offices to respond to this suggestion, for anthropology as a discipline, and the anthropologist as a specialist, have not yet arrived in the planning centres of the less developed countries. Anthropology is still a relatively new subject in these areas. For example, the Planning Commission of Pakistan, a highly prestigious and established division of government, does not hire a single anthropologist or sociologist to help it formulate its national plans. One may expect a response from the relief agencies with their vastly superior resources and presumably superior attitudes to knowledge and development.

Planning Commissions in less developed countries are invariably overstaffed with 'transport economists', 'regional economists', 'agricultural economists', and economists of other varieties. This plethora of economists in Pakistan is a result of the Planning Commissions in the sixties when the Harvard Group, and other such groups were influential in shaping the intellectual mould of the planning processes in Pakistan.

It was heartening to note that a traditional stronghold of the economists, the World Bank, has finally been breached by the social scientists and a post of Senior Sociologist created. If it has taken the World Bank, with its sophisticated data, equipment and approach, so long to recognize the importance of sociology, then one can only conjecture how far behind are other less sophisticated planning institutions. In the meantime, a great deal of time and effort will be lost for the relief of the Afghan refugees which could have been salvaged to some extent by the inclusion of social scientists.

NOTES

1. For a discussion of tribal groups that spans the Muslim world, see Ahmed and Hart, (editors), op. cit., 1984.
2. For a comprehensive discussion see Ahmed, op. cit., 1980.

11

Baluchistan: Land and People

During the last hundred years, Russian moves in Central Asia have been watched with wariness from the citadels of power in South Asia. Two opposed theories have dictated South Asian foreign and frontier policies. One advocated, and was called, 'the Forward Policy', the other 'masterly inactivity' The first suggests that the Russians are hell-bent on pushing down, through Afghanistan and Baluchistan, to the warm waters of the Arabian Sea. They must be stopped at all costs. Major campaigns have been fought on this assumption. The Great Game between Imperial Russia and Imperial Britain was played on the high plateaus, deserted valleys, and among remote tribes in Central Asia. Some of the most evocative British writings and Imperial names are associated with this school: Lord Roberts of Kandahar, Kipling, General Kitchener, Lord Curzon and, in Baluchistan, Sir Robert Sandeman (after whom Fort Sandeman, the district headquarters, now Zhob, was named). The second theory, less adventurous, suggested South Asia build strong defences around its northern borders and dig its heels behind them leaving outsiders to their own devices.

Now that the Russians are in Afghanistan, supporters of the first theory watch developments in and around the Baluchistan Province of Pakistan with great interest. Today, they argue, if the Russians reached the coasts of Baluchistan they would paralyse the shipping lanes bringing oil from Iraq, Iran, and the UAE to the West, threaten the Strait of Hormuz, and be poised to strike at Saudi Arabia. The entire geopolitical balance between East and West would be dramatically and permanently changed.

In Pakistan, the problem with Baluchistan is its size and, partly because of that, its sparse population. Population density is 12 people per square kilometre in Baluchistan. Demographic figures in Baluchistan translate easily into political arguments. For instance, the Baluch have a thin edge over the Pathan population in the Province being just over 50 per cent of the population of about 4.5 million. In Pakistan, Baluchistan accounts for 44 per cent of its total area of 800,000 square kilometres, but only for 5 per cent of its 90 million people. 57 per cent of Pakistan's population live in the Province of Punjab but it has only 26 per cent of the area. Its population density, 230, explains its needs to push into other provinces.

Large Baluch areas also exist in Iran and Afghanistan. There are about 1 million Baluchis in Iran. Indeed Baluch leaders like the Khan of Kalat, claim that Baluchis live in an area of over 3 million square miles, the core of which is Baluchistan itself, and total about 20 million. Together, this area and population form 'Greater Baluchistan'.

Baluchistan is a dry, arid, seemingly unending mass of desolate mountain and desert. There is no vegetation, rainfall a scant 5 inches. Freezing in winter—in places—40°F—and hot in summer—130°F—it is a formidable place to live in; those who live here are formidable people. 'The lofty heights are our comrades and the pathless gorges our friends', goes a sixteenth century war ballad. Their traditions speak of migration from the lands of, and affiliation with, the Kurds. At least one major tribe, controlling the Bolan Pass, retains the ancestral name, Kurd. Both, Baluch and Kurd, are Sunni Muslims, fiercely tribal, and straddle three countries creating international political problems for each. The Baluch have always had problems with Iran. First with the Shah, who banned their dress and customs as barbaric and now with Imam Khomeini.

Intellectuals go to lengths to establish Aryan origins, innocent of the havoc modern Aryans were playing in Europe only a generation ago. In particular, the Brahuis, who consider themselves the elite Baluch tribe, are indignant that they were considered autochthonous or Dravidian by the British. For the Baluch, the pain of the harsh environment is attenuated by the tribal code, its mythology, and its structure.

The tribe is a self-contained world. At its centre is the Sardar or chief of the tribe. Tall, full-bearded, in flowing clothes and heavy turban, the Sardar is not unlike Sean Connery playing a tribal chief. He symbolizes Baluch custom and tribal tradition. Honour, hospitality, and bravery are displayed in his behaviour. The tribe revels in his glory. The word of the Sardar is law, his authority total. In an area threatened by nature and, often, invading tribes unity under the Sardar became the key to survival. The Baluch have a saying 'the Baluch will swear on the Holy Quran but never on the head of the Sardar'.

In turn, Sardars had, over them, Nawabs or Khans who headed tribal confederations. The Khan of Kalat, a Brahui, was, historically, the most important of these. His ancestor had welded the Baluch into a state half-a-century before Ahmad Shah created Afghanistan. But it is a state with fluctuating borders. Baluch society was essentially nomadic. It produced no great cities, no marble wonders, no centres of learning. It was also fiercely inturned and isolated. But the romantic images of tribal life cannot conceal the extreme poverty and harsh living conditions. In particular, women suffer, performing, in an endless cycle of drudgery, the daily chores. They enjoy no rights whatsoever. But Baluch society is changing.

The factors of change are external and hence create acute tension in society. Of these three are worth noting. First, the abolition of the Sardari system by, and the politics of, Mr. Zulfikar Ali Bhutto in the seventies. Mr. Bhutto hoped to end the Sardari system with the stroke of a pen. But in the end he had to call in the army to support his action. The years 1973-7 when Bhutto fell from power, are called the 'War Years' in Baluchistan. Along with abolishing the Sardars he attempted to encourage the growth of an alternative leadership within the tribe. A variety of development schemes, hospitals, schools, roads, were also initiated; hitherto inaccessible areas were thus penetrated.

The second factor of change lies in the large numbers of Baluch who are working across the thin divide of the Gulf in the Arab States. These Baluch turn the wheels of the Arab Gulf States. They, with their hardy northern neighbours, the Pathans, are the two most prominent ethnic groups. They are to be seen working on the toughest physical jobs like the construction of roads. The Baluch return with money in their pockets and other goodies in their possession. A Baluch elder told me 'once we were obsessed with the FCR (Frontier Crimes Regulation) but now we are obsessed by the VCR'. Quetta now boasts Burger and Video Game Centres. These Baluch, mostly from junior lineages or families, also bring back new ideas. They desire status and to be heard in society.

The third factor is the situation in Afghanistan. Only a few years before the Russians entered Afghanistan in 1979, a vigorous Baluch movement existed. Opinion in it ranged from demands for autonomy to independence from Pakistan. This is now subdued. Events have overtaken it.

Some 700,000 refugees, mostly Pathans, have fled from Afghanistan into Baluchistan. The demographic balance between Baluch and Pathan is thus affected. If the Afghan refugees stay on, as many fear they will, Pathans will finally be in the majority in Baluchistan. All sorts of political ramifications will result. To start with the name Baluchistan, the land of the Baluch, will no longer apply.

The Baluch have encouraged Afghan Pathans to settle in the Pathan districts adjacent to Afghanistan and the North-West Frontier Province. They are quick to point out that the camps of the refugees, Afghan Tented Villages — a name coined by Pakistani bureaucracy — are neither tents nor villages. For example, Surkhab, in Pishin District, with an official

population of about 130,000, looks like a large town with
clean mud houses endlessly and neatly placed together.

The Afghan refugees will thus do what Pathan martial
prowess failed to do: convert Baluchistan into a Pathan
majority area. Why did the Pathan momentum lose steam
and end where it did? Firstly, Pathans tended to settle in the
better irrigated, cooler, higher, districts. But apart from
ecology there were other reasons. Blocking their path were
the two fiercest tribes among the Baluch, the Marri and the
Bugti. These tribes, themselves, have a history of conquest.
Baluch invaders have annexed adjoining lands in Sind and
in the Punjab.

Baluchis suffer from a sense of deprivation. They feel
Islamabad has given them a raw deal. They point to their
own Provincial Government. In 1985 3 of the 14 Secretaries
and only 1 of the 4 Commissioners were Baluch. Baluchistan
has the lowest literacy rate, lowest life expectancy, and
lowest income per capita of the four provinces of Pakistan.
Extreme Baluch, represented by the Baluch Students
Organization, see Islamabad as colonizers. They say that as
an answer to legitimate demands Islamabad has only sent in
troops. Islamabad points to the millions of rupees poured
into the development effort; also to corruption (much of
the money finds its way into private pockets), harsh conditions, poor communications, illiteracy, and the Sardars as
hindering development.

The literature on Baluchistan, both in Iran and Pakistan, is
limited but of high quality. It includes works by academics
like Professors Stephen and Carroll Pastner, Robert Pehrson,
Philip Salzman, Brian Spooner, and at the Institute of
Oriental Studies, Moscow, Professor Yuri Gankovsky. Selig
Harrisons's recent book, as the title indicates, *In Afghanistan's
shadow: Baluch nationalism and Soviet temptations*, supports
the thesis which sees Russians pushing through Baluchistan
to the Arabian Sea. In 1962, on a mission to Pakistan for
President Kennedy, Henry Kissinger, then a Harvard
Professor, on being briefed about Baluchistan had said

impatiently, 'I wouldn't recognize the Baluchistan problem if it hit me in the face'. Today, whichever theory one upholds it is clear that developments in Baluchistan will determine the shape of things to come in South Asia and the Middle East.

12

Gilgit: High in the Karakorums

When Pakistanis put on a show they do it well. The Conference on Karakorum culture is one such example. Officially called the 'First International Conference on Archaeology, Ethnology, History, Art, Linguistics, Languages, Folklore, and Social Condition of Northern Areas of Pakistan', it was held in Gilgit, in September 1983.

Gilgit is 5,000 feet high, surrounded by mountains 10 to 11,000 feet high, and situated by Gilgit river. This is where 'three Empires'—Russian, Chinese, and British—met, and their representatives played the Great Game. The lives of the 'characters' in the Gilgit drama were full of dash and courage. Sir Francis Younghusband and Sir George Robertson provided models for the fictional heroes of Kipling and Masters, to whom Gilgit was the epitome of the Great Game.

The place names are evocative: Hunza, Skardu, and Chilas —and beyond the borders—Yarkand and Kashgar in China. The Silk Route, Pamirs, Wakhan, and the Hindu-Kush are all related to this area.

Its great geopolitical strategic importance closed it to 'foreigners' but did not discourage scholars. Chinese scholars like Fa Hien, in the fifth century and Hiuen Tsang, two centuries later, recorded their observations on their way to pilgrimage in India.

The area was visited by Sir Aurel Stein. He last visited Chilas at the age of 80. Scholars like Lorimer, a Political Agent, Gilgit, Leitner, and Morgenstierne contributed to studies of the region. Joseph Wolff, an American missionary, crossed the Hindu-Kush stark naked. The visitor had to be eccentric or brave. The terrain discouraged travel.

The Karakorum mountains are among the highest in the world. The Godwin Austen, popularly known as K-2, after geometrical figures and second to Everest, is 28,251 feet. Two Italians conquered the K-2 in 1954, shortly after Everest was conquered. These mountains are also among the most difficult to climb. Nanga Parbat—the naked mountain—is 26,600 feet high. It has a treacherous and fatal reputation. The world's largest glaciers outside the polar regions are also found here and have earned it the title of 'the third pole'. Hispar—and there are more like it—is about 40 miles long and 3 miles wide. It moves slowly, a few feet a month. The yak roams these mountains and so does, according to legend, the Yeti, the abominable snowman.

The relationship between ecology and society is vividly illustrated. The people are hardy. The need to resist invasions resulted in state formation. Tiny dynastic states, such as Nagar and Hunza, were scattered in the area and ruled by Mirs and Rajas. At least five major distinct languages are spoken, Shina being dominant.

Shina contains many words similar to Pukhto: *zai*, place; *sorey*, man; *brastan*, quilt. So remote are these people that until recently some tribes claimed they were descended from Abu Jahl, one of the Holy Prophet's most implacable enemies. Their wooden graves were marked with birds. Abu Jahl, they claimed, became a bird and flew here from Arabia. Only recently did elders become conscious of the implications of the name. Do these Pukhtun and Arab associations hint at the origin of these people?

Today, their total population is about half a million of which over 50 per cent are Shias. Gilgit has a concentration of Ismailis.

The single most important factor in the history of this region is the Karakorum Highway (KKH). It is destined to change social and economic life. For example, tea followed the KKH. This highway connects Islamabad to the Pakistan-Chinese border at the Khunjrab Pass via Mansehra, Thakot, Besham, Chilas, and Gilgit (about 600 miles).

After Thakot, the KKH runs along the river Indus, rising and falling with the mountain contours through deep gorges and over high passes. It is a miracle of engineering—some enthusiasts call it the eighth wonder of the world. Sheer rock masses, 3 to 4,000 feet high, hang over the KKH with imposing but deceptive beauty.

Signs warn travellers: 'Notorious killing zone. Stones fall without notice'. The bridges and culverts are Chinese. Their exquisite dragons still sit over bridges. The construction of the KKH is said to have cost anywhere over 500 lives, one human per mile, at least. There is a Chinese cemetery and garden in Gilgit to commemorate the Chinese who died during construction.

The KKH reflects the geopolitical needs of Pakistan in a different era. Today, with the Soviets at the Khyber Pass, and Pakistan cut in half, the geopolitical balance of South Asia has changed. The KKH was begun in Ayub Khan's days, when friendship with the Chinese was seen as a keystone in foreign policy.

The KKH thus negated the philosophy of the British political officers whose aim was to keep out 'foreigners'. Some would be turning in their graves at the thought of the Conference in Gilgit.

The Conference was organized by Professor Karl Jettmar, of Heidelberg University who has been working here for the last two decades, and Professor A.H. Dani of Quaid-i-Azam University. It highlighted the collaborative work of Jettmar and Dani, under the auspices of the Pak-German Anthropological and Archaeological Research project. The work of these scholars represents a happy union between Anthropology and Archaeology. Some 125 delegates were invited from 15 countries.

The Germans, who have a head start because of their project, were most prominent; about 24 came. Among the distinguished guests were Professors Anne Marie Schimmel, Klaus Ferdinand, Gherardo Gnoli, and Hermann Berger. The last is one of the world's authorities on the Burushaski language, one of the rarest languages of the world, spoken in Hunza and near the Chinese border.

The Mir of Hunza was also present. In addition, several Ambassadors, Generals, and senior civil servants attended. Also present were two Conservative leaders from Britain—Julian Amery, M.P., and Colonel Neil McLean, ex-M.P.

At least one Buddhist monk in sacred robes and with shaved head was to be seen. There were some touching moments. Pat Emerson read her husband's paper based on his field work in Baltistan. Professor Richard Emerson who had died recently was scheduled to speak at the Conference. As a gesture to the Buddhist heritage of the area the monk was asked to recite from the sayings of the Buddha when the Conference was formally closed.

Funds came from UNESCO and the Government of Pakistan. It was the first international conference held in Gilgit and of its kind in Pakistan. It was also the biggest collection of foreigners the Northern Areas have seen.

With many of the world's most recognized experts present, the papers were of high quality. Professor Georg Pfeffer, who flew in from the IUAES Conference in Vancouver, stated in his speech they were of a much higher quality than the ones he had heard in Canada. Unfortunately, the papers had to be rushed due to the number of speakers.

Above all, it was a unique opportunity to hear experts and meet them in rather unusual circumstances. And perhaps this was the main strength of the Conference. It allowed people from different countries but in related fields to meet each other. Professor Schimmel felt it was the most important international conference in this field in decades.

In terms of method, the Conference underlined the importance of the interdisciplinary approach to the study of Karakorum culture. Linguists, anthropologists, archaeologists, art historians, and that dying—or perhaps dead—

breed of political officer who wrote about his charge (like Lorimer) all have to learn from each other. Here there is layer on layer of great world cultures and great world religions: Islam on Hinduism, Hinduism on Buddhism, and so on (for example, the swastika motif in the wooden mosques which goes beyond Hinduism to Buddhism).

The Conference was a credit to the Government of Pakistan. The arrangements were meticulous; just the logistics of travel and accommodation were a nightmare. Gilgit laid out the red carpet. Buntings and banners welcomed the delegates. Folk dances and dinners were laid on. And a special match of Gilgit polo. The game in Gilgit is played with wild vigour and few rules

After special permission was granted by the President of Pakistan, since the area is strictly off-limits to foreigners, the delegates were taken to the Khunjrab Pass. They lunched with the Mir of Hunza, and spent the night at Gulmit, just short of the Pass.

Hunza is the Shangri La of western writers. They fell in love with the idea of Hunza. It was a convenient myth. Europeans and Americans, sick of over-civilization, looked for unspoilt places and people. Best sellers were written on Hunza. Here was a valley, high up in the highest mountains of the world; isolated and scenically beautiful forming perfect picture-post-card scenery. Its people were fair and healthy. There was no crime or conflict. People were content. There was even a legend that gave them a European connection. They were said to be descended from Alexander's troops. And they enjoyed, extraordinary longevity and excellent health. The people of Hunza, along with the ruler, the Mir of Hunza, did not discourage these stories. I was told of an old man about 80, Jano, who was produced for foreigners with the claim that he was well over a 100 years.

Westerners came to Hunza to learn its secrets of longevity. Was it the apricot? The glacial water? (Muddy, but said to contain minerals, like iron.) The climate? Or, the local wine, 'Hunza water'? Perhaps these physical factors are a red herring. The explanation may lie in social behaviour and organization. Traditional life is relaxed (wine and dances), there is no coercive authority (no state police or army), no one is excessively rich or poor (average landholdings are about 1 to 2 acres per household), the population is small (50,000), and the community is homogeneous (the Ismaili sect of Muslims). Women do not wear '*parda*' and mix quite easily with men. One has only to visit Swat to witness opposing social factors on every count and therefore a tense society. But the question is: why did Hunza alone capture the imagination of the world? Perhaps the single most important factor is the Ismaili belief of Hunza.

I suggest a team of social and medical anthropologists undertake a study in Hunza to examine these questions. Apart from telling us about Hunza society it will also throw some light on why people visiting Hunza need the myth of longevity.

The Aga Khan is a regular visitor to and source of strength for Hunza. His patronage ensures national and international support for his followers. In turn, they are devoted to him. When he visits Karimabad as many as a 100 marriages take place so that the couples may be blessed by him.

The Mir supports the Aga Khan who in turn supports him politically and financially (presently with a very active Aga Khan Rural Support Programme).

The Khunjrab Pass, and the drive up to it, is Central Asian fantasy. Professor Schimmel, whose Sufism is never far from the surface, was in an ecstatic trance: 'this is the seventh heaven', she kept murmuring.

Chinese border guards greeted the delegates, a minor army in a dozen vehicles, who took photographs for over an hour. The height of the Pass, over 16,000 feet, causes dizziness for lack of oxygen.

On the way up is Indira Nala and Indira Qila—named after Hindu gods, and long before the Indian Prime Minister.

Marco Polo sheep, named after the Italian traveller, the ibex and the yak are found here.

The rock engravings, so far seen mainly along the river Indus, reveal a rich source of Buddhist, Hindu, and prehistoric art. One is just outside Gilgit at Kargah, a perfect standing Buddha.

There is enough here to fire the imagination of the scholar. This is virgin territory for anthropologists and archaeologists with a sense of adventure. And a reputation may be made here.

13

The On-Farm Water Management Project:
Honour, Power and Agnatic Rivalry
in Rural Pakistan

Agrarian economic development schemes do not operate in a vacuum, but are embedded in the social structure and are influenced by the social organization of the community. The discussion that follows, suggests that beneath the diverse cultural and structural forms of Pakistan, a tribal structure may be perceived. The structure possesses two characteristic features: life is based on some understanding of the notion of honour (especially related to women), and on rivalry that is largely expressed through agnatic or cousin enmity (called *tarboor* in the NWFP and *sharika* in the Punjab, this cousin is usually the father's brother's son). The desire for honour and agnatic rivalry are converted into a desire for power. It is a zero-sum situation: the more power cousin A has the less his rival, cousin B, will have. Every power unit added to A subtracts power from B. In certain places, as in the NWFP, this is the only model (see also Part One, chapter 3 and Part Two, chapters 5 and 8); in other areas, as in Punjab, this pattern is blurred, while in Sind it is fused and sometimes converted into a feudal order. Irrigation schemes, including the On-Farm Water Management Project (OFWMP), affect such traditional structures and organizations and, in turn, are affected by them.

Also influencing development projects is the administrative apparatus that deals with issues of law and order, revenue collection, and water distribution. For this project, the administrative structure incorporated the On-Farm Water

Management Project. The latter was indeed an important factor. To assess the impact of the Project, it is necessary first to deal with the social structure and administrative framework.

My questionnaire elicited information focusing on the following issues in society: the code of behaviour; the concepts of 'tribe,' 'caste,' and ranked hierarchies; memory of agnatic ascendants (in support of lineage status); prevalence of endogamy and exogamy (marriages are almost entirely homogamous); household composition; physical description of respondents; emigration; and the role of religion in decision-making. The questions were structured to throw light on larger issues. For instance, the code is consciously upheld by senior lineages who maintain memory of their ancestry and who also maintain group purity through endogamy. These groups look and appear better fed and healthier than junior or depressed lineages. It is these groups who can afford to emigrate.

Related studies have been conducted previously. Although they are based mostly in one Province – Punjab, they contribute to our understanding of the problems. However, in some of them, important conceptual errors have been introduced, such as the common use of 'caste' for tribal or occupational groups.[1] 'Caste' has specific associated religio-cultural characteristics in South Asia, which include commensal rules.

The question when dealing with a large and socially complex nation like Pakistan is: can we talk of one universal structure? The administrative structure is indeed central and identical in all parts of the country. It is divided in a series of descending hierarchies. The key figure is the District Commissioner, a mid-level career official, and the key unit is the district under his charge.[2] (See also Part Two, chapter 5.) Although the administrative structure is central, locating a common social structure presents problems. Before dealing with the major ethnic zones separately, we will briefly present an all-Pakistan picture.

Pakistan

Pakistan is an agricultural country with more than three-quarters of its population directly dependent on agriculture. Pakistan may be viewed socio-culturally as a single unit; this assessment is supported by its geography and its predominantly agricultural economy, which interlock the various regions. The river Indus and its supporting irrigation networks constitute the core agricultural area of Pakistan, an area with complex and extensive irrigation systems and fertile lands. In this area lie most of the estimated 87,000 watercourses of Pakistan. The area is largely coincidental with, and a consequence of, the Indus river basin. The water improvement projects I visited were in this core area of Pakistan. The other areas of Pakistan are peripheral to this core area. In the core area, access to irrigation is the key to social status and economic wealth. As we will demonstrate in the following sections, it also provides a critical vehicle for the articulation of the primary theme of village society in Pakistan: the concept of honour, known as *izzat* and *ghairat*.

Since Pakistan's creation in 1947, an entire generation has come of age within its present boundaries. This generation shares major historical experiences and, above all, a common language, Urdu—however imperfectly it may be employed in the hinterlands. It is partly because of these similarities that common problems of the project are found throughout the land. Whether a Sindhi or NWFP landowner, members of this generation will respond along similar lines to the questions posed to them: the head-enders are less satisfied with the project than the tail-enders; the representative of the senior lineage wishes to manipulate his role of Chairman of the Water User's Association to strengthen his position against his lineage rivals.

However, distinct structural and organizational differences lie beneath the socio-cultural and, to an extent, the linguistic similarities. These must be understood to make sense of how and why people behave as they do. It is essential to differen-

tiate between tribal and peasant characteristics to avoid mis-
using the concept of 'caste'. Tribal society is organized on
segmentary principles, and decisions are made on the basis
of kinship—one characteristic of segmentary societies is that
lineage memory is important as a diacritical feature. NWFP
tribesmen will recall five to six generations of male ascendants whereas Punjab villagers have little memory beyond two
to three ascendants. In contrast, peasant society is based on
villages that are largely socially and economically self-
sufficient. One characteristic of village society is its encapsulation within larger state systems and its domination by their
official representatives.

The North-West Frontier Province (NWFP)

In the Tribal Areas, the NWFP provides us with excellent
material for the conceptualization of the least encapsulated
society. The international border tribes such as the Afridi,
Mohmands, and Wazir are included in this area. Here people
are free to organize their lives as they will. The criminal and
revenue laws of Pakistan do not apply. The people live
according to a traditional tribal code which has been called
for centuries the *Pukhtunwali*, or the Code of the Pukhtuns.
They are egalitarian in the extreme. Hospitality, revenge, and
courage are primary features of their code, which is often
articulated through agnatic or cousin rivalry and situations
involving the honour of women. Death may be the result in
some cases involving the code: a wife or sister suspected of
infidelity may be peremptorily shot. This society can be
considered to be *nang*, or honour-based.[3] (See also Part One,
chapter 3.)

In contrast, the Pukhtun tribes in the other half of the
NWFP operate within the administrative structure of Pakistan.
While upholding the code, they encounter the laws of the
land. A wife or sister cannot be shot without invoking the
Criminal Procedure Code. In addition, social and economic

hierarchies based on vast irrigated landholdings have emerged within tribal groups, displacing the original egalitarian tribal structure.

With the disturbance of the essential egalitarianism of the Tribal Areas, social relations have come to be based on land-ownership: those who own land and those who work on the land paying *qalang* (rent and taxes). This group can be called the *qalang* society. Charsadda and Mardan, the richest areas of the NWFP, provide the base for the *qalang* group. The Yusufzai are the dominant tribe here. However, the situation is more complex than this. Between the *nang* groups in their barren mountains and the *qalang* groups on their vast irrigated demesnes are another emerging group: those who own and work 1 to 10 acres of land and who can be called peasant farmers. These are based largely in the Peshawar valley and are a mixture of various tribes such as the Khattaks, Mohmands, Afridis, and even such non-Pukhtun tribes as the Awans. (See also Part Two, chapters 6 and 9.) Irrigation schemes early in this century and the introduction of ferti-lizers and better seeds have benefited these tribes, who form a hardworking, economically independent group.

Punjab

Although it is tempting to suggest that in Punjab, the *nang-qalang* tribal categories give way to a peasant or agricultural one, it would not be an entirely accurate statement. Tribal structures are perceptible beneath the otherwise schematic and tidy 'model' villages of Punjab. Rivalries are often based on agnatic tensions or on local understanding of honour, whether one is a Rajput or Arain. In certain villages, agnatic rivalry expresses itself through the establishment of separate mosques, even though both rival parties belong to the same sect.

Change from a tribal model came about through the intro-duction of the pioneer agricultural community that was settled here by the British in the last century. The British simply moved in with maps and rulers and demarcated 25 acre squares called *chaks* within which farmers were settled. The British thereby created a new community of small to medium sized farms that was not based on religion or tribes. The land was supported by a complex and extensive system of canals. The famous canal colonies of Punjab had their origin here.

For the British, Punjab was a model province. It was a colonial experiment in agricultural organization that worked. The idea behind it was simple. When they conquered Punjab from the Sikhs, the British inherited a vast, sparsely populated, but potentially rich land. Because the post-Mutiny (War of Independence) era after 1857 required a new approach to India, the British decided to experiment. Irrigation schemes were launched, and lands were allotted in neat parcels to various categories of loyal subjects, irrespective of their religion or caste (although the caste schema was maintained in the village). Three features characterized the experiment: the opening of new lands (the canal colonies); the ethnic and religious mix of the population (Sikh, Hindu, and Muslim); and the high turnover of ownership (as sons drifted to urban centres). These features, which are still recognizable today, contrast with conditions in the NWFP and Sind.

However, an older tribal structure is clearly perceptible in Punjab. This older structure, which provides the base for the *qalang* groups, is led by traditional (Rajput) families and provides men for high offices in Pakistan.[4] The other group, the small independent, industrious peasant-proprietor working his few acres, is the backbone of the agriculture of Punjab. The Rajputs, who were once the warrior aristocracy of northern India, have a saying that provides insight into their behaviour: *jan jae par izzat na jaee* (one should lose one's life rather than one's honour). But the majority of members are not entirely motivated by a tribal *nang* code. In the act of becoming settlers and farmers, their memory of a tribal code suffered. Their code is now that of the peasant farmers, not of the *nang* tribesmen, and the rhythm of their lives takes its cue from the agricultural seasons.

A good example, because it is so visually striking, of the structural and organizational differences between the two categories in Punjab is found in the *chaks,* fields of Zafarabad, near Sahiwal. Those fields owned by the Rajputs, large landlords living in Sahiwal or Lahore, are neglected. The watercourses are crooked, untidy, and, in some places, 10 to 12 feet deep. Almost 10 to 15 per cent of the land is lost to wild grass. The landlords are jealous of their feudal privileges, but in a changing world they do little else but hunt and show hospitality. They prefer to live in the towns. Across the canal are the lands of the small Arain farmers whose lives are a complete contrast. They cultivate their own lands, and the watercourses are neat, tidy, and well-maintained. The farmers themselves point out the differences. 'Those people', they observe pointing across the canals, 'kill themselves for honour, hospitality, and enjoyment. We work our own lands'. (See also Part Two, chapter 9.)

The small farmer is industrious and law-abiding. It is this group that is the secret of the success story in Punjab. Their average landholding in one of the most fertile districts, Sahiwal, is 6 acres, whereas in Punjab, the average is 13 acres. In my interviews with them, I learned that they lived on the land and worked it themselves and, therefore, spoke from experience. They also appeared highly responsive to suggestions for improvements in yield and quality of crops. Although the traditional tribal code is clearly subordinate to the agricultural one, the picture is not quite so simple. The Punjabi farmers' agricultural drive is not entirely the result of the Protestant ethic; in certain cases agnatic jealousy helps motivate individuals. (In one village, Christians abandoned their code to adopt one based on agnatic rivalry, and the split marred Christmas festivities and Church organization.)

A typical *chak* village in Punjab is neatly structured, with three distinct categories living in three areas reflecting social status and function. The first are the agriculturists, the *zamindars,* or owners of land. Social and economic positions here coincide (*qalang* Khans, like Choudries in Punjab, mean owners of land).[5] These are members of the dominant tribes of the Punjab, the Rajput, Gujar, or Arain. Among these are the Choudry (or Choudries) the informal elder or head of the community, and the *lambardar,* the officially appointed village representative whose main duty is to collect revenue. The *lambardar* was given one *moraba* (25 acres) by the British as a sign of their favour to use as long as he lived.

The second group may be called the Muslim religious group. Traditionally, they do not own land and remain neutral in agnatic politics. The group is a living reminder of the duties of religion. It consists of holy lineages like the Sayyeds (descendants of the Prophet). The *Mullah,* or religious functionary, who supervises *rites de passage* and lives in the mosque, is another member of this group. However, during the colonial period, the British had placed him in the third category, that of the non-landowning *kammis* (from *kam* or work) occupational groups, a deliberately insulting action.

Kammis do odd jobs and serve as the tenant force for the *zamindars.* Of these, the most important are the carpenters,

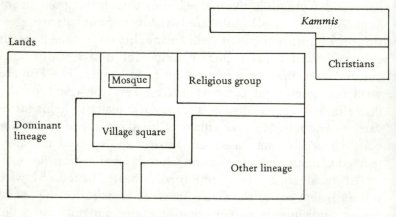

Figure 13.1: Picture of an Average Village

the barbers, and the blacksmiths. Also included in this group are the Christians, many of whom converted from low caste Hindu groups. Punjab villages have 10 acres of land set aside (previously, they had one *moraba*) for the use of this group as long as it serves the village. Payment to this group was traditionally made in kind rather than cash. The politics of the last 10 years has transformed them into an assertive class-conscious group rejecting its inferior social status.

The changes in attitude of the *kammis* have resulted in the *zamindars* becoming more self-reliant. Sons and cousins who would have drifted to towns now stay to work on their lands. Life for the *kammis* is hard. The life of the South Asian peasant was once idealized in studies of village life. The villager was seen as an uncomplaining, sturdy, contented fellow living within a self-sufficient universe. When we attempted to discover this purer, happier life in the village, we found that this is not a true picture. Recent studies point out the harsh realities: the insecurity, rising prices, and changing social conditions. These studies express 'the peasant view of the bad life'.[6]

Sind

In terms of cultural complexity, Sind presents the most interesting picture. It has a history dating back to Mohen-jo-Daro (2500 BC). Its conversion to Islam came with the dramatic incursion into South Asia by the Arabs, led by their general, Mohammad bin Qasim, in 712 AD. It was ruled by Sindhi dynasties and the Baluch Talpurs before the British annexed it. The continuing social complexity of Sind results from its mixture of a large indigenous Hindu population (about 1 million) speaking Sindhi, and a larger refugee population (about 6 million) who arrived in 1947. Language became a key feature of group-boundary maintenance between them. These two groups form a large percentage of Sind's total population of 13 million.

Sind's vast desert areas with their limited irrigation facilities have led to a crude method of survival of the fittest: the dominant groups are placed along the watercourses. These lands have supported a distinctly feudal social structure. The lords of the lands (*Rais* in Baluchi groups and *Vadera* in *Sammat* Sind groups) fit the classic *qalang* mould. Their tenants, the *haris,* are a mixture of ethnic groups, poorer fellow-tribesmen, nomads, and Hindus. The *haris* share the crops they produce on a fifty-fifty basis. They also tend to stay located on one estate and, in spite of working the land, are barely able to make both ends meet. The barren landscape and proximity of large cosmopolitan urban centres tempt the *qalang* lords to leave their lands in the charge of a trusted servant, the *kamdar.* The *kamdar,* for a fixed pay and certain other benefits, administers the lands for his absentee master. Paradoxically, Sind provides a good example of successful water improvement projects. As the holdings are large and the ownership rests with one person, the levelling, straightening, and maintenance of the course present no problems. Problems will arise, however, if the *kamdar* should become indifferent to his master's interests (indeed, we saw some poorly maintained watercourses on such estates).

The interaction of administrative and social structure is clearly illustrated in the water problems here. A 'difficult' *hari* will find himself involved in a false criminal case with the police. The lord, who engineered the drama through informal contacts, will then intervene to extricate the *hari.* He will provide sureties for his tenant, so the *haris* is now bound to future good behaviour.

Needless to say, the village structure here does not follow the schematic pattern of Punjab depicted earlier. Settlements are divided into permanent and central ones of the lord and clusters of temporary mud huts of the *hari* in the fields.

Another relevant element of the cultural context of the OFWMP in Sind relates to the role of the Sufi — an ascetic, mystical Muslim sect. Sufi organizations have traditionally provided a 'safety valve' for the depressed in Sind society. It is no wonder that the great Sufic poets of Sind, who were widely venerated in the countryside, couched their message in a populist idiom. Their leadership, example, and language still provide a potent and coherent sense of identity for the non-privileged of the land. The Sufis have traditionally challenged the tyranny of the rich and privileged. The contrast between Sind and Punjab (and the Peshawar valley agriculturists) in this regard is pronounced. Cultural themes dominate economic ones. There is a deep Sufic influence — intensely religious, other-worldly, ecstatic behaviour — in Sind. The Sufi — or his tomb — provides a deeply emotional point of social focus. Sufi ideology, articulated in themes of universal populism, dominates social life. The Punjab farmer is, in comparison, more pragmatic and his interests primarily focus on issues of crops and yields.

An interesting study could be based on the question of whether the Sufi orders of Sind have converted into economic organizations such as the notably successful Bamba of Senegal (in their ground-nut schemes) or the Tijanyya of West Africa (monopolizing trade), and if not, why not?

Hydraulic Society Concept

Although there is not sufficient space in this volume to treat it, the OFWMP offers a point of contact with the so-called 'hydraulic society' — a society structured around large irrigation works — and suggests a subject for further investigation.

The central agricultural region of Pakistan, especially Punjab, provides perhaps the most successful example of the 'hydraulic society' created by the British in the last century in their Empire. The interesting process whereby vast, irrigated, land systems created and supported an organized and centralized bureaucracy and state, termed 'Oriental Despotism'[7] was here reversed. The British, through their organized bureaucracy, created extensive irrigation systems when they opened the canal colonies of Punjab and brought a hydraulic society into being. As mentioned earlier, the older tribal lines are still perceptible despite more than three generations of this society. The 'Occidental Despotism' thereby raises fascinating issues with far-reaching social and political ramifications. One characteristic of hydraulic societies is their malleability when confronting centralized authority. The individual whether he be an Egyptian *fellah* by the Nile or a peasant by the Euphrates or the Yangtze is vulnerable and helpless when confronting the power of the state. He submits easily to authority. This attitude is in sharp contrast to that of the *nang* tribesman who possesses the capacity to pack and move into the interior, thereby escaping the state. He is mobile, unlike the peasant whose land defines and binds him.

It would be instructive to examine similar hydraulic societies in a global context, especially societies that approximate village life in Pakistan in ecological or historical background such as east Punjab in India or parts of Egypt. Do traditional codes survive hydraulic societies? If they do not, can they re-emerge in situations of change? If we were to attempt such an exercise, we would be able to develop universal models which would illuminate not only social structure and organization in rural society but also could interpret processes of change.

NOTES

1. Merrey, D.J., *Irrigation and Honour: Cultural Impediments to the Improvement of Local Level Water Management in Punjab, Pakistan,* WMT Report No. 53, Colorado State University, 1979; Mirza, A.H., *A Study of Organization Factors Affecting Water Management Decision-Making in Pakistan,* WMT Report No. 34, Colorado State University, 1975; and Mirza, A.H., and Merrey, D.J., *Organization Problems and Their Consequences on Improved Watercourses in Pakistan,* WMT Report No. 55, Colorado State University, 1979.

2. For a discussion related to this point in the context of what I call 'the Islamic district paradigm,' see Ahmed, op. cit., 1983.

3. Ahmed, op. cit., 1980.

4. Pettigrew, J., *Robber Noblemen: A Study of the Political System of the Sikh Jats,* Routledge and Kegan Paul, 1978.

5. Barth, op. cit., 1972.

6. Bailey, F., *The Peasant View of the Bad Life in Peasant Societies,* Shanin, T., (editor), Penguin Books, 1971.

7. Wittfogel, K., *Oriental Despotism,* Yale University Press, 1971.

14

Nomadism as Ideological Expression: The Gomal Nomads

Data for this case-study were gathered during the period I was Political Agent in South Waziristan Agency (1978-80), where some groups of the nomadic Suleman Khel and Dottani tribes live. These tribes have traditionally used the Gomal route to enter Pakistan, along the Gomal river which flows from Afghanistan into the Agency to join the Indus near Dera Ismail Khan. Over the last two generations some members of these tribes have decided to settle along the Gomal. Indeed, their association with the Gomal, reinforced by the presence of those who settled here created a name for them. They are known—and refer to themselves—as *de Gomal khalq,* 'the people of Gomal'. In this chapter, I will, therefore, refer to the two tribes under discussion as the Gomal nomads.

Nomad ethnographies have traditionally, and perhaps correctly, placed an emphasis on the dominant role of ecology as a factor shaping society; indeed, comparative studies have almost come to regard nomadism as an ecological adaptation. Climate and terrain, availability of pasture and water, and types of animals herded, are seen to influence patterns of movement and forms of herding and camping associations.[1] Thus nomadism is treated as a 'trait of cultural ecology', characterized by 'lack of interest in fixed property and fixed resources'.[2] Political structures, too, are seen as related to ecology.[3] Reflecting another view, Bates[4] and Irons[5] supported Lattimore's argument[6] that nomadism may also be seen as an adaptation to the political rather than the natural environment. Although sufficient literature exists on the above themes, there is a conspicuous lacuna on the ideological/ cultural content of nomadic life as it relates to concrete administrative/political zones. The Gomal nomads exhibit a defined ideological position which instructs daily life. This ideological position offers additional significant explanations for understanding Gomal nomads and phases of their sedentarization.

While agreeing with the main body of literature on nomadism, perhaps, we may usefully examine ideology as an additional factor to ecology in explaining nomadism. My data from Waziristan indicates that we should examine ideology with specific reference to and within administrative zones more closely as an explanation of and for nomadism. It is argued here, that the Gomal nomads live in the administrative and social interstices of the larger states not by accident but by choice, not as victims of ecological conditions but as part of a political strategy which expresses explicitly a desire to live freely. This feature is perhaps most characteristic of those nomadic tribes crossing administrative/political borders in South Asia. The state in South Asia is traditionally highly centralized, monolithic, and bureaucratic (the Mughal matrix being still visible). For the often illiterate, traditional, generally poor nomad, the state characterizes vast powers, corruption, and impersonal administration. He wishes to remain free of its tentacles. He can do so only by movement.

In addition, nomadic life may be seen as an ideal cultural expression or statement of the larger tribal group — usually sedentary — to which the nomads belong. Through a nomadic existence, certain key features of the larger society are translated, expressed, and perpetuated. Nomadism may thus be seen as an ideological expression and social extension of Pukhtun society reflecting the two major systems within which the Pukhtun organizes his life, *Pukhtunwali*, the Code of the Pukhtuns, and Islam. Gomal nomads themselves emphasize these sets of ideologies, which presume and presuppose each other, in explaining their style of life. Indeed.

there appears to be a conflation of these two systems as reflected in the key features of Gomal life.

There are two key features of the Gomal ideology: *azadi*,[7] political freedom—owing allegiance to no political system or man—and thereby underscoring the unique and direct relationship with the one God; and *tor* or safeguarding honour of women. Together these two features permit the Gomal nomads the fullest possible expression of ideal Pukhtun values.

Azadi may be understood—as it is understood by the Gomal nomads—in terms of administrative borders and structures.[8] In this regard, a serious methodological criticism may be levelled at much of the literature on nomadism which ignores the existence of the administrative structures within which nomads operate. The nomads appear to make moves and counter-moves as a response to seasonal/ecological factors solely. They seem to operate in an administrative vacuum. However, transition from one administrative zone to another is a key factor in migration implying vastly differing personnel, rules and procedures. One major factor in migration is the attempt to escape or, where possible, exploit the administrative structures. Mobility allows nomads freedom inconceivable to peasant or settled groups. For instance, the Tribal Areas in Pakistan, where government presence is minimal, allow the nomads almost complete freedom to transport and sell prohibited commodities. In contrast, this is more difficult in Punjab due to different administrative arrangements. The escape from and exploitation of these administrative webs within which other groups live allows nomads cultural and political freedom. Their names appear on no revenue forms for taxation or police records for identification. Settled Pukhtuns who may be somewhat dismissive about the ignorance and poverty of nomads, such as the Gomal group, nonetheless recognize them as an expression of *azadi* which contrasts with their trapped situation within administrative and political webs. Their migrations and activities are thus viewed as 'escaping' between and from different zones rather than as response to herding needs.

Migration may thus be seen as a political or cultural escape, both in a real and symbolic sense, from political zones. Indeed, this is how they perceive themselves. Their very names *powindah* 'one who travels on foot', and *kochi* 'one who travels', both derived from Persian, support this. I will also argue, as others have done, that to place nomads in a discrete social category with rigid boundaries may create methodological problems. Nomadism remains and reflects an aspect of its own desire to remain desedentarized. The sedentarization process, perhaps inevitable in the last half of the twentieth century, may be a logical state in social and economic progress but it also creates serious dilemmas for the Gomal nomad. For a start, his understanding of *azadi* – the fundamental nomadic concept – is compromised.

Gomal Ethnography

Let us examine the ethnographic data.[9] The Suleman Khel and Dottani, the Gomal nomads of this study, are two of the smaller tribes of South Waziristan Agency. The Suleman Khel number some 1,513 and the Dottani 2,383 souls, according to the Pakistan Census 1972.[10] The tribes are organized along segmentary principles familiar in the literature. That is, they exhibit 'nesting' attributes, are acephalous, egalitarian, trace genealogical links to an apical ancestor and are characterized as *nang* or honour-based groups.[11] The tribes are found in South East Afghanistan, where their major population lives, and also further south east towards the Indus near Dera Ismail Khan. The basic socio-economic – indeed political – unit appears to be the nuclear family, around the household head which includes his wife/wives and offspring organized as a 'tent-camp'. The number of this unit is usually between 12-15 souls. During and for the purposes of migration other such units related in the patrilineage join together.

Pastures in Pakistan are either those reserved by the government for the nomads, called *chiraghan* or *melagah,* or during migration those allowed by local tribes. Migration down the Gomal river and into Pakistan takes place annually in autumn and they return to their pastures in Afghanistan in early spring. Travel is calculated on the basis of a *parowa* or daily span of about 8-9 miles. Their animals are camel, sheep, and goat. Horses are rarely used. Although the Gomal nomads are reluctant to mention the fact, there is an increasing tendency, over the last two generations, to 'settle' one male sibling as owner of joint property—usually 1-4 acres—along the Gomal river. This sedentarization, paradoxically, assists in the *azadi* of the nomads. The sedentarization of one member of the family allows them the best of both worlds. To enquiring officials, males are perpetually 'out' on migration while the Gomal house is a useful 'hide-out' in times of trouble across the border.

Both tribes are marginal to the political life of the South Waziristan Agency which is dominated by two powerful cousin tribes, the Wazirs and Mahsuds, and their intense agnatic rivalry[12] (see also Part Two, chapter 5). Indeed, the intensity of the Wazir-Mahsud agnatic rivalry draws in the political administration of the Agency; their *azadi* is thus compromised. In contrast, the Gomal nomads live outside the sphere of the administration.

The traditional stronghold of the Gomal nomads is the Zarmelan plain. The plain is an arid, dusty bowl of rock and sand surrounded by desolate and barren mountains. It is perhaps for this reason that the Wazirs and Mahsuds have allowed the Gomal nomads ownership of Zarmelan. They also live along the banks of the Gomal river which allows them to cultivate one crop of wheat and barley.

An important event tying the Gomal nomads to the fixed administrative structure of the Agency was the nomination in 1980 of the Suleman Khel elder, Zarif Khan Kamrani (whose genealogy is given on page 218) to the prestigious Agency Council. He was the first Gomal nomad to be appointed and in time a vocal representative of their needs in Council meetings. He was nominated in the hope that, through more active involvement in Agency affairs, the Gomal nomads could legitimately demand and obtain more facilities from government. The connection would also serve the nomads well in the times of trouble that lay ahead in the region. I was not to be disappointed. Schools, tube-wells, and roads were high on their list of demands—as they were on mine for these tribes. Another important development directly related to the emerging political situation in the region was the establishment of a Scouts[13] post on the point where the borders of Afghanistan, Baluchistan, and the North-West Frontier Province meet, on the banks of the Gomal river. Zarmelan today is thus 'penetrated'. The Zarmelan post situated on the vital route used by the Gomal nomads will surely affect their traditional movement; it detracts from their *azadi*. It also illustrates what is one of my major arguments in this study, which is to underline the consequences of larger political developments on nomadic ideology and life.

Gomal Genealogy

The Suleman Khel are one of the larger and better known tribes of the Ghilzai confederation—the total population of which was estimated to be about a million by Robinson[14] and which is now estimated to be more than doubled, between two to three million. The Ghilzais, who have provided ruling dynasties in India (1290-1320), and Persia (1722-1729), retain a somewhat exaggerated sense of social importance. The Dottani, on the other hand, are not Ghilzai.

The origin of the Ghilzai remains obscure, some commentators claiming holy Islamic descent for them while others point to a Turk origin. Robinson, following Dorn and the Mughal historians, relates the story which gives them the holy descent and also their name: Shah Hussain, a noble born but impecunious Persian, married Matu, daughter of Sheikh Bitan, a tribal chief in Afghanistan, after making her pregnant. The boy 'being the fruit of a clandestine amour, was called

Ghilzye. Ghil, in the Afghan language, signifying a 'thief', and 'zye', 'born, a son'.[15] The Gomal nomads reject this story and explain the name as deriving from 'khals'—or land they owned in Afghanistan—hence 'khalszoi'—'sons of the land (of khals)'. This, in time, became Ghilzai. Ghilzai, in turn, had a son Ibrahim from whom descended Suleman Khan. Lodhi is appended to Ibrahim—from loe dey—'he is the eldest'—after Ghilzai pronounced Ibrahim as the 'eldest' of his sons.

The story of Ghilzai origin establishes two interrelated social facts: first, their 'holy' descent and second, their 'non-Pukhtun' ancestry. As a consequence of these facts, the Ghilzai are inclined to underscore their 'Islamic' character.

The Ghilzai have traditionally been rivals to the ruling Durrani dynasty for political power. Consequently, the Durrani have constantly sought to weaken and divide the Ghilzais, especially the Suleman Khel. Amir Abdur Rahman, the Iron Amir, is said to have deported about a thousand families from each of the leading divisions of the Ghilzai to Afghan Turkistan.[16] It is perhaps no accident that the first non-Durrani to rule Afghanistan after the overthrow of the Durrani rule in 1978 was Noor Mohammad Tarraki, a Ghilzai. Some observers note that Tarraki's purge of Durranis reflected a zeal which was more ethnic than ideological.

Genealogy assumes an exaggerated importance for Gomal nomads because of their mobility and the span of their migrations. Unlike settled Pukhtuns, they cannot identify with known and fixed geographical features such as a valley or mountain. Even the Gomal river—which recently has given them a geographical association—symbolizes a form of freedom, winding its way, as it does, through two countries and numerous administrative/political zones. Genealogical memory, oral and imprinted in the minds of the elders, is thus a key to identity. Almost all the males I talked to, who held positions of authority in their camps (elders, sons of elders), could trace their ancestry to Suleman Khel. The Gomal nomads express their Islamic associations tracing the conversion of Quais, their putative apical ancestor, by the Prophet himself. After converting, they explain, he changed his name to a more 'Islamic' name, Abdur Rashid.

Below is the genealogy of Zarif Khan Kamrani, the Suleman Khel elder. The genealogical links to Isa Khan (Isa is spelt as Azi) from Suleman Khel, are also provided by Robinson.[17] The genealogical table makes two points: the importance of generation recall to Gomal nomads—up to 14 generations linking Zarif Khan with his ancestor Shah Hussain—and the suggestion of non-Pukhtun origin of the tribe. The latter point, after Ghilzai's many centuries of assimilation and association with *Pukhtunwali*, is not sociologically important. The first point is important: genealogy remains a diacritical feature distinguishing Pukhtun from Pukhtun, and Pukhtun from non-Pukhtun.

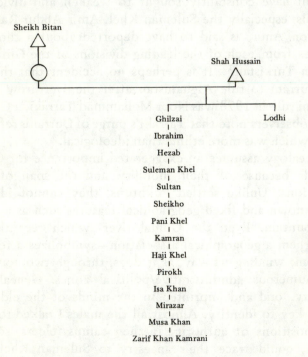

Figure 14.1: The Genealogy of Zarif Khan Kamrani

Daily Life

Let us briefly examine the daily activities of the basic unit. The basic unit, as stated earlier, is socially, economically — indeed to a large extent politically — self-sufficient. The rhythm of daily life appears to be unchanged since the last two generations at least.[18] Adult males on the move or in seasonal camps are involved in trade deals, temporary manual labour, and conducting various forms of politics. The household head is the decision-maker and does not hold any official or administrative position. Women, as in other Pukhtun tribes, lead an exceedingly busy physical life. They cook, clean, sew, wash for the household, and also tend the animals. Children, from an early age, assist their parents — in the early years the mother, and later, the boys are attached to the father. Although on the surface life is physically hard and unsettled, in the daily routine it assumes steady and known patterns. Authority is clearly demarcated, as are job roles. Each member knows his position in society.

For other needs, such as making cots, shoes, etc., the *qasabgars,* or service groups, have been affiliated to the tribe. *Qasabgars* are various supporting professionals such as cobblers, goldsmiths, barbers, and carpenters. Ideally, there is no intermarriage between *qasabgars* and the major host tribes. The *qasabgar* does not 'carry the gun' and does not own land, diacritica which distinguish him from Pukhtun. In time, some *qasabgar* groups, especially among the settled Dottanis, have merged with the host tribe assuming their name and creating fictitious genealogical links. Genealogy thus remains an important diacritical feature for tribes like the Suleman Khel who wish to distinguish non-Suleman Khel. We saw above the capacity of elders, like Zarif Khan, to recall male ascendants up to the apical ancestor of the tribe.

Life is hard and luggage is kept — almost by nomadic definition — to a minimum. The daily budget is spent largely on food items of which the main are tea, sugar, meat, pulses, flour, and kerosene oil. The average family — or basic unit —

is estimated to spend between 50 to 60 rupees (5 to 6 dollars) daily. Milk and firewood are free for the nomads.

The major expenditure revolves around the *rites de passage.* Marriage is the major and most expensive of these, in part due to the actual bride-price payment, followed by rites of death, birth, and circumcision. The pattern for the *rites de passage* are familiar from other comparative data on Pukhtun tribes.[19] The low daily budgets and expenditure on *rites de passage* are a consequence of the nomadic life; one that lends itself to easy movement at short notice across changing borders and zones in South Asia. A factor that supports their movements and assists them in mapping strategy is the recent arrival of the radio among the Gomal nomads. Almost every family unit possesses the radio and the family head is an avid listener to national and international news.

The Ideological Content of Gomal Nomadism

Turning to a discussion of the ideological content of nomadic life, it is seen that the influence and presence of Islam permeates life among the Gomal nomads. Indeed, as they see it, Islam is visibly interlinked with their ancestry — traced to their holy ancestor Shah Hussain — and their tribal mythology. For instance, the Gomal nomads explain the downfall of the Ghilzais by a story involving a *Pir* — saint — and his 'curse'. Apparently, an ancestor of the tribe had displeased the *Pir* who cursed the tribe through *khayray,* or *'badoa'* ('bad prayer'). For seven generations, he had predicted, the Ghilzais would be dominated by their rivals, the Durrani. A Ghilzai proverb claims *Badshahi da Durrani, tura da Ghilzai* — kingship belongs to the Durrani, but the sword (power, honour, etc.) belongs to the Ghilzai. The story reflects interestingly on history as Durrani rule began in Afghanistan about seven generations ago (allowing about 30 years for a generation). Religious mythology was again sustained for the Ghilzai when Noor Mohammad Tarraki, in 1978, came to power in Kabul displacing Durrani rule. Their tribe, the Ghilzais, the

Gomal nomads point out, have provided a Muslim dynasty in India. They have carried the banners of Islam to far points of South Asia. Islam and tribal identity appear interlinked to them.

In contrast to the observations of other anthropologists[20] I found the Gomal nomads firm in their allegiance and—where locally understood-practice of Islam. Robinson also notes, 'They are generally strict in the performance of religious duties'.[21] For instance, almost every nomad I checked wore a religious talisman—*taweez*—usually verses from the Holy Quran—around his neck as a visible symbol of his faith and protection against unspecified dangers.

It appears that a certain myth about Muslim nomads possessing 'a reputation for being poor Muslims'[22] prevails in nomadic studies in spite of general, though scattered evidence to the contrary.[23] My observations corroborate those of Evans-Pritchard[24] who noted that laxity in practice of the Cyrenaica Bedouins was not to be understood as irreligiosity. Nomads translate various aspects of life into Islamic idiom. For example, Lancaster notes the Rwala Bedouin's adverse reaction to sedentarization is seen in primarily 'religious' terms.[25]

Some observers point to laxity in practice as a proof that nomads are 'poor Muslims'. It is noted that fasting during the month of *Ramazan*—one of the five compulsory features of Muslim life—is suspended. It is my observation that the question of fasting has been misunderstood by many observers of Islamic groups. According to Islamic tradition and customs, the fast may be legitimately postponed if the person is 'travelling' (on *safr*—journey). The Gomal nomads who do not fast if the month of *Ramazan* coincides with their migration appear to compensate—under Islamic practice—the days missed once they have camped for the season. When travelling the nomads drop the *nafil* in their daily prayers. They explain this as a special dispensation deriving from the time of the Prophet.

A more useful discussion than the 'poor Muslims' *versus* 'good Muslims' one (and where does that lead us to?—few

Muslims—however 'poor' in practice—will admit inferiority)
would be to examine the pre-Islamic organization, values,
etc., that may have been 'Islamized' and retained. We may
thereby learn more about the ideological adjustments between
Islamic universalism and nomadic particularism. An extension
of this enquiry relates to the question of tribe and state in
the Muslim world. As we know the relationship is sometimes
uneasy and largely undefined, which creates certain tensions
in the contemporary world. Nationalist governments sometimes behave as if they possess a monopoly on culture and
religion. The issue is farther obfuscated by the 'romantic'
view of nomadic life against the 'realist' view.[26] The 'romantic'
image, deriving from the 'noble savage' prototype, perhaps
does more harm than good to the object of affection. We
may avoid this trap altogether if we view nomadism as an
ideological expression of certain ideals of the larger settled
group. The nomad, then, may be seen, as reflecting the higher
ideals of society and not as a cultural aberration left high and
dry by the ebb and flow of historical progression.

The nomadic interpretation of Islam may be seen literally
and simply, as the Gomal nomad sees it, as the submission to
the one God. Any other relationships makes him uneasy. To
assert the freedom this relationship implies he must keep
moving; he must also possess, what Robinson so aptly terms
'restlessness in his blood'.[27] Matters pertaining to geographical
locality and social relationships are the exclusive domain of
the camp elder. Through them he ensures his freedom.

Let us briefly examine how the Gomal nomads may interpret the laws of *tor* distinctly from other Pukhtun groups. As
we know *tor,* which suggests the violation of the honour of a
woman, may be converted to *spin*—or white—only by death
(of the couple involved). *Tor,* it is locally argued, is both
Pukhtun and Islamic in concept. The courts and law of
Afghanistan and Pakistan often take a lenient view of *tor*
cases; the accused is considered by the Criminal Procedure
Code in Pakistan as having acted under 'grave provocation'.
Nonetheless, tribesmen are sometimes involved in lengthy

and expensive court cases. In the Tribal Areas, the matter is simpler. Society allows killing—usually by the father or brother of the person—in *tor* cases. However, there are various escape routes which men often utilize.[28] New ideas and new money have further influenced people on *tor* cases.[29] In contrast the nomads, living within a whole, viable, defined, and recognized universe—conceptualized as the basic socio-economic unit and during migration the tent-camp—can order the speedy implementation of the punishment. Society will explicitly approve. Moving from zone to zone, it is easy to elude entanglement with local people and administration. Few questions are asked and fewer answers provided. The nomad carries his secrets with him. *Tor* punishments, are rigidly implemented. Otherwise, it was argued, not only morality but social morale, the ideological component of society, and ultimately discipline in the unit would suffer. The last, it was argued, was not possible for the efficient organization of a nomadic camp.

What remains of interest in the situation of the Gomal nomads is the pattern of their migrations. They traditionally crossed international borders and widely differing ecological zones. From the central zone of Afghanistan in autumn, south-east across the mountain ranges, along the Gomal river, into the plains of Punjab, sometimes further south towards Delhi and Calcutta, and some, it appears, as far south as Australia.[30] Winter was spent under tent-camps or in neighbouring villages working as part-time labour. The transition from Central Asia into South Asia was signified by the compulsory surrendering of arms at the check-posts on the borders between Afghanistan and British India. This chapter emphasizes the presence of these administrative structures and zones as they are not sufficiently dealt with as a factor in nomadic life. They are a real and integral part of nomadic life; migration routes and camping sites are often selected with administrative borders and their personnel in mind. Some of the latter are to be avoided altogether, some negotiated, and some circumvented. The nomadic encounter with the personnel of the state, especially on the outskirts or border zones, is fraught with possibility for both sets of actors.

Awareness of their passages through traditionally difficult administrative areas, and of the potential to mobilize migratory tribal networks for the Great Game, played between Imperial Russia and Britain, was fully exploited in the last and present century. Rudyard Kipling's horse-trader from Kabul, in *Kim,* personified the tribesman who represented a link with Central Asia and the nomadic life.

Conclusion

Perhaps the greatest threat to the life-style of the Gomal nomads has little to do with the traditional factors of change, analysts discuss[31] and traditional processes of sedentarization.[32] In the case of the Gomal nomads, geopolitical decisions made by heads of government have affected their life. In the early sixties, President Ayub Khan of Pakistan, reflecting the deterioration in the relationship with Afghanistan, ordered the closing of the border to the *powindahs.* This resulted in severe dislocation and hardship for them. The Gomal nomads, nonetheless, managed to migrate to Pakistan through unfrequented paths such as the Gomal route. Their span of migration, however, was shortened. While they could pasture freely in the Tribal Areas of the Frontier where there are no police, fewer reached the Punjab with its complex and developed administration networks. When the Russians entered Afghanistan in 1979, the Gomal traditional life-style was once again severely affected. Until that year, their life was largely traditional and unchanging in spite of the inconveniences of Ayub Khan's ban on their entry. Even labour opportunities in the Arab States, which through remittances sent home are affecting other tribes,[33] were largely ignored. To my mind, 1979 is the most critical year — and a turning point — in the recent history of the Gomal nomads. It is unlikely that their traditional life will be restored fully. Their capacity to express their needs for political freedom by shifting across borders will be impaired. This event may enforce sedentariz-ation of the Gomal nomads. Nomadism, in any case, is not a total social category. A sloughing-off process, as we saw earlier, was clearly at work among the Gomal nomads.

However remote from political life they may have kept themselves in the contemporary situation, the Gomal nomads find their traditional life disrupted. Apart from a general unrest and tension in the country which disallows normal migration, many have expressed a desire to take part in the holy war—*jihad. Azadi* is now translated in a directly religious idiom which encompasses total social life. Many adults leave their families with their kin along the Gomal route and—in rotation with agnatic kin—take turns with their dated 303 rifles to wage *jihad* in Afghanistan against a supreme military power of the age. This gesture in itself, it could be argued, reflects the idealistic content in nomad life and translates as the desire to maintain *azadi.*

NOTES

1. Johnson, D.L., *The Nature of Nomadism: A Comparative Study of Pastoral Migrations in Southwestern Asia and Northern Africa,* Department of Geography, Research Paper 118, University of Chicago, Chicago, 1969; Krader, L., 'The Ecology of Nomadic Pastoralism', in *International Social Sciences Journal,* 11, pp. 499-510; Rubel, P., 'Herd Composition and Social Structure: On Building Models of Nomadic Pastoral Societies', in *MAN,* 4, 1969, pp. 268-73; Spooner, B., *The Cultural Ecology of Pastoral Nomads,* Reading, Massachusetts, Addison-Wesley Publishing Co., 1973; and Sweet, L.E., 'Camel Pastoralism in North Arabia and the Minimal Camping Unit', in *Man, Culture and Animals: The Role of Animals in Human Ecological Adjustments,* Leeds, A., and Vayda, A.P., (editors), American Association for the Advancement of Science, 1965, pp. 129-52.

2. Spooner, op. cit., 1973, pp. 3-4.

3. Barth, F., *Nomads of South Persia: The Basseri Tribe of the Khamseh Confederacy,* 1961 and 'Nomadism in the Mountain and Plateau Areas of South West Asia', in *The Problems of the Arid Zone: The Proceedings of the Paris Symposium,* Arid Zone Research 18, UNESCO, Paris, 1962, pp. 341-55; Black-Michaud, J., *Cohesive Force: Feud in the Mediterranean and the Middle East,* Blackwell, Oxford, 1975; Salzman, P.C., 'Political Organization Among Nomadic Peoples', in *Proceedings of the American Philosophical Society,* III, 1967, pp. 115-31; and Sweet, op. cit., 1965.

4. Bates, D.G., 'The Role of the State in Peasant-Nomad Mutualism', in *Anthropological Quarterly,* 3, 1971, pp. 109-31.

5. Irons, W., 'Nomadism as a Political Adaptation: The Case of the Yomut Turkmen , in *American Ethnologist,* I, 1974, pp. 635-58.

6. Lattimore, O., *Inner Asian Frontiers of China,* American Geographical Society, New York, 1940.

7. Not all anthropologists heed Mauss that the anthropologist has 'to be also a novelist to be able to evoke the life of a whole society', Mauss, M., *Manuel d'ethnographie,* Payot, Pauline D., (editor), Paris, 1947, p. 8. Novelists, on the other hand, with sometimes a sharper eye for cultural forms and comparisons than anthropologists who are necessarily confined to focusing on social features such as structure and organization, have perhaps best portrayed the feeling of freedom, *azadi,* of the nomads (among others Rudyard Kipling, John Masters, and James Michener). The following paragraph captures this aspect, *azadi,* of the nomad: 'Across the scrub-covered plain approached men with camels. The men had the faces of eagles and walked with long, slow, lifting strides. One of them looked up as he passed by. Anne smiled at him, expecting the *salaam* and the answering smile of an ordinary Indian wayfarer. But this was not India. The man stared her down, from pale green kohl-rimmed eyes. He carried a long rifle slung across his shoulders; a woman, shapelessly swathed in red and black cotton, swayed on top of the camel that he led; a lad of fourteen walked behind the camel; the lad had no beard, but his stride was an exact imitation of his father's insolent lilt, and he too carried a rifle.

'Pathans Aka Khel Afridis' Major Hayling said. Anne stared after them, a little angry, a little frightened', Masters, J., *The Lotus and The Wind,* Harmondsworth, Penguin Books, 1956, p. 9. Here I am tempted to follow Meeker's use of 'heroic' for such groups as suggesting political independence. See Meeker, M.E., 'The Twilight of a South Asian Heroic Age: A Rereading of Barth's Study of Swat', in *MAN,* (N.S.) 15, 1980, pp. 682-701.

8. Both nomads and administrators recognize the *azadi* of nomadic life. The *azadi* of another nomadic group, the Gujars, had struck me when I was a young administrator (26) and in charge of Mansehra Sub-Division, as Assistant Commissioner in 1969. In an impressionistic essay I wrote of them: 'There is an indescribable and unfettered freedom about them. . .they laugh and march. Some nights camping by a grove of olive trees that protects a grave-yard, some nights under the shelter of jutting rocks by the road side; sometimes on the road in the month of *sawan* and its playful mists and rains; sometimes returning in September with trees along the road and in clumps turning autumn gold and yellow. . . . But always drifting, always free'. See Ahmed, op. cit., 1974.

9. *Notes on Nomad Tribes of Eastern Afghanistan* written by a British political officer who served in the Agency about two generations ago—for the purpose of discouraging such groups from disrupting civil life in British India by petty theft, smuggling, or even kidnapping—remains nonetheless a reliable document for the examination of the Gomal nomads. I was able to locate the descendants of some of the names mentioned by Robinson—and utilize his excellent genealogical charters.

10. These figures are somewhat suspect. Tribal enumerations are based on what are officially called 'estimates'. The migratory nature of these two tribes makes the actual figure permanently living in the Agency even more difficult to assess. The continued deliberate vagueness of the tribesmen regarding such information further supports my argument: they do not wish to engage modern administrative apparatus as they feel it would compromise their freedom.

11. Ahmed, op. cit., 1980.

12. Ahmed, A.S., 'Order and Conflict in Muslim Society: A Case-study from Pakistan', in *The Middle East Journal,* Vol. 36, No. 2, 1982, pp. 184-7, and op. cit., 1983. See also Part Two, chapter 5.

13. The Scouts are a para-military force that guard the borders in the Tribal Areas.

14. Robinson, J.A., *Notes on Nomad Tribes of Eastern Afghanistan,* Nisa Traders, Quetta, Pakistan, 1934, reprinted 1978, p. 55.

15. Ibid., p. 53.

16. Ibid., p. 57.

17. Ibid., pp. 200-1.

18. Ibid.

19. Ahmed, op. cit., 1980.

20. Barth, op. cit., 1961.

21. Robinson, op. cit., 1934, p. 9.

22. Tapper, R., *Pasture and Politics: Economics, Conflict and Ritual among Shahsevan Nomads of Northwestern Iran,* Academic Press, New York, 1979, p. 2.

23. Ahmed and Hart, op. cit., 1984; Cole, D., *Nomads of the Nomads: The Al Murrah Bedouin of the Empty Quarter,* Aldine, Chicago, 1975; Ibrahim, S.E., and Cole, D., *Saudi Arabian Bedouin,* papers in Social Science, Cairo, 1978; Pastner, S., 'Ideological Aspects of Nomad-Sedentary Contact', in *Anthropological Quarterly,* Volume 44, No. 3, July 1971; Salzman, op. cit., 1967; Irons, op. cit., 1974; and Lewis, I.M., *A Pastoral Democracy,* Oxford University Press, 1961.

24. Evans-Pritchard, op. cit., 1973.

25. Lancaster, W.O., 'Review of Ibrahim and Cole', in *Nomadic Peoples,* No. 5, Commission on Nomadic Peoples, IUAES, 1980, pp. 20-7.

26. See ibid for a good example of the one confronting the other with reference to the Bedouins in Saudi Arabia.

27. To illustrate the cause of this restlessness is to reflect on nomad character: 'As an Afghan once told Mr. Elphinstone, "We are content with discord; we are content with alarms; we are content with blood; but we never will be content with a master"'. See Robinson, op. cit., 1934, pp. 2 and 8.

28. Ahmed, op. cit., 1980.

29. Ahmed, A.S., 'The Arab Connection: Emergent Models of Social Structure and Organization among Pakistani Tribesmen', in *Asian Affairs,* London, 1981. pp. 167-72.

30. Robinson, op. cit., 1934, p. 26.

31. Stanford, S., 'Pastoralism under Pressure', *O.D.I.* No. 2, London, 1976.

32. Salzman, P.C., (editor), *When Nomads Settle: Processes of Sedentarization as Adaptation and Response,* Praeger, New York, 1980.

33. Ahmed, A.S., 'The Arab Connection: Emergent Models of Social Structure and Organization among Pakistani Tribesmen', in *Asian Affairs,* London, 1981; 'Mullah, Mahdi and Mosque: Emergent Trends in Muslim Society', paper presented to SSRC Conference, South Asian Islam, Philadelphia, May 1981 and op. cit., 1983.

15

Can Pakistan be Japan?
Social Factors in Economic Development

The President of Pakistan, General Zia-ul-Haq, visited Japan in July 1983 and was visibly impressed with what he saw. Before General Zia other visitors, ranging from noted world economists like Veblen and Rostow to experts—India's Madan[1] and Rustomji and Spare;[2] America's Christopher,[3] Dore,[4] Franko,[5] Mendel,[6] Reischauer[7] and Vogel;[8] and Singapore's Swee[9]—have been equally impressed by the Japanese model of development. And like many foreigners General Zia asked why his country, Pakistan, cannot be like Japan?[10] The question raises important issues of a sociological nature in order to explain Japan's economic success.

What impressed General Zia? Lessons of high productivity, high profits, discipline, and loyalty in firms? Or, like any one visiting Japan from South Asia, was he struck with the series of contrasts in social and public life: the politeness, the orderliness, the cleanliness, and the appearance of formality or properness in Japan? It is difficult not to be moved like General Zia on a first visit to Japan.

In dress, in standard of living, in their economy, the Japanese are like, or better than, most Europeans. Nowhere in Asia or Africa can their organization and standards be equalled. For Asians, Japan's highly developed world comes as a cultural shock; the thought that these are, after all, Asians remains in the mind. They are not masquerading as a developed nation, they are a developed nation.

The statistics available for the two nations provide further dramatic points of comparison.

Japan and Pakistan: Comparisons

The national statistics—taken almost at random—indicate the contrast between the two nations. Japan's average annual per capita income is about 7,000 and Pakistan's 350 dollars. Japan has some 40 million motor vehicles, Pakistan not quite 1 million; Japan has a hospital bed for 92 persons, Pakistan has one for every 2,000; Japan has a physician for 782 persons, Pakistan one for 3,655;[11] Japanese live until 77 years, Pakistanis 54; Japan's literacy rate is almost 100 per cent, Pakistan's about 20 per cent. The better figures for Japan are in spite of the fact that its 120 million people live on 377,682 square kilometres (spread over four main islands) over 70 per cent of which is mountainous (314 persons per square kilometre)—Pakistan's 90 million people are spread over 796,095 square kilometres (112 persons per square kilometre).

These statistics may be translated as indices of immutable economic differentiation and for Pakistan of irreversible despair. Is there, then, some structural flaw in Muslim society and inherent advantages in Japanese society? No. Not so. I shall make a brief and schematic presentation of some historical dates and events in support of my answer to the question.

The diametrically opposed paths the two societies took will be illustrated by these key dates and events in the recent history of South Asian Muslims and Japan. They will also help us understand both Muslim and Japanese society in better perspective.

The year 1603 has been a critical one for Japanese history. In this year, Ieyasu Tokugawa, consolidated his authority and established the shogunate and the Tokugawa dynasty. Japan was ending centuries of what its history had been until then, political turmoil and civil strife between competing war lords. In contrast, Akbar, the great Mughal Emperor, still ruled South Asia. He was to die two years later in 1605. It was the zenith of the Mughal Empire. Mughal India then was among the most powerful economic and military nations of the world. Only a few years before Akbar died, Elizabeth, the

Queen of England, granted a charter to the East India Company to trade in India. By 1857, the Company would be the direct cause of the termination of the Mughal dynasty in India.

As also, the middle of the nineteenth century when both societies, Tokugawa Japan and Mughal India, were dying. In Japan, the vigour of Tokugawa rule was long exhausted and, in India, the authority of the Mughal Emperor was restricted to his quarters in the Red Fort in Delhi. Great events took place which would shake the foundations of both societies and determine the directions they would take in the coming century. In Japan, in 1853, Commander Perry forced his way into the Tokyo harbour with his gunboats. In India, in 1857, the Mughal Emperor in Delhi became the rallying point for the widespread rebellion against the British. As a direct consequence of these events, one emperor lost and the other gained an empire. The last Mughal Emperor was deposed by the British in 1857, and the rule of the Meiji dynasty began in Japan in 1868.

Both, Muslim society in South Asia and Japanese society, in the middle of the nineteenth century, faced difficult and complex choices. Were they to become as much as possible like the aggressive and dominant western powers, the British in the case of the former and the Americans in the latter, who had forced themselves in or were they to shut their doors and preserve traditional life and thought? We know that both societies made opposite choices. The Muslims, with notable exceptions such as the College at Aligarh, preferred not to adopt the ways of the British in India. The Japanese, on the other hand, threw themselves into learning what the West had to teach. After careful research they selected the best each nation had to offer: their navy was modelled on the British, their law on the French, and their monetary and banking systems on the USA. The Prussians provided models for an Imperial Constitution and Army High Command which, it has been argued, perhaps set the Japanese on the road to Imperial conquests.

Less than a century later, in the forties, again two diametrically opposed pictures are presented by Japanese and Pakistani societies. The old Japan was almost hammered to death by bombing in 1945 by the victorious Americans. In 1947, Pakistan, a new nation, was born from British India with high expectations and hopes.

By the early sixties, Pakistan was considered a model developing country. It was the largest Muslim country in the world enjoying its longest period of political stability. Its progress in industry and agriculture was considered satisfactory. The Integrated Rural Development Programme in Comilla, (formerly East Pakistan now Bangladesh), attracted world attention, including that of countries who would themselves become models in the coming decades, like South Korea. Japan was then in the process of rising—strong and renewed—from the ashes of the Second World War. Symbolically, it was just breaking into the world market with its Toyotas and Hondas.

In the eighties, once again, two opposed pictures emerge: Japan among the richest (as we saw with a per capita income of 7,000 dollars), and most literate (literacy about 100 per cent) nations of the world, second in economic power perhaps only to the USA—and Pakistan, emerging from the political trauma of 1971 during which it was separated from its eastern wing, among the poorer (with a per capita income of 350 dollars), and less literate ones (literacy about 20 per cent).

These snapshot contrasts raise a number of questions. What are the factors responsible for Japan's remarkable success? What were the social and political pre-conditions necessary for these factors to become operative? Can we put our finger on one secret?

One simple answer would be to say that Japan was never colonized, at least not quite like India, and thus blame it on the Europeans. This is, I fear, a superficial solution. Or to discover the Japanese secrets of development, do we examine aspects of contemporary Japan which are said to contain them: management technique, educational system, or diet? These aspects in themselves are effect not cause of what we are seeking.

It is hard to make up one's mind but to the social scientist perhaps the mystery is not so very great. We will, therefore, look for more convincing answers in Japanese society and history.

Japanese economic development can largely be understood through Japanese social structure and organization formed over the last centuries. The argument presented here is that the nexus between an act and its consequences, or between the failure to perform it and another set of consequences, is dictated not by nature but is the consequence of a given social structure. In particular, the code, bushido,[12] which sustained, defined and interpreted that society must be clearly understood. Let me get to the very heart of the Japanese matter by discussing the essence of bushido.[13]

Bushido: The Way of the Samurai

The main features of bushido derive from Confucian and Buddhist preaching and therefore reflect their values. These like duty and loyalty to parents and seniors, correct behaviour, and acceptance of fate, are Confucian. Frugality, simplicity, discipline, and meditation, are Zen Buddhist. During the Tokugawa period, from the seventeenth to nineteenth centuries, other characteristically feudal features were added to the code. These were haji, shame, yuki, bravery, and the cult of katana, the sword.[14] The social behaviour of the ideal samurai approximated to the bushido.

In South Asia, two groups, one feudal and the other tribal, approximate in their codes, which emphasize honour, and martial prowess, to bushido. These are the Rajputs[15] and the Pukhtuns.[16] In particular, Pukhtunwali, the Code of the Pukhtun, with its emphasis on honour, bravery, and tura, sword; or, more recently, topak, gun,[17] resembles bushido.[18]

However, there is one critical feature in *bushido* which does not exist in *Pukhtunwali*. This is the concept of *chu* or loyalty to the master. In Pukhtun society, every man considers himself a Khan or chief. Except to God Almighty he reserves his *chu*. Group loyalty or discipline are therefore hard to sustain among Pukhtuns.

The code of *bushido* was a highly developed social philosophy practised by the *samurai*. It emphasized learning, *bun*, and the martial arts, *bu*, equally. Thus *bun-bu* practised together pointed to *ryo-do*, or both ways, on which the ideal *samurai* travelled. If the sword symbolized *bu*, the elaborate tea ceremony symbolized *bun*. Both concentrated the mind, provided balance, and illustrated form. At the heart of *bushido* was honour.

The cult of honour was highly developed in Japanese society. With honour was associated the concept of death and with that the sword. Mishima was to echo Jocho Yamamoto (1659-1719) in the line that caught the imagination of modern Japan: 'I found that the way of the *samurai* is death'.[19] It is significant that expressions of direct affection between man and woman, love or *ai*, is a recent import from and after the American occupation. In the world of the sword, there was little room for love.

Death, even in suicide, was not a simple or haphazard affair. Death, according to *bushido*, involved elaborate ritual (as Mishima was to illustrate through his own dramatic suicide in 1967). Through ritual suicide or *seppuku* — commonly called *hara kiri* or belly slitting — honour could be redeemed. Thus *bushido*, in its most dramatic manifestation, was equated to the cult of the sword.

The sword was an integral part of social behaviour and organization. The way a *samurai* sat, or placed his sword, indicated his relationships. If the sword was placed on the right hand side, it indicated a friendly or social conversation. Only the *samurai*, who wore two and his lady who carried a small one to safeguard her honour, were allowed swords. The sword was always at hand whether sleeping, talking, or negotiating. A folk saying declared: 'the sword is the soul of the *samurai*'. Folk-tales and literature are associated with the sword. One of Rohan's most famous stories is *hitofuri-ken* (The Sword). The sword of the *samurai* became a metaphor for Japanese society.

Even today, the fascination with the sword is barely disguised.[20] The West, and particularly the Americans, meeting the Japanese in the middle of the last century for the first time, in what would become complex military and economic relationships, saw only the *bu* or martial arts in *bun-bu*. The stereotype has not quite died. The western definition of the *samurai* only mentions *bu*. For example, *The Concise Oxford Dictionary* defines *samurai* as a 'Japanese army officer' and, historically, 'member of military caste in Japan'.

Bushido inspired austerity and simplicity in other aspects of life: Tokugawa architecture consists of straight lines and rectangular shapes; the food is simple, raw fish and vegetables;[21] physical fitness[22] and cleanliness[23] are almost a social obsession. Greys and blacks were – and are – preferred, for instance, in architecture and clothing. *Bun-bu* balances frugality and masculinity, action and contemplation.

We may refer to our own Japanese model as that of the *samurai*. This model helps explain Japanese society, its failures and its successes. But this is not, let me hasten to explain, the stereotype model. In the way I wish to employ it I have made adjustments in the model. Along with *bu* I wish to emphasize *bun* in my *samurai* model to explain the Japanese. So although the *samurai* represents a man with a capacity for violent action, he is also a man capable of writing, thinking, and with a sense for aesthetic beauty. The *samurai* model is for the individual, a source of strength, discipline, frugality,[24] and, above all, loyalty (to the master, later nation). It equipped the Japanese to deal stoically with the earthquakes, typhoons, and storms that occur so regularly in Japan.

It is not difficult to see these characteristics reflected in the modern Japanese, whether fighting the Americans in the

Second World War or, in their large industrial organizations today. Just as the strength, frugality, and loyalty that *bushido* inculcated, served to make them formidable warriors the same characteristics drive them in the large economic enterprises today.

Not only activist intellectuals like Mishima live by *bushido*. Men like Nitobe, who became a Christian, wrote of and supported the concept.[25] Nitobe's influential work[26] dedicated to his uncle, acknowledged his admiration for 'the deeds of the *samurai*', revealing the themes of *bushido*: 'courage' (chapter IV), 'honour' (chapter VIII), 'loyalty' (chapter IX), 'suicide' (chapter XII), and, of course, 'the sword, the soul of the *samurai*' (chapter XIII).

For the earliest great classical writers such as Saikaku (1642-93) to modern ones like Nitobe or Mishima — or those writing today like Fujiwara, including the poets[27] — the themes of *bushido*, the essence of the *samurai* model, are central to life and society.[28] On television, in plays, and in dramas, the *samurai* fascinates Japanese audiences. The *samurai* theme has been popularly translated in the West through films like *The Magnificent Seven* and novels like *Shogun*.[29]

The *samurai* cult inspires society from the profound to the pop level: from the ritual suicide of Mishima to the hairstyles of Sumo wrestlers and toys for children.[30] At all levels of society the *samurai* model is evident.

Through the *samurai* model, we may understand a range of Japanese activities from Iwo Jima, where during the last days of the war on a small island, 8 square miles, almost 23,000 Japanese died rather than surrender to the Americans, who suffered about 20,000 casualties; to the *kamikaze*, the suicide pilots, or the Japanese aggressive competitiveness in the world of high technology today.

It is also the *samurai* model that explains the complex and special relationship the Japanese have with the Americans. The Americans physically and militarily beat the Japanese. They, therefore, deserved honour[31] (their physical size and white colour also impressed the Japanese).[32] However, the short history of the Americans and their lack of developed culture invited contempt by the Japanese. It is a love-hate relationship.

The ambivalence for things American is a feature of Japanese society. Japanese female models, whether on posters or in stores, look as closely American as plastic surgery can make possible. Jeans and sneakers are worn by the young generation. Signs of golf practice nets, perched on roofs and between buildings, Coca Cola, and Kentucky fried chicken are everywhere. The daily English press advertises plastic surgery, George Washington societies, and Jeanne Dixon horoscopes. In a sense, the *samurai* acknowledged the superior warrior but, being Japanese, Japanized the warrior's customs and values to make them acceptable. The American victory was a military not political or cultural conquest. But *bushido* and *bun-bu*, the core of the *samurai* model, were the consequence not the cause of a certain kind of society. Let us briefly examine that society in the Tokugawa period, from 1603 to 1868 and its transformation in the Meiji Restoration from 1868 to 1945.

The Tokugawa and Meiji Periods: Sociological Foundations of Modern Japanese Society

The serious ethnic tensions in South Asia — and anthropologists claim that they are the main feature of the region[33] — have not marked Japanese history. In South Asia, ethnic tensions have often been a prelude to political movements leading to independent states (as in Bangladesh). In Japan, the distinction is between a Japanese and non-Japanese, rather than ethnic or sectarian. The Japanese are a distinctively homogeneous nation. The answer to this lies as much in the ideological foundations of Japanese society as in Japanese history[34] — and we have available extensive archaeological and anthropological studies of the Japanese from prehistory[35] to contemporary society.[36]

Japanese society could be usefully conceptualized along the pattern of the classic segmentary model of tribal societies.[37] A tribal network relates members of society, irrespective of class, to each other and, through ascendants, to the founding member of the tribe (Figure 15.1). Through a complex series of relationships each household worships the hierarchically established number of gods. These gods acknowledge the ancestor of the Emperor, Amaterasu, as the main god. The Emperor, called Tenno, (*Ten* sky, *No*, Emperor of), is descended from Amaterasu and remains the keystone to the ideological foundations of society. Tenno was also an essential part of the structure of Shintoism, the traditional religion. For example, the editing and maintenance of the main holy book, *Kojiki*, which sanctified the authority of Tenno as invested from heaven, was supervised by him. *Kojiki* reorganized native myths regarding creation, death etc., into a systematic genealogy relating Tenno to the Japanese people. He also appointed priests at the various categories of shrines.

The Imperial family spoke an exclusive language and was entirely endogamous. They were the 'dwellers above the clouds'. For the Japanese, a healthy Emperor meant a healthy Japan and this critical equation was embodied in prayer.[38]

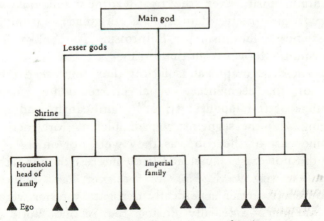

Figure 15.1: Ideological Foundations of Society

Tenno, thus, assumes the significance in segmentary tribes of the eponymous ancestor who lives in and through his descendant the current chief. He is the head, the font, and the symbol of the tribe.

It is significant that the rebellions in recorded history were mainly of oppressed farmers against *daimyos* (there were at least a thousand revolts during the Tokugawa period) or to restore the Emperor (during the Meiji period). *Ishin* and *Sonno-joi*, the cries of modern Japan, were a longing for a past long dead, before the *shoguns* assumed power. Literally, they meant 'restore the Emperor and expel the foreigner'. To the end (of the war) the Japanese fought fanatically for the honour of the Emperor. Their main aim was to save him, if he was demolished their ideological world would be devastated.

Shintoism, 'the way of the gods', itself was a religion of the living. Its emphasis on fertility, pleasure, rituals based on rice-wine, and abhorrence of death provided society with a worldly, here and now, ideology. Its Shamanism, and its animism, did not encourage speculation of unseen future worlds. Its easy eclecticism allowed it to absorb foreign or non-local values and customs. Gods were freely and easily created; a revered parent, a favourite dead wrestler, a mountain spirit. Even the post-war new religions, *shinko shukyo*, are easily identified as originating from either Christianity, Buddhism, or Shintoism. The Sokka Gakkai, for instance, derives from Buddhism.

Japanese geographical isolation thus reinforced the concept of the segmentary tribal charter which identified members of the Japanese tribe.[39] Significantly, and again in keeping with the segmentary principle, no foreigners could become part of the tribe; as they were not on the charter, they did not exist. Japan had little interest or sympathy for them. The very word *gaijin*, for foreigner, has a connotation of contempt. Other specifically derogatory terms were used for foreigners — especially during the Second World War — such as 'demon' for the British, 'domestic animal' for

Americans, and 'lice' for Koreans. To the Japanese, human beings were clearly those on the Japanese charter. Those not on it were simply not human.

It was this attitude which made the Japanese so insensitive to the people they conquered and colonized in the Second World War. Once beaten in war, according to the *samurai* model, the loser could only redeem his honour by ritual death. The Japanese were disgusted with the Asian peoples they overran. The vanquished, neither committed ritual suicide in shame for surrendering nor offered resistance. Worse, their officers were white Europeans who talked of the *Geneva Convention*. It was for this reason, the Japanese did not appreciate the concept of surrender and the *Geneva Convention* of rights for prisoners of war. It made them harsh rulers, and memories of their brief incursion into South East Asia are still alive and bitter.

Thus, we see that a conflation of ideology and society created a unified social order. But within Tokugawa society classes were well-developed.

Society itself was divided into neatly functional and recognized classes. Above every individual stood Tenno, the Emperor, descended from the sun goddess and divine. His status and position in the ideological world of Japan were unquestioned.[40]

The Emperor, in turn, authorized the *shogun* to administer the land. The *shogun*, ruled through *daimyos*, who headed the districts (in the late Tokugawa period there were about 260 such districts). Each *daimyo* maintained around him *samurai* to enforce law and order and administer smaller units. Each unit was run with revenue losses and gains balanced annually by a hierarchy of *samurai*. The *samurai* depended for their upkeep, mainly rice, on the *daimyo*. This encouraged frugality, and loyalty, among them.

The *shogun* kept a careful eye on his immediate subordinates, the *daimyos*. Outgoing women and incoming weapons would mean conspiracy was being hatched. A complex system of checks and balances restricted the power of the *daimyos*: marriage could not be contracted without permission of the *shogun* as political alliances were feared; roads and bridges between districts were discouraged to maintain their isolation; *daimyos* had to spend almost half the year at the capital and when, at home, had to leave behind the family as hostage. Fearing assassination attempts the rulers took ingeneous precautions: the floors of the palaces were 'nightingale floors' concealing devices which squeaked when walked upon and sliding doors hid armed guards when receiving guests.

The last link from the *shogun* down was the *daikan*, chief magistrate, also a *samurai*, who administered at the village level. These rulers belonged to one class.

Underneath the ruling class, the men who wore swords, were the farmers. The farmers were compelled to hand over about 40 per cent of their produce for the upkeep of the *samurai*. Under the farmers were the artisans, and under them the merchants, and beneath them all, the *eta*, tanners and scavengers who dealt with the disposal of executed bodies. The *eta* were not unlike the untouchables of India.

The Japanese class system was peculiar to Japan. It never degenerated into the Indian caste system. Firstly, there was a regular upward mobility marked in the later Tokugawa period through talent or adoption; secondly, the *samurai* remained strong enough in society to fulfill their obligations such as maintaining law and order, and ensuring prosperity in the districts. By fulfilling their function they maintained their own superior position. The class structure was no longer tenable by the end of the Tokugawa period as we shall see later.

What was Tokugawa life like? To the Japanese, space was limited, it always is on an island. And therefore, space was as defined as it was economized. Japanese utilized space in society economically and functionally at every level. Domestically, every inch in the home was—and is—used. Bedrooms and dining rooms were converted by bringing in beds (on the floor) and tables (food is eaten sitting on the floor).

Miniature plants, *bonsai*, which take up only a few inches were cultivated in homes. The domestic economy reflected *bushido*.

Society defined boundaries between groups, ages, and sexes, and evolved a rigid set of rules for eating, speaking, and walking. Clothes, food, marriage, and manners were regulated according to class and seniority. Each *samurai* was distinguished by his mail armour, emblem, and flags. Family heads were required by law to post the family position and status on the door. Proper behaviour, 'face',[41] was thus important in society. It was a world of established social hierarchy and rules of behaviour[42] — a formal, unsmiling, hierarchical, and demanding world. The main themes of society were complete obedience, immediate punishment, death, and honour. They created a need to conform, a desire for perfection in individuals.

This publicly accepted structure and order perhaps explains the absence of men of charisma. No Chenghiz, Napoleon, or Hitler have emerged in Japan.[43] Decisions were made on the basis of accepted authority or, as today, consensus.

The length of the Tokugawa period, which spoke of a kind of stability, produced an important shift in the understanding of *bun-bu*. As the *samurai* was not occupied with *bu* his emphasis on *bun* increased correspondingly. Art, education, and literature were thus developed by him.

Tokugawa society in some aspects, forecast the modern state in all its essential ambivalence, the apparatus of repression on the one hand, and the provision of social welfare on the other.

It was a tidy world for the Japanese. Everyone knew his place in society and the space allotted to him. And for the ruling class it was a comfortable world.

However, three sources could challenge and upset the tidy world of the ruling class. First, an organized church. We know how the church *versus* state struggles in medieval

Europe drained the energies of society. It was only after this struggle had been resolved that the Renaissance began in Europe, in the fifteenth and sixteenth centuries. The Renaissance lead to the Industrial Revolution of the seventeenth and eighteenth centuries which, directly affected the outcome of the colonial encounter between Europe and the rest of the world. In Japan, no such struggle between church and state took place. The *samurai*, combined at one and the same time, aspects of the warrior and Zen priest. We have already seen how groups in society were related to the Emperor through a complex network of shrines and ideological myths. The Emperor himself was head of the nation—the *shogun* ruled on his behalf—and the very core of religion. The religion of Japan in the main was and remains Shintoism (at various stages 'foreign' religions—such as Buddhism and Christianity—have been savagely persecuted, their priests killed, and their places of worship destroyed).

The second could have come from the Emperor himself, wishing for more direct involvement in administration. The relationship between the divine Emperor, Tenno, and powerful military dictator, *shogun*, is a complex one. By controlling the purse strings of the Emperor, the Tokugawa *shogun* could play politics in the Imperial palaces and effectively restrict his role in administration. Nonetheless, the *shogun* relied for his legitimacy on the authority of the Emperor.

Thirdly, a threat to the established order could come from outside in foreign ships. This, the Tokugawa set about to prevent by cutting off Japan from the world. To build a boat became a crime in Tokugawa Japan. A Japanese returning from a foreign country could be killed according to official instructions contained in the 'Seclusion Edicts'.

By the middle of the nineteenth century, the Tokugawa dynasty ended. Why was the Emperor restored and given full authority? Firstly, the Tokugawa dynasty had long faded away in its vigour. The *samurai* were heavily in debt to the emerging merchant class, who in turn, demanded change in society and expansion of their interests. And the threat to the Tokugawas came — as the founding fathers always feared — from outside. After 1853, it was becoming increasingly difficult to ignore the outside world.

The restoration of the Emperor in 1868, must be understood in the context of the ideological foundations of Japanese society, which we have discussed earlier. The Revolutions of France in 1789, Russia in 1917, and Iran in 1979, terminated Imperial dynasties and either killed or exiled the Emperor. In Japan, the Emperor was 'restored' and given for the first time in almost a thousand years, executive authority. On the surface, dramatic events were unfolding: Buddhism, the shogunate, the *samurai* — as institutions — were rejected. But, it was precisely the vast body of poorer or more progressive *samurai* who provided the base and vigour for the developments in the Meiji era. These *samurai* entered commerce, business, education, government, and the army, in big numbers. With them they brought the philosophy of *bushido*. Better established *samurai* or *daimyos* became governors and ambassadors. The younger members of the Tenno's family, too, wished for change. Consensus not conflict was inherent in social change. Meiji rule was thus neither a revolution nor a break with the past. It was more, perhaps, a shift and realignment of authority and power within Japanese structure.

How was this transition from the feudal to the modern phase conducted so successfully and so swiftly? The answer to this key question lies in the central figure of Tenno. Tenno himself was fully committed to change and the nation responded unreservedly. The Tenno's leadership gave change in Japanese society both a structural and ideological base.

The middle of the nineteenth century to the first quarter of the twentieth, was an exhilarating period for Japan. Its national insignia, depicting the rising sun, was appropriately chosen. Indeed, Japan could do no wrong. And, in the midst of the great drive to catch up with the world, was the figure of the Emperor. Although a young man at the Meiji Restoration, the Emperor remained the central figure in the modernization drama. He was surrounded, by a group of younger *samurai* determined to modernize – not necessarily western-ize, an important distinction – Japan. In his western hair-style and clothes he symbolized Meiji Japan. Women, too, contribu-ted to the new thinking.[44] Side by side with these devel-opments, there emerged a great sense of nationalism for Nippon or Japan (Figure 15.2).

Let us not forget that the turn of the century was the high noon of modern Imperial Europe. The world for the European was racially a simple place. The whites were superior to the other races – black, brown, or yellow, whom they ruled in their vast empires. Rudyard Kipling was the acknowledged troubadour of the British Empire. The brown 'wogs' in South Asia, or the yellow 'chinks', and 'Japs' in East Asia were simply inferior racial species, according to the Imperial vision. But it was during this high noon that the Japanese, yellow and Asian, beat the Russians, white and European, in a military encounter in 1905. The Japanese forced the Russians to sign a humiliating agreement which

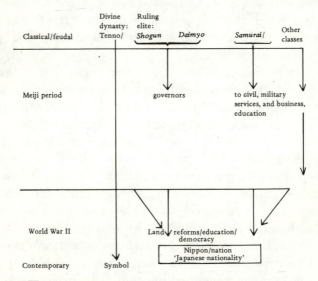

Figure 15.2: Japanese Social Historical Sequences

neither Napoleon nor Hitler could do. A racial thrill ran through Asia. Not unnaturally, the West saw every Japanese as an aggressive *samurai*. During the war with Hitler's Germany, the swastika motif, imported centuries ago from India, did not help matters for the Japanese.

Notably, Japan was dominated by the *samurai* ethos. The world was divided according to the *samurai* social system. There were nations, in particular, Americans, British, and Germans, who were social equals. They were worthy of emulation. And then there were the others, the poor, the weak, and the struggling, like those in Asia. These were equated with the lower social orders who must obey the commands and acknowledge the superiority of the *samurai*.

In a broad sense, to the Japanese, the world was simply divided between white Europeans, who were worthy competitors, and black Africans who were seen as inferior. The brown races—Middle East Arabs, for instance, rarely came into contact with the Japanese. Islam was a blank for them, and vice versa.[45]

Japanese history may be read as both simple and complex. On the surface it is simple. A thousand years of society closed to the outside world. And then, in the last hundred years, a speeded-up version of the history of most modern nations: the demise of feudalism, emergence of an autocratic, militaristic monarchy, colonial empire, war, defeat, democracy, and rapid industrialization. These sequences show unique and dramatic ups and downs: the defeat of Russia in 1905; the atom bombs dropped on Hiroshima and Nagasaki (the only such bombs used against mankind in history, a fact which rankles in Japan[46]). They also explain some of the complexities of Japanese history and society. The great tension in society is a consequence of these developments in recent history. It is the trauma of this rapid change which partly explains the need to preserve the *samurai* model. The model provides continuity in society and affords the individual an opportunity to contemplate honour in rapidly changing, and sometimes degrading, times.

Contemporary Japanese Society

On the surface, the hundred years since the Tokugawas were deposed, have brought a social revolution in Japan. But if, Tokugawa life is viewed through what we are calling the *samurai* model, a remarkable continuity may be perceived. This continuity, the Americans as victors of the war and during the American Occupatioɪ (1945-52) had deliberately set out to destroy.

The target of the Americans was the old culture at the heart of which stood the *samurai* model. Possession of *samurai* swords was made illegal and *samurai* exercises were forbidden. Shintoism, too, was officially discouraged. Drastic land reforms, constitutional rights, and new values (mass democracy, women's rights etc.,) were introduced. Having little choice but, to accept these changes, the Japanese responded by extending the *samurai* model from the preserve of one class to that of the entire nation.

The Japanese nation became the *samurai*. The virtues that characterized the *samurai* would assist to reconstruct Japan from the ashes. *Chu* — loyalty — was transferred from the immediate master to the nation, for instance.

It was Mishima who symbolized the re-emergence of the *samurai* model in Japanese society. No longer was the Japanese, apologetic or embarrassed by his past. In his books, Mishima castigates intellectuals and scholars, baseball players, and television stars for succumbing to western materialism and as symbols of decadence. For him, only the way of the *samurai* could restore classic Japanese honour and this, he set out to do by his own death. Mishima's writings, the ideas contained in them, and his death reflect the *samurai* model. His popularity and elevation to a cult figure, emphasize the strength of the model in society.

The model was never far beneath the surface, either in the perception of the Japanese or, those who interacted with them. Two of the most popular films depicting the encounter between Japan and the West during the Second

World War, *Bridge on the river Kwai* and the contemporary *Happy Christmas, Mister Lawrence*, employ *bushido* to define the Japanese. The films of Kurosawa and Oshima work around the theme of *bushido*. But, because they are Japanese, they balance *bun* with *bu* rather than just depict the martial aspects of *bu*.

We may trace much of contemporary Japanese society to the *samurai* model and its symbolism: the director of the multinational who commits *hara kiri* to redeem his honour when exposed in a bribery case; or the name given to a university student who fails, *ronin*, a masterless *samurai*, one who has no base, or the stoicism in confronting failure or success or even the emphasis on physical fitness.

Fortunately, the model is universally accepted in Japan. Partly because of this Japanese society is homogeneous. In contrast to Japanese society which is homogeneous and has historically discouraged immigrants and outsiders, Pakistan society neither discourages nor disrespects outsiders, particularly if they are Muslims. Historically, many lineages claim descent from areas outside Pakistan. The Sayyeds, claiming to be descended from the Holy Prophet are from Arabia, as also are the Qurayshis, Ansaris, and Siddiqis. The Gilanis claim to have come from Iraq, the Isphanis from Iran, the Durranis from Afghanistan, and so on. The creation of Pakistan brought an influx of millions of refugees from varying social backgrounds and ethnic regions of India. Many of these refugees rose to high positions in Pakistan, even becoming heads of state. Today, too, there are almost 3 million Afghan refugees living in Pakistan. (See also Part Three, chapter 10.) Although there is evidence of sporadic, and sometimes physical, confrontation between refugees and locals, on the whole, Pakistan has been generous to its refugee population. No such waves of immigrants flowed into Japanese society. The only large groups of immigrants, the Koreans, who came as cheap labour, still remain foreigners in the most profound sense in Japan. Japanese society was, and is, in an ethnic sense, monolithic.

The world exists in, and for, Japan — this fact confronts a visitor to Japan. All signs for public transport, advertisements in public parks, and television programmes on the numerous channels etc., are in Japanese.

The key social unit was, and is, the nuclear family. Because of the intense sense of competition and pressures to remain within the proper bounds of society, known and acknowledged by all, individuals often break under the pressure. The suicide rate is therefore high. However, traditional methods of upward mobility provided a safety valve and allowed a dynamic merit-based elite to emerge. Adoption of talented young men, irrespective of family, was an established method to recruit talent in Tokugawa Japan. Today, too, large firms and government select the best and the brightest. It is the pragmatic way to maintain quality in life.

The Japanese, above all, are a pragmatic people. They confront a foreign phenomenon and if they acknowledge its value, they make it their own. But only after Japanizing it. From the early centuries, especially after the seventh, the Chinese influenced Japan in thought, art, literature, and language. The rulers of Japan accepted foreign values. For instance, after Buddhism was introduced in the sixth century, the Tenno's family accepted its principles. But both, Buddhism and Confucianism were synthesized with the indigenous religion, Shintoism. As we know, these religious philosophies provided the major elements in *bushido*.

The Japanese ideological and religious world emphasizes ritual rather than eschatological or philosophical concerns. Eclecticism ensures consensus and continuity. The Japanese Muslim eats pork. Pig, cow, or snake, none of these are religiously taboo in Japan. Japanese temples house Sanskrit Hindu demons, Buddhist images, and conduct Shinto rituals. The Japanese, Christian or Buddhist, is married as a Buddhist at a Shinto shrine with Shinto rites, but, is buried as a Buddhist. 'On the 25th of December', there is a saying, 'all Japanese become Christian'. As we know, the Japanese genius for adapting was displayed at its fullest· in the nineteenth century.

Society, like religion, is amorphous, flexible, and eclectic. It engages foreign ideas in a most interesting manner: it simply swallows them. Once swallowed, they are regurgitated and emerge unmistakenly as Japanese. Coca Cola, base-ball, hamburgers, go-go bars, bunny girls, the Eiffel Tower, Disney-land—all of western origin, are today an integral part of Japanese culture. Even foreign words are Japanized, for instance *shokku*, from shock, or *kisso* from kiss. A senior Japanese diplomat summed up: 'the Japanese developed a skill at learning and adapting while keeping their own cultural identity'.[47]

It is this pragmatic ideological flexibility and eclecticism which allowed Japan to survive the traumas of change; it also partly explains how the rigid social code of the *samurai* model was maintained. Indeed, the weaker a rigid ideological code, the stronger the social one.

But, it is not entirely a rosy or positive picture. There are dark spots in it. Paradoxically, the problems of Japanese society rise from its phenomenal economic successes. The *samurai* model is under attack at its most vulnerable point: the home. Disturbing, but little known accounts, of bored wives becoming alcoholic while waiting for husbands who stay late at factories are merging. Stories of sons beating their fathers and rejecting the work ethos are also told. The younger generation, born after the traumas of the war, have high material expectations and wish to put in little of their time achieving them. In a deliberate act of rejection they block their ears and minds to the world with their Walkman sets which are common and popular. There appears to be a sense of discontent with the directions in which Japanese society is moving.

In some groups, the discontent expresses itself in the dress and behaviour of the *take-no-ko-zoku* or the tribe of bamboo shoots. These young people who look, behave, and dress like western youth, dance and sing their time away. Wearing black leather clothes, and with their hair combed back, they look like early Elvis Presleys, but their skins are yellow and their eyes slanted. These Japanese youth are mutants of the Japanese-American encounter.

There are also signs of another disquieting, more serious, element. This is the distinct emergence of the *bu* spirit in Japanese society after lying dormant for almost a generation, or assuming other forms. *Bu* will once again propel Japan into becoming a military power. Intellectuals in society, sense the stirrings of crude forms of *bu* and hear Mishima's voice talking of *bushido*, honour, and death. Japanese intellectuals recognize that 'in an extremely modern period, something extraordinarily traditional always begins to revive'.[48] The best known Japanese anthropologist warns of the 'danger' inherent in Japanese society[49] which could lead to, among other things, 'war'. These are serious matters which will affect Japanese society in the coming years. And there are no easy solutions in sight.

Let me sum up the discussion so far by attempting to define what constitutes the Japanese mind today. It is a composite of three distinct but interlocking and overlapping socio-historical categories (Figure 15.3). The contemporary mind overlays the strong feudal base and both are suffused with the ideology and mythology of ancient Japan.

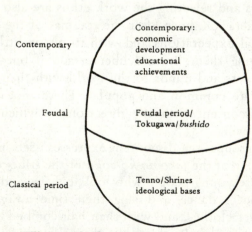

Figure 15.3: The Contemporary Japanese

The Secrets of Japan's Development

At the risk of over-simplification, let me employ the *samurai* model to help us understand Japan's development success. The *samurai*, motivated by the core elements of *bushido*, discipline, austerity, loyalty, determination — challenges all competitors from outside. His skills and high motivation to win assure him victory. In place of his sword is technical knowledge (and in keeping with the model, not necessarily Japanese but often borrowed). He must export, not import (foreign cars are conspicuous by their absence in Japan compared to the large numbers — especially Japanese — seen in the USA or England). The strong *samurai* has little sympathy for the weak or poor of the world (Japanese aid remains small to developing nations; its attitude to charity, as in the case of the Vietnamese Boat People, disappointing). It is, once again, a contest between Japan, the people of the island, and the world. It is the Japanese model, the Japanese secret.

What lessons does Japan teach us? Particularly those which developing nations, like Pakistan, could learn and follow. Can we successfully pinpoint the conflation and coincidence of factors which provided a base for development? Five factors emerge clearly.

The first, and possibly the main factor, is Japan's education policy. Over a hundred years ago, in 1872, education was made compulsory. There were estimated to be 54,000 elementary schools and almost a thousand academies teaching both commoners and *samurai*. The base existed in the temple schools in almost every village. Where did Japan produce the enormous number of teachers required for this task? The answer is to be found among members of the *samurai* class already familiar with learning and the acquisition of knowledge.

The first lesson, then, is the emphasis on mass education. Today, Japan is one of the most literate nations in the world. The circulation of daily papers, always a reliable index of national literacy, is estimated at 60 million. The number of newspapers sold per 1,000 people is 569, the highest in the world (it is 453 in Britain and 282 in the USA).

The second, is that of birth control. The population growth during the Tokugawa period was already controlled at about 1 per cent a year. Scarcity of land and controlled production and distribution of rice for political purposes, as we have seen, ensured small families.

The third, is of respect for civil and political rights. Japanese society, in spite of a divine Emperor and a feudal base, is today a working democracy. Elections, a free press, and public expression allow society to remain dynamic and cohesive. Merit is rewarded and talent recognized irrespective of class or ethnicity. The title, *sensei* – like South Asia's *ustad* or *guru* – is given to masters of craft. *Sensei* are widely respected.

The fourth, is the creation and maintenance of a homogeneous society in ethnic and administrative terms. The Ainu, in the northern island, are the major distinct group in Japan, but provide few ethnic or political problems. The concept of Nippon or Japan overrides other loyalties in society. In contrast, South Asian political borders are flexible and ethnic divisions sharp. In 1947, Pakistan was born from India and, in 1971, East Pakistan became Bangladesh. Geography has reinforced Japanese nationalism.[50] Japan, being an island, has been a geographical and political unit for at least a thousand years. Pakistan retains a complicated category of administrative units inherited from British India: Tribal Areas (federally administered), Tribal Areas (provincially administered), Frontier Regions, Settled Districts, and Northern Areas.

Finally, planning for and development within the framework of traditional values and customs. Ritual and custom bind society together and provide continuity to it. Traditional values – frugality, loyalty, face – assist production and unity in the large firms. Traditional proper behaviour has been adapted to the needs of modern life. Popular books like *How to be Considerate* by Suzuki and *Anthology of Office*

Lady Common Sense issued by the Sumitomo Corporation show the way. It was precisely the rejection of religious and traditional values by nations wishing to modernize in a hurry, like Turkey, which created acute problems for them.

The mainstream of the Japanese development argument is both compelling and cogent. And it is easy to romanticize the Japanese success story and be blinded by its material achievements. I have certain doubts and queries alongwith other recent commentators, Japanese and non-Japanese.[51]

The Japanese developmental model raises immediate moral and ethical questions for those interested in imitating it or learning from it.[52] There are two major structural flaws in society. Both of these characterize and derive from the *samurai* model.

Firstly, the lack of a moral or spiritual content in society based on a universal philosophy; a philosophy preaching the brotherhood of man irrespective of caste, class, or race. *Bushido* provided society with a charter for social action not moral philosophy. There appears to be little moral content in society; but there is abundant energy and forceful direction in industry and business. The emphasis is on action, the material, here and now. This is also as we saw earlier, the essence of Shintoism, the Japanese religion. And Shintoism was created by Japanese society, not the other way round. It does not claim to be, like Islam, a revealed religion from a supreme being. Partly as a consequence of the lack of spirituality and morality in society, is the unconcern with the afterworld. This central issue in its relationship to society is not satisfactorily explained in studies of Japanese religion.[53]

The absence of a universal philosophy is directly related to the absence of great original philosophers or prophets in Japan. It is remarkable for such a literate and talented nation not to have produced a first rate, towering, figure in history preaching a philosophy based on brotherhood or love. There are elements of Buddhist, Taoist, indeed Christian, thinking in Japan but no Buddha, Lao-tsze, or Christ. Neither has modern Japan produced an Iqbal, a Tagore, or a Gandhi.

Secondly, the intense and, sometimes aggressive, concepts of race and nation—and the two are interchangeable in Japan—raise problems both for the Japanese and those who deal with them. The world is divided into Japan and—or *versus*—the rest. There is no concept of a universal brotherhood transcending role and nationalities such as one based on religion, as in Islam or Christianity, or one on ideology such as the Communists propagate. In the twentieth century, when destinies of nations are becoming increasingly interlocked this aspect can become a major barrier to international harmony. Japanese nationalism rapidly, and violently, degenerates into crude xenophobic exhibition. Elements of xenophobia are never far from the surface. As an example, although English is taught at high school level for a number of years, the average Japanese is reluctant to speak it. Japan and things Japanese are exclusively preferred. Both these major ideological and social flaws present continuing and complex problems for Japan in its dealings with the world; both reflect aspects of the *samurai* model.

Conclusion

Of the great civilizations of the world, Japan is perhaps the most notable in its almost total absence of contact with Islam. Apart from a few isolated and individual cases no relationships—either trade, or war, or diplomatic—existed between the world of Islam and that of Japan. The two, Islamic civilization and Japanese, were, on the surface, diametrically opposed in their system of ideology, beliefs, and values.

Consider an important example, the attitudes to life and death. For the Japanese life is, as we have seen, here and now. It is a physical and material existence. The afterworld is dark and remains a frightening question mark. The Japanese therefore concentrates his energies in securing this world.

This aspect of Japanese ideology partly explains Japan's remarkable material achievements. For the Muslim, on the other hand, this world, *dunya* is a preparation for the next.[54] (See also Part One, chapter 4.) Through practice of *din* or religion the Muslim may secure the afterworld. The ideal Muslim balances *din* with *dunya*.

Consider too, God: for the Muslim, God is one Supreme, Omnipotent, being. The Japanese god is amorphous—part emperor, part divine, part nature, part nation. In Islam, nothing stands between man and God, except, perhaps, the intercession of the prophets (also human). For the Japanese, god is linked with each household and shrine through a hierarchy and rituals.

A stock-taking of our situation is suggested. Muslims are groping around for competing models which may instruct them in contemporary problems of development. For them, contemplating such models is often a poignant journey into the past. The President of Pakistan in a speech to an international conference of Islamic scholars—still with Japan on his mind—compared the Japanese schools to the *madrasahs* of classical Islam (Organization of Islamic Countries, Standing Committee on Science and Technology in Islamabad, in December 1983). Education, as we learned from Japan above, was the first major factor in its development. Islam, perhaps more than any revealed religion, emphasizes the value of learning. The word *ilm*, knowledge, is the second most used word in the Holy Quran after *Allah*. 'Go to China to acquire learning' and 'the life in pursuit of knowledge is one spent in *jihad*, or struggle for *Allah*', are two well-known *hadith*, sayings of the Holy Prophet. The President was therefore right in picking out education. But only partly. Islamic society has many other lessons to teach Muslims.

Perhaps, not Pakistan society *as it is* but an Islamic society *as it should be* has the answers. And perhaps we may find these in the sociology rather than the theology of Islam, although they reflect each other. Let us see what these are?

The positive key social elements of *bushido* and the *samurai* model are found in the Holy Quran: emphasis on the unity of the group or community,[55] care of parents,[56] balanced speech,[57] modest bearing and walk,[58] physical fitness,[59] and physical cleanliness.[60]

These virtues in society are reinforced by the *hadith*. See Muslim's section on 'good manners and joining of the ties of relationship'.[61] Also caring for parents,[62] caring for the sick,[63] humility and rights of neighbours.[64]

Some of the positive and key elements in the *samurai* model are reflected in the life of the Holy Prophet. In particular are his frugality, austerity, humility, and courage. These characteristics became values of ideal Muslims.

Even the Japanese factor of a balanced and frugal diet can be traced to early Islam. Examples of such a diet, based on milk, dates, and honey, abound from the life and times of the Holy Prophet.

We may thus conceptualize the ideal Muslim *mujahid*, one who embarks on *jihad*, as a sort of Islamic *samurai*. He represents the finest ideals of his religion and culture. However, Muslims have sometimes taken the meaning of *jihad* literally.[65] *Jihad* is interpreted as physical war. But in its essence, the concept of *jihad* is to be understood in terms of striving, and provides a general base for commitment and dedication.

Theologians have emphasized ideology and ritual in Islam. Equally important are the social and physical injunctions in the Holy Quran and *hadith*. These, as we see, are reflected in *bushido*. Perhaps they have not been sufficiently stressed in Islamic teaching. The problem is, of course, that the ideals of Islam and the behaviour of empirically observed Muslim society do not always coincide. The result is, as a Japanese long employed at the Pakistan Embassy noted, 'although Islam is great, Muslims are not so good'.

The interesting—and unexpected—conclusion is that some of the secrets of Japan's development may be found in Pakistan's own backyard. We may, therefore, conclude by re-phrasing our question, 'can Pakistan be Japan?', to the more legitimate question 'can Pakistan be Pakistan?'.

NOTES

1. Madan, T.N., 'Westernization: An Essay on Indian and Japanese Responses', unpublished paper, 1983.

2. Rustomji, M.K., and Sapre, S.A., *The Incredible Japanese*, Macmillan Ltd., India, 1982.

3. Christopher, R.C., *The Japanese Mind: The Goliath Explained*, Linden Press, Simon and Schuster, New York, 1983.

4. Dore, R.P., 'Reflections on the "learn from Japan" boom', *International House of Japan Bulletin*, Vol. 3, No. 2, Spring 1983.

5. Franko, L.G., *The Threat of Japanese Multi-Nationals: How the West can Respond*, John Wiley and Sons Ltd., England, 1983.

6. Mendel, D.H., 'Japan as a Model for Developing Nations', in *Japan's Modern Century*, Skrzypczak, E.R., (editor), The Voyager's Press, Tokyo, 1968.

7. Reischauer, E.O., *Japan, Past and Present*, Alfred A. Knopf, Inc., New York, 1964; 'Special Features in the History of Japan', talk on 8 August to the National Association for Research on Education in History, 1964; and *The Japanese*, Charles E. Tuttle Co., Tokyo, 1977.

8. Vogel, E.F., *Japan as Number One: Lessons for America*, Harvard University Press, 1979.

9. Swee, G.K., 'The Meiji Road to Development', *Far Eastern Economic Review*, 8 December 1983.

10. The wish to become like Japan is not new in South Asia. Forster, E.M., in *A Passage to India*, Penguin Books, 1961, p. 262, concluded, two generations ago, India, to progress, 'must imitate Japan'.

11. *Statistical Yearbooks*, Statistics Bureau of Prime Minister's Office, Tokyo.

12. *Bushi* for *samurai* and *do* for 'the way of' or 'code'.

13. By emphasizing *bushido*, I run the risk of simplifying what is a complex matter. I am interested in building a simple, schematic model to understand Japanese society holding other variables constant and focusing on *bushido*.

14. Benedict, R., *The Chrysanthemum and the Sword*, Houghton Mifflin Company, Boston, 1946; Mishima, Y., *On Hagakure : The Samurai Ethic and Modern Japan*, Basic Books, New York, 1977; Nakane, C., *Japanese Society*, University of California Press, Berkeley, 1970; and Nitobe, I., *Bushido : The Soul of Japan*, Kenkyusha, Tokyo, 1935.

15. Hitchcock, J.T., 'The Idea of the Martial Rajput', *Journal of American Folklore*, July-September 1958.

16. Ahmed, op. cit., 1980.

17. Ibid.

18. The striking similarities between certain aspects of *Pukhtunwali* and *bushido* will be examined in a joint paper: Ahmed, A.S., and Matsui, T., '*Pukhtunwali* and *bushido*: The Social Consequences of two Asian Codes of Honour', (forthcoming). It is not surprising in the context of the two codes that the only Asian legend to emerge from the Japanese-Asian encounter was that of Zarak Khan, the Pukhtun. The story of Zarak Khan has been made into films and become part of South Asian folklore. Zarak Khan died living up to his own Code: the *Pukhtunwali*, which as much as *bushido* emphasized honour, bravery, and courage. Both codes helped to create, in a profound sense, a man's world with its characteristic features (including, for instance, homosexuality; see Mishima op. cit., 1977). The important question is raised as to why Japan developed so rapidly and Pukhtun society remains a closed and, in economic terms, backward one? This is dealt with in the joint paper.

19. Mishima had given his generation this famous line: 'I found that the way of the *samurai* is death', dramatized by his own dramatic ritual suicide which caught the imagination of Japan. Mishima was inspired by Yamamoto the *samurai* —turned-priest of the Tokugawa period. Mishima kept the original Hagakure written by Yamamoto with him for inspiration.

20. When I visited Osaka in November 1983 the main castle—from the Tokugawa shogunate—was drawing endless crowds to see a major exhibition of *samurai* swords. Appropriately a glistening, glinting *samurai* sword provided the backdrop to introduce the cast of *Shogun*, the popular TV serial based on the book: Clavell, J., *Shogun : A Novel of Japan*, Atheneum, New York, 1975.

21. Japanese diet established since the Tokugawa period is medically the best modern dieticians can recommend. Fish, often raw, vegetables, and sea-weeds, form Japanese diet. Little salt or sweets are eaten. It explains the statistics for the Japanese being the longest living people in the world.

22. Not even in the United States of America, now going through the throes of a passion for physical fitness, have I seen pull-up bars and instructions for exercises provided with rest facilities along the highways.

23. Japanese are among the cleanest people in the world. The family hot bath is a daily ritual. So particular are they about dirtying themselves that they eat the Japanese form of *halwa*, sweets, with wooden forks. These forks are also part of the traditional tea ceremony and, once used, thrown away. It is for reasons of cleanliness they do not touch or shake hands. A good national illustration of their cleanliness is the Ethnological Museum in Osaka which I compared to the best known ones in the West, in Cambridge (Massachusetts), and Oxford. So new is the Osaka Museum that its artefacts depicting ancient objects not only look new, but, also *smell* clean.

24. An important element of *bushido* is contentment with little. A famous *samurai* saying illustrates how to pick teeth to show to the world a full belly when it may be empty. It also illustrates the importance of 'face'.

25. Nitobe is to be honoured officially when his face appears on the new 5,000 yen note.

26. Nitobe, op. cit., 1935.

27. Ueda, M., *Modern Japanese Poets and the Nature of Literature*, Stanford University Press, 1983.

28. Not all accounts of *bushido* are laudatory. For instance, Saikaku, who belonged to the merchant class, wrote of the inhumanity and cruelty of *bushido*.

29. Clavell, J. *Shogun: A Novel of Japan*, Atheneum, New York, 1975.

30. May 5 is called *tango-no-sekku*, boys holiday. Households, with boys, decorate warrior dolls with armour, swords, and bows and arrows. A popular present for boys is the toy helmet or sword of the *samurai*. My friends Professors Mitseo and Hisako Nakamura presented me with a realistic toy *samurai* helmet for my son as a souvenir.

31. General MacArthur, the Commander of the American Occupation Forces, was seen in the mould of a *shogun* in the popular mind. See James, D. Clayton, *The Years of MacArthur*, Vol. 2, Boston, 1975.

32. The Japanese seem almost obsessed by physical sizes. Height and weight are cited in the press to indicate the nation is growing taller. In particular, younger members of the royal family are observed as being taller than their elders. A spate of letters followed President Reagan's visit to Japan in 1983, in the Japanese press (for instance, a letter by SoMiyamoto, *The Emperor*, in *The Japan Times*, 2 December 1983). Their arguments were that size does not indicate greatness. They repudiated stereotypes of the 'short and frail' Emperor alongside a tall and vigorous Reagan (or earlier MacArthur). Gandhi was quoted as part of their arguments. Colour, too, is important to Japanese. A folk saying testifies to this: 'with women, as with wine, the whiter the better'.

33. Geertz, op. cit., 1973.

34. Benedict, op. cit., 1946; Dunn, C.J., *Everyday Life in Traditional Japan*, C.E. Tuttle Co., Tokyo, 1969; Jansen, M.B., *Japan and its World: Two Centuries of Change*, Princeton University Press, 1980; Lehmann, J-P., *The Roots of Modern Japan*, Macmillan, 1983; Sansom, G., *A History of Japan 1615-1867*, The

Cresset Press, London, 1964; and Storry, R., *A History of Modern Japan*, a Penguin Original, 1960.

35. Aikens, C.M., and Takayasu Higuchi, *Prehistory of Japan*, Academic Press, New York, London, 1982.

36. Benedict, op. cit., 1946; Buruma, I., *A Japanese Mirror: Heroes and Villains of Japanese Culture*, Jonathan Cape, 1983; Fukutake, T., *The Japanese Social Structure*, Dore, R., (translator), University of Tokyo Press, Tokyo, 1982; Hasegawa, N., *The Japanese Character : A Cultural Profile*, Bester, J., (translator), Kodansha International, Tokyo, 1982; Hirashima, S., 'Growth, Equity and Labour Absorption in Japanese Agriculture', in *Labour Absorption and Growth in Agriculture : China and Japan*, ILO and ARTEP, Bangkok, 1982; Ishida, E., *Japanese Culture : A Study of Origins and Characteristics*, Kachi, T., (translator), University of Tokyo Press, Tokyo, 1977; Kato, S., *Form, Style, Tradition: Reflections on Japanese Art and Society*, Bester, J., (translator), Kodansha International, Tokyo, 1981; Nakane, op. cit., 1970; and Norbeck, E., *Changing Japan*, Holt, Rinehart and Winston, USA, 1976.

37. Fortes, M., and Evans-Pritchard, E.E., (editors), *African Political Systems*, Oxford University Press, 1970.

38. In a ritual drama of fertility, Tenno would sleep briefly, then awaken, symbolizing the passage from barren winter to a fruitful spring.

39. The concepts of *ouchi*, 'us', *versus soto*, 'them', are easily transposed from small groups such as the nuclear family to other relations, as the Japanese acknowledge. (*Human Relations in Japan*, film, Foreign Ministry, Japan.) International relations may be conceptualized thus, too: Japan is *ouchi*, the world *soto*.

40. When I asked my Japanese academic colleagues why the *shogun* could not kill the Emperor and take his place I revealed my South Asian and Muslim origin. Muslim history is replete with examples of Commanders-in-Chief overthrowing their Emperors and assuming the title themselves. In Japan, the Emperor is divine and such a gesture would have been meaningless in terms of securing power. The legitimacy of the Emperor rested in religion and history. Even the term *shogun*, literally 'barbarian-subduing generalissimo' meant Commander-in-Chief of the army who was appointed by the Emperor himself.

41. See the *samurai* saying in note 24.

42. The first thing a Japanese does after introductions is to exchange calling cards. These immediately 'place' a man according to his seniority and status and help to determine relationships.

43. The absence of a single Japanese from compiled lists by authors of the most influential persons in history (for instance, Hart, M.H., *The 100 : A Ranking of the Most Influential Persons in History*, A & W Visual Library, New York, 1978), supports my point. The group—transferred in the nineteenth and twentieth century to the nation—and not the individual explain the dynamics of Japanese society. In contrast, South Asia has six names in the list, including three 'interesting misses' of whom the most prominent is Mr. Gandhi (ibid). The only Japanese to appear in the book is Meiji Tenno, the Emperor Mutsuhito, who is mentioned as an 'interesting miss' (ibid).

44. Sievers, S.L., *Flowers in Salt : The Beginnings of Feminist Consciousness in Modern Japan*, Stanford University Press, 1983.

45. Japanese Ambassadors in Cairo confirm that Muslims were simply disinterested in Japanese history. See Mendel, op. cit., 1968, p. 207, f.n. 36.

46. Takayama, H., *Hiroshima in Memoriam and Today*, Daigaku, Letter Press Co., Hiroshima, Japan, 1973.

47. Yanai, S., 'Tradition and Transformation : Salient Features of Japanese History upto 1868', unpublished paper. Also published as 'The Secret of Japan's Rapid Economic Growth', *The Pakistan Times*, Magazine Section, 24 February 1984.

48. Hasegawa, op. cit., 1982, p. 59.

49. Nakane, op. cit., 1970, p. 151.

50. In contrast to the intense nationalism and unity of the Japanese in the face of foreigners, Pakistanis are divided by sects and ethnicity. So notorious has their own lack of unity become that they tell jokes about it. When Dr. Muhammad

Afzal, the Education Minister, launched my book, Ahmed, op. cit., 1983 on the nineteenth of November in Islamabad, he stressed the need for unity and recounted one of these jokes. Some visitors were being shown around hell. The angels pointed out the large cauldrons as belonging to this or that particular nation. Each cauldron was guarded by angels with spears. These angels would push back sinners into the fire if they tried to escape. But there was one unguarded cauldron which intrigued the visitors. 'Oh, that', explained the angels, 'is for the Pakistanis and we have no problems there. Everytime a Pakistani manages to reach the top the others drag him back into the cauldron themselves'.

51. Kawasaki, I., *Japan Unmasked*, Charles E. Tuttle Co., Tokyo, 1969; Morishima, M., *Why has Japan Succeeded?* Cambridge University Press, Cambridge, 1982; Nagai, Y., ' "Inspite of" or "because of"? Japan's success and Japanese Culture', Speech at the International Affairs, Harvard University, 21 October 1982; Taylor, J., *Shadow of the Rising Sun*, Morro, 1983.

52. An eminent Indian academic who lives in Japan enumerated some of these for me. First, Japan has a recent colonial past with a record of brutality to colonized people. Second, contemporary politics is marked by corruption which is seen in society in terms of *chu* —loyalties—and is therefore, condoned and acceptable. The current controversy regarding the charges of corruption surrounding Kakuei Tanaka and his continued power as the 'shadow *shogun*' illustrate this point. The electorate in his constituency disregarded the charges and returned him with a large majority recently. Third, ancestor worship, astrology, and palm reading—at which modern Indians scoff—are still practised in public and private life. What is of interest to us is that the three contemporary features derive from the *samurai* model.

53. Bellah, R.N., *Tokugawa Religion*, The Free Press, Illinois, 1957; Earhart, H.B., *Japanese Religion: Unity and Diversity*, Dickenson Publishing Co., Belmont, 1969; Kitagawa, J.M., *Religion in Japanese History*, Columbia University Press, New York, 1966; and Norbeck, E., *Religion and Society in Modern Japan*, Tourmaline Press, Houston, 1970.

54. Ahmed, A.S., 'Death in Islam: The Hawkes Bay Case', in *MAN: Royal Anthropological Institute Journal,* Vol. 21, No. 1, March 1986. See also Part One, chapter 4.

55. The Holy Quran, *surahs al Imran* : 103-5; *al Haj* : 78; *al-Room* : 38; and *al Hijrat* : 9 and 10.

56. Ibid., *al Ahqaf* : 15; *al Baqra* : 83 and 215; *an Nisa* : 8.

57. Ibid., *an Nisa* : 8; *al Furqan* : 63; and *al Luqman* : 19.

58. Ibid., *al Furqan* : 63; *al Luqman* 18 and 19.

59. Ibid., *al Dahar* : 28.

60. Ibid., *al Baqra* : 125 and 222; *al Maidah* : 6; *al Haj* : 29; and *al Mudathhir*: 4 and 5.

61. Muslim, I., *Sahih Muslim*, Siddiqi, A.H., (translator), Vol. IV, Book XXX, Sh. M. Ashraf, Lahore, 1981.

62. Ibid., ML III.

63. Ibid., ML XIII.

64. Ibid., MC XII.

65. For a fresh discussion of *jihad*, see Ahmed, op. cit., 1983.

Index